Whose Child Am I?

The publisher gratefully acknowledges the generous support of the General Endowment Fund of the University of California Press Foundation.

Whose Child Am I?

Unaccompanied, Undocumented
Children in U.S. Immigration Custody

Susan J. Terrio

UNIVERSITY OF CALIFORNIA PRESS

University of California Press, one of the most distin-
guished university presses in the United States, enriches
lives around the world by advancing scholarship in the
humanities, social sciences, and natural sciences. Its
activities are supported by the UC Press Foundation and
by philanthropic contributions from individuals and
institutions. For more information, visit www.ucpress.edu.

University of California Press
Oakland, California

Library of Congress Cataloging-in-Publication Data

Terrio, Susan J. (Susan Jane), 1950– author.
    Whose child am I? : unaccompanied, undocumented
children in U.S. immigration custody / Susan J. Terrio.
        pages   cm
    Includes bibliographical references and index.
    ISBN 978-0-520-28148-6 (cloth)
    ISBN 978-0-520-28149-3 (pbk. : alk. paper)
    ISBN 978-0-520-96144-9 (ebook)
    1. Unaccompanied immigrant children—Government
policy—United States—Case studies.   2. Illegal alien
children—Government policy—United States—Case
studies.   3. Juvenile detention—United States—Case
studies.   4. Immigration enforcement—United States—
Case studies.   5. Mexicans—United States—Case
studies.   6. Central Americans—United States—Case
studies.   I. Title.
    JV6600.T47   2015
    325—dc23
                                        2014042624

Manufactured in the United States of America

24   23   22   21   20   19   18   17   16   15
10   9   8   7   6   5   4   3   2   1

In keeping with a commitment to support environmen-
tally responsible and sustainable printing practices, UC
Press has printed this book on Natures Natural, a fiber
that contains 30% post-consumer waste and meets the
minimum requirements of ANSI/NISO Z39.48–1992 (R
1997) (*Permanence of Paper*).

Contents

4/17 YBP 85.00

Illustrations

Acknowledgments

In researching this book, I have acquired a number of debts. I am immensely grateful to the Radcliffe Institute at Harvard University whose exploratory summer workshop program helped me launch this project on unaccompanied, undocumented children in U.S. immigration custody. The three-day seminar assembled practitioners and academics with expertise on child migration, refugee populations, and U.S. immigration law. I would like to thank immigration attorneys Barbara Hines, Christopher Nugent, and Aryah Somers and legal scholar Jacqueline Bhabha; migration experts Elzbieta Gozdziac, Susan Coutin, and Cecilia Menjivar; child refugee expert Olivia Faries; child psychiatrist Stuart Lustig; and former chief immigration judge Michael Creppy. I also thank Chief Immigration Judge Brian O'Leary, who approved my request to observe immigration court hearings around the country. I also thank my colleague Andy Schoenholtz for allowing me to audit his course on U.S. immigration law and policy at Georgetown Law School in 2010.

A number of practitioners provided invaluable assistance at the outset and throughout my research, steering me to the right sources and contacts. They include immigration judge Dana Leigh Marks; attorneys Michelle Brané and Olga Byrne; child refugee experts Olivia Faries, Hilary Chester, Connie Daniels, Kimberly Haynes, Natalie Lummert, Chak Ng, Kristyn Peck, Anita Prasad, Laura Schmidt, and Dawnya Underwood; consultant Susan Schmidt; and child psychologist Judy Okawa.

Between 2009 and 2012 I made sixteen trips in the United States to visit federal facilities, observe hearings in immigration courts, and attend conferences on undocumented children. The following attorneys at legal service agencies were extremely helpful guides to U.S. immigration courts and the law: in Phoenix, Arizona, Sara Lofland and Alejandra Valdez; in California, Gladys Molina, Kristin Jackson, and Angie Junck; in Miami, Florida Deborah Lee and Michelle Abarca; in New Orleans, Hiroko Kusuda and Laila Hlass; in Chicago, Sarah Diaz, Anita Maddali, and Maria Woltjen; in Boston, Jane Rocamora; in East Lansing, Michigan, David and Veronica Thronson; in Newark, New Jersey, Elissa Steglich and Barbara Camacho; in New York, Abigail Cushing, Alison Kahmi, and Mario Russell; in Harlingen, Texas, accredited representative Lauren Fisher and attorney Carly Salazar; in Houston, Anne Chandler, Dalia Castillo-Granados, Maria Mitchell, and Yasmin Yavar; in San Antonio, Jonathan Ryan; in Seattle, Rebekah Fletcher and Juli Bildhauer; and in Washington, DC, Larry Katzman. I want to express my heartfelt thanks to attorneys Megan McKenna and Daria Fisher Page at Kids in Need of Defense for their help in connecting me with young interviewees and to Wendy Young for sharing her unerring insights and invaluable expertise. I am especially indebted to attorneys Michelle Brané, Jessica Jones, Jennifer Podhul, and Emily Butera, whose ongoing assistance has been indispensable to the success of this project. I interviewed many other attorneys who requested that I not quote them by name. I thank them all for their professionalism, knowledge, and unswerving dedication to serving a vulnerable population.

The Executive Office of Immigration Review—the federal agency that oversees the federal immigration courts—does not permit sitting judges to speak publicly. Nonetheless, a number of judges discussed, under the cover of anonymity, the challenges of working in the immigration court system and of adjudicating juvenile cases. Their perspective is a critical addition to this study.

I want to express my gratitude to Maureen Dunn, then director of the Division of Unaccompanied Children's Services at the Office of Refugee Resettlement (ORR), who approved my request to visit federal facilities and to interview staff members. I also thank her colleagues Elaine Kelley and Jallyn Sualog, who assisted with the logistics of on-site visits. Communication liaison Lisa Raffonelli provided comprehensive statistics on ORR admissions, staffing, and release for 2012 and 2013. I interviewed supervisors, case managers, clinicians, teachers, and youth care workers acting under contract to the government. I appreciate their time and candid commentaries on everyday life in the custodial system. Most of them declined to be quoted by name, so I identify only those staff members who had retired or changed jobs or specifically agreed to be identified.

I am particularly indebted to the social workers from the Safe Haven program at the Lutheran Immigration and Refugee Services who worked under contract to the government until September 30, 2010. They drove me to far-flung facilities, explained arcane regulations, and permitted me to observe the interviews they conducted with detained youth. For their extraordinary generosity I would like to acknowledge Jasmin Hernandez, Zrinka Ivkovic, Aileen Moore, Alexandra Peralta, Annaken Toews, Michaela Vergara, and Lauren Wichterman. I am also indebted to the many child welfare experts I interviewed at the United States Conference of Catholic Bishops. I also want to thank the directors and staff of federal foster care and unaccompanied refugee minor programs in Phoenix, Arizona; Worcester, Massachusetts; Grand Rapids and East Lansing, Michigan; Richmond, Virginia; and Seattle and Tacoma, Washington, who graciously agreed to organize my on-site visits and arranged for interviews with local foster parents, formerly detained young people, attorneys, social workers, clinicians, and school officials.

The heart of the book comes from the stories of young people who braved nearly insurmountable obstacles to get to the United States. Only one youth wanted his real name to be used: Modesto Boton-Rodriguez. His story of educational and professional accomplishment is what I would wish for all young people who seek refuge and opportunity in this country.

I am immensely grateful to the Woodrow Wilson International Center for Scholars for funding a 2012–13 fellowship that provided the time and space for me to write the book. I had the companionship of an exemplary class of Wilson Center fellows from across the academy, journalism, and government service, as well as permanent scholars and administrators. I would like to recognize Cynthia Arnson, Kim Connor, Rob Litwak, Helma Lutz, Cornelia Pillard, Andrew Seele, Josh Stacher, Philippa Sturm, and Gail Triner. The law study group organized by Philippa Sturm was a wonderful venue in which to share work in progress. The Wilson Center assigned me an exemplary student research assistant, Melody Ojeda, who gathered reams of valuable government data. Finally, I owe special thanks to Wilson Center director Jane Harman for supporting a special Wilson Center program in February 2013 that gave three undocumented Georgetown students—Citlalli Alvarez,

Francisco Gutierrez, and Kim Maima—the opportunity to share their stories. Working closely with those young people to organize the event was one of the highlights of my 2012–13 fellowship year.

Generous support for research travel was provided by Graduate School Summer Research fellowships in 2009, 2010, and 2012 and five years of grants-in-aid from Georgetown University. Additional writing support came from a 2012 National Endowment for the Humanities Summer Fellowship and a 2013 Senior Faculty Fellowship from Georgetown University. Four Georgetown students provided indispensable research support. Laura Brace transcribed recorded interviews, Jennifer Lizbeth Vargas conducted interviews and shared her story, Citlalli Alvarez proofread the entire manuscript, and a recent graduate of Georgetown Law School and undergraduate anthropology major, Eleanor Hagan, researched all the case law sources, thus saving me the embarrassment of incorrectly citing references or confusing citation styles.

For their helpful comments on fellowship applications and book chapters I would like to thank my academic colleagues Fida Adely, Peter Baker, Susan Coutin, Debbie Boehm, Denise Brennan, Rochelle Davis, Elzbieta Gozdziak, Susan Hirsch, Joanne Rappaport, and David Rosen. I am indebted to all those who shared data, suggested reading, provided contacts, and sent postings from television, radio, print, and social media: Harold Arteaga, Susan Carroll, Elliott Colla, Shalyn Fluharty, Elzbieta Gozdziak, Lauren Heidbrink, Robert Juceam, Elizabeth Kennedy, Laurie King, Ken Mayeaux, Elizabeth Stephen, and Marjorie Zatz.

Just as I was searching for a book cover I had the good fortune to make contact with an extraordinarily gifted photojournalist, Michelle Frankfurter. She has spent the past two decades documenting the journeys of Central American and Mexican migrants to the United States. Michelle graciously allowed me to use her beautiful, haunting photographs for the cover and the interior of the book. They illustrate perfectly the treacherous journey young migrants make in search of a safe harbor.

Finally, I am extremely fortunate to work with a wonderful editor at the University of California Press, Maura Roessner, whose guidance and excitement about this book spurred me to finish ahead of schedule. On the production side of the press, Jack Young has been a model of efficiency and responsiveness. I am deeply grateful to Susan Coutin and Marjorie Zatz, superb law and migration scholars who reviewed the finished manuscript and made excellent suggestions for its revision.

I must also recognize my Radcliffe sisters, Tera Hunter, Salem Mekuria, Eve Trout-Powell, and Betty Shamieh for their unquestioning love and support since we met at Harvard in 2005. They are among the first friends I turn to when I feel the need to complain, celebrate, or mourn. As always my deepest gratitude and love go to my husband Steve, daughters Kristin and Stephanie, and grandchildren Syd, Gabe, Noah and Ben, and close friends who support my work but also entice me to put it down and spend time together enjoying good food, red wine, and plenty of laughter.

The American Dream

That American dream of a better, richer, and happier life for
all our citizens of every rank . . . is the greatest contribution
we have yet made to the thought and welfare of the world.

—James Truslow Adams, *The Epic of America*

On September 5, 2012, Benita Veliz, an undocumented youth advocate from San Antonio, Texas, took the podium during prime-time coverage of the Democratic National Convention. She made a plea for immigration reform and urged fellow Latinos to reelect President Barack Obama because, she said, "he fought for my community." Benita was brought to the United States as a child "like so many Americans of all races and backgrounds." Unlike most of her U.S. citizen peers, Benita graduated at sixteen as the valedictorian of her high school and finished college at twenty with a double major, a record that would have made her eligible for citizenship if the Dream Act had passed in the U.S. Senate in 2010. First proposed in 2001 by Illinois senator Dick Durbin with bipartisan support, it was designed to give legal status to young immigrants who had entered the country before the age of sixteen and completed college study or military service. Benita explained, "I feel just as American as any of my friends and neighbors. But I've had to live almost my entire life knowing that I could be deported." She reminded her listeners, "When Congress failed to pass [the Dream Act], President Obama . . . took action so people like me can apply to stay in the country and contribute." On June 15, 2012, late in the presidential campaign and under pressure from Latino groups, Obama issued an executive order that offered a temporary reprieve from deportation and short-term work authorization to young immigrants like her.

Benita vowed that Dreamers would continue to fight for permanent legal status, but "while we do we're able to work steady, to pursue the American Dream."

At a San Diego federal detention center for unaccompanied minors the same summer, Elizabeth Kennedy, a graduate student volunteer, asked the five kids in the English-language class she taught to write a story describing what the American Dream meant to them. The children had not been brought to the United States like Benita but came from their home countries in Central America and Mexico on their own or with smugglers, risking their lives to cross the treacherous border terrain. They were all apprehended within hours by U.S. immigration authorities, scheduled for deportation proceedings, and detained in a closed federal facility pending a hearing in the San Diego immigration court. After screening by staff and local attorneys under contract to the government, they would be released to approved U.S. sponsors, sent back, or, if no sponsors were available, held in custody until they turned eighteen or they requested voluntary departure. The new arrivals were young, between thirteen and seventeen. They had left home with idealized visions of life in the United States wrought from media images and migrants' tales of the plentiful work and easy money to be made. In detention too the American Dream narrative was all around them in cheerful images, inspirational messages, and group activities.

The children wrote that they missed home, but few wanted to return because they were sure that life would be better on this side of the border. They would be loved and want for nothing. They dreamed of going to school, landing good jobs, and having a middle-class life. They were optimistic about the future in spite of the poverty, abuse, and neglect many had suffered. A number of the children made the journey to join a parent who had migrated in search of work and to be part of the families their parents had established in the United States. Others came in search of refuge and new attachments after violence back home tore their families apart. One thirteen-year old girl I will call Juanita wrote:

> I have always dreamt of being in the United States with my dad. I came because I want to know my dad because he loves me and to see my brother and sister who are here. I will realize my dream of being a legal secretary, to study English and music, to have my legal papers, get a car, and to continue studying hard. I don't want to suffer anymore in Guatemala. I haven't seen my brother in eleven years and my little sister was born here.

Juanita's fourteen-year-old classmate named Pedro explained:

> I would like a pretty house with a pool and a park. I would like to be a licensed linguist. I would like to have a dad. My family and my grandparents have all died, my dad left with another woman, and my mom looked for another man. I would like a family and to have peaches to eat every day.

A serious fifteen-year-old named Jesús said:

> We come for different reasons, but we all have high hopes and ideas. My biggest dream is to go to school.

DREAMERS AND DETAINEES

Dreamers like Benita have been the poster children for immigration reform because their work ethic and sacrifices earned them scholastic achievements that appear to defy the odds. Sen. Dick Durbin, their long-time supporter, has taken the Senate floor every year to urge passage of the Dream Act. "These kids didn't make the decision to come to this country," he said on one such occasion. "It was a decision made by their parents and if they were breaking the law, I don't believe the children should be held responsible."[1] The Dreamers' stories tell the wrenching tale of children raised in the United States by parents of humble origins who arrived with little money but great faith in the opportunity for a better life. These young people embody American values and confirm the promise of the Dream yet live under the constant threat of deportation. The underlying message is that they should be awarded the political recognition of citizenship, unlike the willful "aliens" who continue to breach the border and threaten national security. Despite the color of their skin, Dreamers can be viewed as honorific Americans because of their command of English, cultural capital, and embrace of mainstream identity.

In contrast to the public attention lavished on Dreamers like Benita, until recently little has been reported in the mainstream media about the thousands of undocumented children like Juanita or Jesús who came alone in pursuit of the American Dream and landed in federal detention. When journalists wrote about undocumented families, they focused on the U.S. citizen children who were caught up in immigration sweeps and mistakenly deported or chronicled the ordeal of living in families where some members have citizenship and others do not. Before 2014 reports on immigration detention exposed the appalling conditions of unauthorized adults but largely ignored the treatment of unaccompanied children in federal custody.

A vulnerable population that has been hidden from public scrutiny and absent from immigration debates for years suddenly became breaking news in 2014, when shocking pictures of kids in detention centers began circulating in the media. The number of children detained at the Southwest border since October 2013 had surpassed 57,000 by July 2014 and was climbing rapidly.[2] News reports since then have galvanized the public, creating both sympathy and alarm. We have heard stories of Central American migrants as young as four or five packed into overcrowded holding cells and witnessed anti-immigrant protesters banning these children from entering their communities by blocking buses[3] or even passing resolutions.[4] Facing what President Obama called an "urgent humanitarian crisis," his administration has been scrambling to set up additional shelters, and the president has promised to "stem the tide" of further migration, asking Congress for emergency funding to aid the effort. Critics of the administration blamed the crisis on lax border security, while advocates described the children forced to flee gang and cartel violence in Mexico and Central America[5] as refugees.[6]

Children migrating alone have compelling reasons to leave home. They see the journey north as necessary—a chance to reunite with undocumented parents "on the other side" or a hedge against domestic abuse, predatory police, forced gang conscription, and drug traffickers. The murder of younger and younger victims by gangs is a major factor fueling the exodus of children from Central America.[7] After a treacherous journey they risk their lives crossing the border through barren desert or the swift currents of the Rio Grande, endure abuse by smugglers or gangs en route, experience coercive arrests by the Border Patrol, and wage a prolonged, uphill battle to stay in the United States legally.

In addition to these new arrivals, increasing numbers of teenagers have been identified and referred to immigration authorities by police, probation officers, juvenile judges, or child protective services because of their unlawful status.[8] Like the Dreamers, they were brought to the United States as young children and grew up here. Unlike the Dreamers, many were designated as unaccompanied because they were too afraid to identify their undocumented family members after they were apprehended. As a result, they were removed from their families, held in federal custody, and put into removal proceedings. Many of these youths face removal from the United States because they are ineligible for legal status. Although like the Dreamers they are culturally American, they are not "good" victims. Both groups—the recent arrivals and the long-term residents—are questionable symbols of vulnerability. Even those who ultimately win legal status and settle permanently in the United States say that the stigma of confinement continues long after their release. They suffer for years from the ill effects of separation from family and the trauma of a dangerous journey.

I became interested in this population after researching youth crime in France in 2000–5 and discovering that almost half of the Paris juvenile court cases involved unaccompanied and separated child migrants from Eastern Europe or Africa. They were forced to steal or to prostitute themselves when their attempts to find legal work or to enroll in school failed.[9] How, I wondered, did we deal with the same vulnerable population? This book answers that question. Based on site visits to twenty-six government-contracted detention facilities and foster care and postrelease programs, 140 interviews with federal staff and immigration authorities, observation of 120 hours of immigration court proceedings, and in-depth interviews of thirty-nine formerly detained youth, I tell the story of how the U.S. government got into the business of detaining unaccompanied children. Using data gathered between 2009 and 2012, the period immediately preceding the current surge, I track the evolution of the custodial system. I focus primarily on six youths—Ángel, Carlos, Corina, Ernesto, Maribel, and Modesto—who describe in their own words the lives they left behind in Guatemala, El Salvador, Honduras, and Mexico, their reasons for migrating, the journey north, and what they experienced in government custody. This is their story, a firsthand account of what became of their American Dream.

"I AM AN AMERICAN AND I MAKE MY OWN DESTINY"

The historian James Truslow Adams popularized the phrase "American Dream" in his 1931 book, *Epic of America:* It is "[the] dream of a land in which life should be better and richer and fuller for every man, with opportunity for each according to his ability or achievement."[10] Adams observed that the dream appealed not only to the native born but to the millions of immigrants who were lured to American shores in a quest for both material plenty and the opportunity to "attain the fullest stature of which they are innately capable,"[11] regardless of birth or position. Since the earliest days of the nation, the American Dream has figured prominently in literature, politics, and popular discourse. It is at the core of our national mythology and is intricately bound up with basic American values such as individualism, meritocracy, achievement, optimism, and faith in progress. It translates deeply held beliefs about the openness of social class, the possibility of upward social mobility through hard work, and, more important, the ability of individuals to achieve success by their own efforts. It glorifies economic success and individual initiative. The American Dream remains powerful because it unifies present and would-be Americans around the promise of a better future and the mythic past of an immigrant nation forged from many origins. As a national narrative it is, and must be, silent on the categories of differences that threaten the arc of progress. It consistently downplays the stubborn persistence of poverty and the entrenched inequalities based on class, race, ethnicity, and gender. It ignores the overwhelming evidence that in the twenty-first century the United States has less equality of opportunity than almost any other advanced industrial country, a particularly salient reality for poor immigrant families and children.

Both the enduring power of the dream and its current fragility were on full display in the rhetoric of the 2012 presidential campaign. In the political theater of the party conventions, both nominees, Mitt Romney and Barack Obama, crafted speeches that drew heavily on the American Dream. In his August 30 speech to GOP delegates, Romney repeated Adams almost verbatim by describing Americans as "optimistic, positive, and confident in the future." "That optimism is uniquely American," he continued. "It is what brought us to America. We're a nation of immigrants, the children, grandchildren, and great-grandchildren of the ones who wanted a better life, the driven ones. . . . They came not just in pursuit of riches in the world, but for the richness of this life." Romney highlighted the immigrant beginnings of his family, who fled to the United States from Mexico during the revolution and were treated as war refugees by the U.S. government. He depicted the founding of his equity firm, Bain Capital, as a risky endeavor that became "a great American success story" thanks to his family's ingenuity and hard work. Downplaying his class privilege, family connections, and private school education, he insisted, "I am an American and I make my own destiny."[12]

Obama's September 6 convention speech repeated the same themes. He evoked the "the basic bargain at the heart of America's story" that enabled his grandparents to go to college and opened the doors of Harvard to him and his wife. The bargain is "that hard work will pay off, that responsibility will be rewarded, and that everyone has a fair shot." This narrative put his white mother and her parents on a level playing field with his wife's working-class African American family. Obama spoke of an inclusive social contract that would strengthen the middle class and lift up the neediest, but he added, "As Americans . . . we insist on personal responsibility, we celebrate individual initiative. We're not entitled to success. We have to earn it. We honor the strivers, the risk takers, the entrepreneurs who have always been the engine behind our free enterprise system."[13]

Despite agreement on resonant American values like freedom and work, both candidates' positions revealed deep ideological divides on the role of government in regulating the market, in addressing economic disparities, and in setting national immigration policy. The promise of a postracial society heralded by the 2008 election of the first African American president was a chimera by 2012. Race shaped political narratives and played a prominent role in voting patterns. The GOP won a majority of white votes, whereas Hispanics, Asians, and African Americans voted overwhelmingly for Democrats. The campaign unfolded in the context of demographic anxiety about the shrinking proportion of whites to minorities—Latinos and Asians—and nativist fears about what the loss of a white America would mean for the national culture. The economic crisis of 2008 continued a long-term trend of downward mobility among the middle class as millions lost jobs, homes, and health care. The downturn had a disproportionately negative impact on underemployed and jobless minorities and on young people, particularly those ages eighteen to twenty-four who are the new face of homelessness.[14] Neither nominee explicitly mentioned race, and both avoided a meaningful discussion of class, ignoring the poor and concentrating exclusively on the middle class. Romney contrasted the dream "of every new wave of immigrants" to build a better future with a new reality: "For the first time a majority of Americans now doubt that their children will be better off than they are."[15] Although the median net worth of whites is roughly twenty times higher than that of African Americans and Hispanics, whites expressed much more pessimism about the direction of the country and their own future prospects.[16] When whites are no longer the majority, will the United States still be the same country? If the institutions of social mobility and national security that whites have always counted on—the schools, the labor market, and the economy—are broken, is the American Dream itself in jeopardy?

RACE, IMMIGRATION, AND THE LAW

Adams's *Epic of America* appeared less than a decade after the passage of landmark legislation in 1924, the Reed-Johnson Act, which ended the era of open immigration from Europe and signaled the beginnings of stringent restrictions.[17] It established for the first time numerical

limits based on national origins and aligned quotas with the racial hierarchies of the time. The law inaugurated a new emphasis on both territorial integrity and muscular control over the nation's contiguous land
borders. It reaffirmed all the restrictions on the admittance of undesira-
bles codified in the Immigration Act of 1907, namely, idiots, imbeciles,
the insane, criminals, polygamists, anarchists, and persons likely to
become a public charge. It took legal practices that had justified racial
discrimination against African Americans through separate but equal
policies and extended them to other ethnoracial groups in immigration
law: Asians, southern Europeans, and those of "the Semitic race."[18]
Most important, the law created a new category of illegal alien[19] that
stood in sharp contrast to the citizen as the only formal bearer of
inalienable rights.[20] Its sponsor, a junior senator, David Reed, shared
his congressional committee's concern with "racial purity" and their
fear that the rising immigrant tide would bring "races that would mon-
grelize and weaken hardy American stock."[21] Writing in the *New York
Times,* Reed warned that the new immigrants could not be expected
to assimilate as their predecessors had: "America can no longer tolerate
the irritation of her 'foreign colonies'—those groups of aliens who
speak a foreign language and live a foreign life and who want neither to
learn our common speech nor to share our common life."[22]

Forty years later, in 1965, President Lyndon B. Johnson signed the
Hart-Cellas Act into law in a dramatic overhaul of immigration policy
that abolished national origin quotas and made family reunification the
basis for legal status. Although widely viewed as a major reform, because
it corrected what Johnson called "a cruel and enduring wrong in the
conduct of the American nation," Hart-Cellas imposed other restrictions
that are still with us today.[23] It extended the principle of formal equality
in admission to all countries and imposed national quotas of 20,000
entrants for each country in the western hemisphere. The unintended
result was that the law created greater opportunities for migration from
Asia and Africa while severely restricting it from Mexico, the Caribbean,
and Latin America. It ended the annual legal Mexican migration of
200,000 bracero workers and 35,000 permanent residents. After 1965,
the majority of Mexican migrants became illegal aliens, and the number
of apprehensions and deportations skyrocketed from 151,000 in 1968
to 781,000 in 1976. These immigration enforcement policies and the
statistical evidence used to support them have created the mistaken
but enduring perception that "Mexican" is a synonym for migrant illegality.[24]

Contemporary warnings about America's "Mexifornias" that are overrun with Spanish-speaking "illegals" who commit crimes, undercut wages, spread disease, refuse to learn English, and produce anchor babies at government expense recall early-twentieth-century anti-immigrant views. Then, eugenicists, politicians, novelists, and even Progressive-era sociologists and reformers decried the dangers of immigrant crime and poverty in crowded tenements and issued dire predictions of race suicide as a result of hereditary defects in the blood of unwanted immigrants. Now, virulent resistance to undocumented immigration is expressed by a combination of unemployed workers, nationalists, nativists, demagogic political opportunists, and conservatives, as well as liberals who fear that these immigrants will swamp the welfare system and swell the ranks of the unemployed. The Southern Poverty Law Center, which tracks hate groups, documented the role of the eugenicist John Tanton in founding the Federation for American Immigration Reform (FAIR), Numbers USA, and the Center for Immigration Studies, all important groups in the anti-immigrant movement.[25] The Latino threat is embodied in the images of the drug runner, the human smuggler, and the gang banger.[26] The stereotypes that underlie these images have been reinforced by grassroots rallies, citizen militias, talk radio, movies, and television shows such as Arizona sheriff Joe Arpaio's three-episode pilot on the Fox Reality Channel. The cable shows *Border Wars, Law on the Border,* and *Border Battles* glorify the enforcement efforts of beleaguered agents struggling to hold back the flood of illegal aliens who wreck havoc on communities.

Terms such as *racial purity* have largely disappeared from public usage, but racial thinking is expressed in coded language about work, education, immigration, and entitlements. During the primaries, GOP candidates advocated a return to the opportunity society and lamented Obama's entitlement society. Newt Gingrich mocked Obama as the "food stamp" president, and Romney's campaign warned that under Obama, "you wouldn't have to work or train. They would just send you a welfare check." "Entitlement society" is racial code for disadvantaged minorities and illegal aliens who get undeserved handouts funded by taxpayers; "opportunity society" refers to the white mainstream population who have to work hard for what they earn.[27] The shrill taunt, "What is it about illegal that you don't understand?," usually targets Latinos— not only the undocumented but also legal residents and U.S. citizens. The Harvard political scientist Samuel Huntington best expressed the racialized anxiety about the loss of national identity in the wake of fears linked to a burgeoning Latino population. In a widely cited 2004 article, he warned against the lump of unassimilated Spanish-speaking immigrants and the threat they pose to the Anglo-Protestant culture that has been central to American identity for three centuries. "There is no Americano Dream," he insisted. "There is only the American Dream created by an Anglo-Protestant society."[28] As comprehensive immigration reform efforts gathered steam in Congress in 2013, racist diatribes specifically targeted undocumented Latino youth. Rep. Steve King of Iowa likened them to livestock, insisting that for every Dreamer valedictorian there were one hundred drug mules who had "calves the size of cantaloupes" from hauling huge bales of marijuana across the desert.[29] When the number of unaccompanied children crossing the U.S.-Mexico border from October 2013 to June 2014 surged to 57,525,[30] moral panic centered on the threat of criminality and disease they posed.

THE STATE OF EXCEPTION FOR UNACCOMPANIED ALIEN CHILDREN

The state of exception legislated for "Unaccompanied Alien Children" (UAC) has an unsettling history.[31] In 1984, during the Salvadoran civil war, there was another large-scale migration of children to the United States as thousands of youth fled violence at home and headed north. Until that time U.S. immigration authorities had routinely released detained children to parents or family members already living in the United States pending immigration court hearings. But citing the need to protect vulnerable children caught up in a humanitarian emergency and using their broad powers to detain noncitizens, in 1984 authorities in the western division of the Immigration and Naturalization Service (the precursor to Immigration and Customs Enforcement [ICE] and Customs and Border Protection [CBP], the immigration enforcement agencies within the Department of Homeland Security [DHS]) made automatic detention the new norm and release the exception.[32] Once the state of exception was firmly established, the rationale for detaining a vulnerable population became both a self-authorizing status and a moral imperative. Federal authorities continued to defend detention even when legal aid organizations in California sued them for confining children under the punitive conditions usually reserved for violent offenders.[33] Children as young as fourteen, who posed no security threat or flight risk, were incarcerated with adult criminals and adjudicated youths, subjected to handcuffing and shackling, and deprived of legal and social services.

A 1985 class action lawsuit challenged the government's indefinite detention of undocumented minors and the harsh treatment they received. After years of litigation, in 1993 the Supreme Court affirmed the government's right to detain undocumented children in secure facilities for unspecified, and sometimes prolonged, periods pending release to approved sponsors and an appearance in immigration court.[34] Faced with continuing legal challenges, the federal government agreed in 1997 to establish minimum standards for their humane treatment, to hold them in the least restrictive setting, and to ensure their prompt release.[35]

Federal authorities have continued to justify detention as a humanitarian response to exceptional conditions of instability and displacement. Intake teams are on standby 24/7 to admit undocumented children who are determined to be unaccompanied because they are under eighteen and without parents or guardians in the United States who are able and willing to provide care. Paradoxically, a permanent state of emergency now exists. Detention is not a temporary suspension of law and policy in crisis situations. Rather, when coupled with selective deportations, it serves as the dominant paradigm for managing the increasing numbers of undocumented Central American and Mexican children who are apprehended annually by immigration authorities.

The federal custodial system is a constantly expanding leviathan that now costs taxpayers close to a billion dollars a year and affects thousands of families.[36] Between 2004 and 2010 the budget for the custodial system soared from $53 million to $225 million and included thirty-seven full-time administrative staff members working with thirteen contracting agencies to oversee thirty-nine facilities with 1,561 beds.[37] Beginning in 2011 the number of arrivals spiked. A new record was set in 2012 when the total admissions reached 14,721, requiring the rapid recruitment and training of additional staff. By 2012 sixty-four federal and contract staff members managed sixty-nine facilities with 2,927 beds.[38] In 2013 there were 25,041 children in eighty-three government facilities and programs with roughly 5,000 beds.[39] Federal authorities projected that in 2014 new admissions of unaccompanied children could balloon to 74,000; a 2015 estimate of 130,000 represents a cost of $2 billion.[40] The estimate for 2014 was subsequently lowered by USCCB, an ORR subcontractor that reported there were 61,340 admissions to 114 federal facilities.[41]

The overwhelming majority of those in federal detention come from Guatemala, El Salvador, and Honduras, a pattern that has remained constant since the 1980s. Children in custody are younger than ever before, with 24 percent under the age of fourteen in 2013, up from 17 percent in 2012. New data analyzed by the Pew Research Center show a 117 percent increase in the number of unaccompanied children ages twelve and younger apprehended at the U.S.-Mexico border to date this year (May 31, 2014), compared to the last fiscal year.[42] The number of unaccompanied teenagers ages thirteen through seventeen increased by 12 percent, and nongovernmental organizations (NGOs) report a dramatic increase in the number of young girls, who now make up 40 percent of the total. Among all countries, Mexico had the highest number of unaccompanied minors apprehended at the border (17,219) in 2013, but in July 2014 far fewer Mexicans (11,550) than Hondurans (13,244) were in CBP custody.[43] Undocumented Mexican children are underrepresented in federal custody[44] because the vast majority are quickly deported after apprehension.

The apprehension of undocumented, unaccompanied children ensnares them in two parallel but separate federal systems: mandatory detention and removal proceedings in immigration court. The children enter a labyrinthine system that encompasses Border Patrol stations, ICE centers, subcontracted facilities and programs for minors in thirteen states,[45] and immigration courts. Federal policy manuals describe custody as necessary to protect a vulnerable population from "smugglers, traffickers and others who would victimize or exploit them" and to neutralize "the danger they may pose to themselves or others."[46] Detaining child migrants is also a guarantee that they will appear at all removal hearings or legal proceedings initiated against them.[47] Huge resources go to electronic detection, risk assessments, psychosocial evaluations, preliminary legal screenings, detention bed space, staff recruitment, immigration adjudications, and deportations, whereas legal representation for all children in immigration court, comprehensive postrelease tracking, and long-term social services are not funded. While the Department of Health and Human Services through the Office of Refugee Resettlement (ORR) assigns itself as the legal guardian for unaccompanied children and operates facilities to hold them, the enforcement branches of the Department of Homeland Security—Customs and Border Protection and Immigration and Customs Enforcement—and the Department of Justice sweep up and prosecute the very same children.

Detention centers are spaces of exception where the competing agendas of humanitarianism and security collide.[48] One agenda, informed by Western child welfare standards, centers on the individual child as a dependent victim and emphasizes compassion and protection. It relies on a conception of children as developing beings who are vulnerable to coercion and in need of protection from the obligations and violent disruptions of adult society. This agenda is centered on trauma, pathology, exploitation, and victimhood. It prioritizes attending to the immediate needs of new arrivals who are hungry, exhausted, disoriented, and, sometimes, ill or hurt. It likewise recognizes the basic rights of confined children to education, visitation, health care, recreation, social services, cultural identity, legal assistance, and safe release. It is designed to facilitate rapid release and reunification with family or approved sponsors. Nonetheless, this agenda does not treat children as autonomous and important participants in the decision to leave home, to cross borders, and to work.[49]

The humanitarian agenda conflicts with a second, more political, and better-funded approach that favors security and punitive enforcement. It is dominated by discussions of accountability and choice and views immigrant children as alternately threatening and burdensome. The priority is to reduce risk, limit mobility, discipline families, and engineer the social body through decisions related to sponsors and residence.[50] These control mechanisms are intended to reinforce security by holding greater numbers of children in highly regulated facilities, isolating suspected offenders and flight risks in secure detention, and removing large numbers of unaccompanied youth, particularly Mexicans, through deportation or voluntary departure.

The regimented custodial care of children stands in stark contrast to the lack of legal protection afforded them in federal immigration courts. Current U.S. immigration law prohibits funding for direct legal representation and competent advocacy for children in removal proceedings. It excludes best interest considerations for minors in court hearings. The U.S. government took a series of "historic steps" in 2014 to fund legal representation for 2,700 undocumented children after their release from custody. This funding will affect only a fraction of those expected to appear in removal proceedings.[51] Most of these children will continue to face immigration judges and government prosecutors without the benefit of legal counsel or a child advocate in backlogged immigration courtrooms.

In immigration law legal status is achieved and held by individuals, not by families. In the absence of parents U.S. immigration law treats children as functional adults in terms of substantive rules, evidentiary requirements, and burden of proof criteria without giving them the necessary safeguards for their developmental immaturity, cultural incapacity, and special vulnerability.[52] They are held accountable in the same way as adults when they are enjoined to find competent pro bono legal representation on their own and to make high stakes decisions with regard to release from custody, family reunification, and return to the home country. Since most child migrants are ineligible for the limited forms of legal relief available under U.S. law, their choices after release involve living in the shadows and risking deportation or agreeing to return to their home countries.

⚹ Like the refugee camp,[53] the closed federal facility responds to problems of public order and border security by creating spaces of exception.[54] Confinement is not a final solution to the dilemmas posed by the lack of legal status but the temporary defense of minimal existence. It is a bare life that is highly controlled and bereft of full social and political rights.[55] The suspension of national and international norms premised on the detention of children is accepted only because it applies to undesirable subjects. A situation that would be considered intolerable if it were applied to white middle-class U.S. citizen children is accepted because of the perceived threat they pose as "illegal aliens."

For years the rights deficits of young migrants without legal status have been blamed on their invisibility. The implication is that public advocacy would generate change if their unique challenges were made known. Jacqueline Bhabha argues that visibility is not the issue. It is rather "an unresolved ambivalence" about the legitimacy of protecting "alien" children that explains persistent policy failures.[56]

DEPORTATION NATION

Over the past twenty-five years, unauthorized immigration has been conflated with crime and terrorism and portrayed as a new and dangerous threat to national security. Fear of "illegals" has produced a public consensus on tighter enforcement as part of any comprehensive immigration reform proposal. Distrust of the undocumented congeals all the familiar racial anxieties, undermining "democratic norms and fostering a punitive state long before the current 'war on terror.'"[57] The immigration and terrorism laws passed in 1996 and again after September 11, 2001, represented a significant shift in the assessment of risk and in the methods needed to contain it. These statutes have curtailed existing personal freedoms, gutted due process protections, given unparalleled enforcement powers to immigration authorities, blurred the boundary between criminal and immigration law, and limited judicial review of detention and deportation decisions.[58] Deportability—the ever-present possibility of being deported—is the condition of both the undocumented and legal residents who, despite some protections, remain removable.[59]

By expanding the categories of deportable offenses to include nonviolent misdemeanors, applying them retroactively to include acts committed "at any time" in a person's life, and eliminating the exercise of discretion by immigration judges in most deportation cases, these laws have allowed the state to wield arbitrary power against groups who are being targeted on the basis of racialized national identities and held to harsh standards of unauthorized conduct.[60] In immigration enforcement, race may be used as a factor in determining whether a person is undocumented. Border Patrol agents typically record the skin color of the people they arrest.[61] "Driving while brown," as one California immigration attorney put it, puts one at risk for traffic stops by police in states on the Southwest border that have large Latino populations. Supreme Court doctrine gives local police wide discretion to follow, stop, frisk, and deploy excessive force against suspects. As a result, a higher body of law "continues to expose African Americans and Latinos to surveillance, harassment, violence—and death."[62] More than border security or social control, current deportation policies are "a living legacy of the ideas about race, imperialism, and harsh government power" that we have grappled with since the founding of the nation.[63]

By the time Benita took center stage at the 2012 Democratic National Convention, a renewed emphasis on enforcement and security had resulted in a militarized southern border and the criminalization of migration through increased apprehensions and prosecutions, robust collaboration between local police and federal authorities to identify undocumented persons, the failure of even modest comprehensive immigration reforms, and the shattering of families after the apprehension and separation of undocumented parents from their U.S. citizen children. The frantic crackdown on the undocumented has channeled huge resources to contain exaggerated sources of harm. In 2010, John Morton, head of ICE, pledged to focus enforcement efforts on criminal aliens. Instead, in the twenty-six-month period from July 2010 to September 2012, ICE deported more than two hundred thousand immigrant parents who have U.S. citizen children, most of whom were charged with minor offenses.[64]

The large-scale deportation regime in the United States created a "formidable machinery" of enforcement that imposes harsh penalties for immigration law violations and relies on a massive and well-funded detention system.[65] The annual total number of detainees increased from 88,730 to 429,247 between fiscal years 1995 and 2011. That dramatic increase mirrors the mass incarceration that grew out of a domestic war on crime. Despite a drop in violent crime that began in the 1990s, the U.S. prison population has risen to a high of 1.6 million, a figure that represents 22.4 percent of the world's inmates.[66] To detect, apprehend, and detain unauthorized immigrants,[67] the government spent a gargantuan sum—$18 billion—on enforcement, more than the total expenditures for all its criminal enforcement agencies combined.[68] Despite a massive investment in sophisticated surveillance technology, fencing, military aircraft, and additional Border Patrol agents to secure the border and wage a global war on terror, the threat from international terrorists has been negligible. Instead, the vast majority of the adults who were apprehended and detained were labor migrants, people crossing the border in the hope of finding work. They found primarily low-wage work as nannies, maids, or day laborers.

During the 2008 campaign, Obama pledged a balanced approach to immigration policy. Instead his administration has focused almost exclusively on enforcement, deporting a record two million undocumented immigrants during his first six years in office. That number was nearly as many as the total deported during the two terms of the George W. Bush presidency.[69] In the 2012 election campaign, Obama promised less enforcement by increasing the use of "prosecutorial discretion" to close the deportation proceedings of immigrants who had U.S. citizen children, strong ties to the community, and no criminal records. This initiative generated great hopes but produced few results. After reviewing 298,173 cases for potential relief, Immigration and Customs Enforcement closed only 5,684, or 1.9 percent, of the total proceedings as of June 28, 2012.[70]

Obama has once again used his executive authority to announce a new deferred action program, this time for the parents of U.S. citizens or Legal Permanent Residents, who will get temporary relief from deportation and work authorization for three years. This November 19, 2014, order also expands the 2012 executive order for child arrivals to include those who were brought to the United States before January 1, 2010. However, the White House insisted that the administration's "aggressive and coordinated Federal response" to the 2014 influx of unaccompanied children to the U.S. border would continue with a focus on "heightened deterrence, enhanced enforcement, stronger foreign cooperation, and greater capacity to secure our borders."[71] The new executive order directed immigration courts to prioritize the removal cases of "recent border crossers," a reference to unaccompanied children and single mothers with young children.

A NEW AMERICAN STORY

This is the story of what happens to child migrants like Ángel, Carlos, Corina, Ernesto, Mirabel, and Modesto who are apprehended and detained every year. To put their stories in the appropriate context, I examine the litigation and legal debates surrounding a federal system that insiders and outsiders alike describe as disjointed and labyrinthine. I explore the contrasting perspectives of staff, attorneys, and youths on "child-centered custody," protection, and risk and follow children into removal proceedings in federal court. They discuss the limited avenues for legal relief available to the "Unaccompanied Alien Child" under U.S. immigration law, as well as the difficult choices these proceedings demand. I provide the differing perspectives of immigration attorneys and judges on the challenges that children face in court and the reforms needed to repair a broken system. Throughout the book, I include extended narratives of youths who attempt to make sense of American notions of justice, law, rights, and accountability as they struggle to realize a version of the American Dream while remaining part of families that stretch across national borders.

In early February 2013 three undergraduate Dreamers from Georgetown University, Francisco, Kim, and Citlalli, told "a new American story" at a public event I helped them organize as a resident fellow in 2012–13 at the Woodrow Wilson International Center in Washington.[72] Their story places Dreamers and detainees within the same narrative of possibility and uncertainty, of hope and loss. Francisco, a senior business major at Georgetown, reminded listeners, "The story of undocumented youth is . . . about the families and homes we've established, about the daily interactions in our immigrant communities, and the interconnected stories between all of us." All three grew up in the United States with parents who encouraged them to believe "that the American Dream belongs to everyone, no matter where they come from." Finding out that they were "illegal" exploded that myth. Kim, a sophomore in the School of Foreign Service, evoked the constant, suffocating ordeal of "a life filled with uncertainty every minute, every hour." Choking on sobs, she added, "It is a story of closed doors, of broken dreams, broken families, split up because of deportation. . . . [I]t is a story of depression, stress, and fear, and the psychological toll of being in this country and not having any of the freedoms that so many people enjoy. . . . [A] pathway to citizenship is just about being human in this country. We have lost the freedom to be mobile, the freedom to provide for our families, our freedom to just feel like we exist."

2

Which Way Home?

Rebecca Cammisa's 2010 Oscar-nominated documentary, *Which Way Home,* follows Central American children on the 1,450-mile journey through Mexico en route to the United States on top of a freight train known as the Beast (la Bestia). The film opens with the image of a bloated corpse caught in the swift current of the Rio Grande. U.S. Customs and Border Protection agents identify the body as that of a minor who drowned trying to cross into the United States. This death marks the end of one child's American Dream. It also serves as a cautionary tale. We meet Kevin, a streetwise fourteen-year-old Honduran, who "has always dreamed of the U.S." so he can find work and help his mother. We are also introduced to his childhood friend Fito whose dream is to be adopted by a U.S. family. Along the way they meet Yurico, a Mexican street kid, who wants "to free himself from drugs" and find a "better life." In a macabre acknowledgment of the lucrative traffic in migrant death, Yurico imagines selling crosses for cemeteries.

Their journeys north, like those of other youths in the film, mostly end in disappointment and a return to the home country—either dead or alive. After he crosses the first time Kevin is apprehended and detained in a federal shelter in Houston, where he feels "cornered and locked up." After two months he is returned to Honduras, where he remains for a year before attempting a second crossing. He is again caught and transferred to a minimum-security shelter near Los Angeles (this is where our paths crossed briefly in 2010). Kevin hopes to get legal status and remain in the United States; Fito and Yurico abandon the journey.[1] Yurico returns to his drug habit and life on the street. In one of the last scenes we see him in the public square high from sniffing glue. He is determined to return to the United States when he turns eighteen.

Cammisa's film is particularly powerful because child migrants speak for themselves and share their views of home, family, and the magnetic lure of El Norte. In this chapter I introduce Ángel, Carlos, Corina, Ernesto, and Mirabel, whose home countries, like 90 percent of the unaccompanied child migrants to the United States,[2] are Mexico, El Salvador, Guatemala, and Honduras.[3] These are countries where social inequality is high, livable wages are scarce, and violence is a scourge in the home and the community.[4] Their stories chronicle the persistence of rural poverty in traditional agrarian areas as well as the appearance of a "new poverty" experienced predominantly by urban dwellers.[5] More of the urban poor are young people who are relegated to long-term job insecurity and reduced social mobility despite higher levels of education. Within excluded populations, youth, women, and indigenous groups remain the most vulnerable. They suffer most from the effects of chaotic urbanization patterns, the lack of public services, and the everyday insecurities that flow from weak state legitimacy and underdeveloped civil institutions.[6]

Punitive U.S. immigration laws, harsh gang abatement policies, and the war on drugs have a corrosive effect on life in Central America and Mexico. Thousands of Mara Salvatrucha and 18th Street gang members in Los Angeles who are deported back to the "home country" reconstitute themselves in El Salvador and spread their operations to Guatemala and Honduras. The exportation of U.S. zero-tolerance policing strategies to Central America alongside the deportation of gang youth fuels more undocumented immigration, this time as a result of the combined pressures from gang, cartel, and state violence. The insatiable demand for drugs in the U.S. market has spawned new criminal cartels, creating murderous competition over smuggling routes and distribution networks. Young people see firsthand the intensification of lawlessness, the political corruption, the extrajudicial killings, and the armed gangs and drug cartels that infect all spheres of social life.[7] Migration is a calculated wager against the certainty of a social or a physical death if they remain at home.[8]

As an expendable, surplus workforce in their home communities, young people understand that selling their labor abroad is the only option.

FIGURE 1. Guatemalan boy shining shoes in the southern Mexican border city of Tapachula. Photo by Michelle Frankfurter.

More than mere survival, they want to thrive and "to be someone." They view honest work as a prerequisite for the blessings and challenges of a normal life. Some insist that their goal is education and self-improvement, but it is impossible to know how important this is for youth who are mistreated, malnourished, forced to leave school and put to work, or left homeless and emotionally starved after the loss of family (figure 1).

These migrants travel alone or in groups, hire smugglers, or venture into uncharted areas without help, often carrying only a change of clothes, a U.S. phone number scribbled on a scrap of paper, and cash hidden in the soles of shoes or sewn inside the linings of clothes. They witness or survive robberies, fall victim to brutal attacks or sexual assaults, and outrun or hide from federal police and Border Patrol agents but also fall prey to criminal gangs and drug cartels whose specialty is kidnapping and extortion. They struggle with hunger, illness, and exposure to the elements and see fellow migrants lose limbs or die while jumping freight trains. To keep fear and loneliness at bay, they bond with fellow travelers and savor the occasional kindnesses offered by strangers. Young migrants escape detection by adopting false identities, disguising social ties, and feigning distance from their real families. This is only a temporary protective shield because it places them outside the law and consigns them to spaces where they do not officially exist. Only later do they realize how necessary it is to establish a paper trail to prove their legal existence and to obtain relief from deportation.[9]

MOTIVATIONS FOR LEAVING: TO BE SOMEBODY

I met Maribel and her social worker at the Richmond offices of Catholic Charities in April 2011, four years after she left her home in San Pedro Sula, Honduras, murder capital of the world. Maribel had her green card and was happily organizing a Virginia wedding to a Guatemalan immigrant from her Hispanic evangelical church. In contrast, her childhood had been turbulent and violent. She and her two siblings and mother were terrorized by an alcoholic father. He abused them and stole the earnings from her mother's struggling grocery store to spend on liquor and women. Her family life was riven by psychological abuse and explosive violence until the 2007 event that was the tipping point.

> I always dreamed of getting away because my father drank a lot. When I lived there it was like a nightmare. I said to myself, "I don't wanna be with my parents, I want to go away." It was the same thing every day. My daddy called us whores and my mom didn't do anything. She was a mom in the old way. Women exist for men, and they do what men say. I had two sisters and I always fight for my sisters. I said, "I can't take it anymore." But then he would say he loved us. When he wasn't drunk I could feel it. But then he drank, he said bad things, he would break things, break the windows. When the bad came I prayed that I could take it. My older sister was sick and my younger sister was too little so I was the daughter to take responsibility. I would always dream that my dad was different, that he had respect for us, but I learned that he didn't change. Because of him I didn't have a childhood. I never had friends come home with me from school. I never had boyfriends. My mom was always pushing me to go out after school, but I was afraid to leave my sister.

Despite this prelude, I was unprepared for what Maribel described next, as she became more agitated and started to sob.

One day I can't take it and I confront him outside the house: "How can you take our money, money that we need to pay bills and for medicine?" He got mad and pushed me down. He held a machete on me, and then he raised it over his head and was about to kill me. A neighbor saw this and she screamed my name and told him, "NO, NO, stop." I saw that he didn't respect my life. I said I can't stay, a father who tried to kill his child? Daddy, how could you do this?

When an uncle offered to pay for a smuggler to take Mirabel to the United States, her mother begged her not to go. Locals are well aware that migrant girls are sexually assaulted and sometimes sold into the sex industry by smugglers. In fact, tales of rape are so common that many girls get birth control injections before they leave home.[10] The trade in children is especially profitable as they can be sold multiple times. "We all know the stories of women who get raped or die in the desert," Mirabel told me. "But I was fed up. I couldn't stay. I had no life there." She told her mother she loved her, boarded a bus with her teenage cousin, and headed north, hoping for a better life in El Norte.

That same spring I met another young Honduran, Ernesto, who also lived in Virginia. He had left behind his mother, eight siblings, and step-father. His biological father, "a rich teacher," had not recognized him when he was born and had never been a part of his life. Ernesto contrasted his deprivation with the advantages enjoyed by his father's legitimate children, noting that they were educated professionals and well-off.

Why did he leave Honduras? He described his family's poverty, explaining that in Honduras "you don't go to school for twelve years and then get a diploma like here. There you go six years, get a degree, study three more years, and then you get a higher degree." Although he finished secondary school in Honduras, he had little faith in the possibilities for social mobility through education. It was dangerous to cross Mexico, but he had no choice. The media images of limitless opportunity and extravagant lifestyles in the United States were an irresistible lure.

> I mean, you just can't care about the odds or you wouldn't do it. You know that 40 percent will die because they get killed or kidnapped. How did I decide? It was the American Dream! In Honduras we think that there is so much money in the U.S. that you can just pick it up in the street.

Ernesto's stepfather forced him to do backbreaking work in the fields, clearing land and planting crops. Vicious beatings resulted if his work was found lacking. Ernesto remembered asking for a toy when he turned five and was elated when his stepfather said yes. "'Here is your toy,' he said," shoving a garden hoe at him. "I had no life there. My mom tried to protect me, but she was afraid because he beat her all the time. She had eight kids with him. She had no choice, she had to stay."

At sixteen, Ernesto had had enough. He considered borrowing the money to pay a smuggler or coyote as a guide. In 2006 when Ernesto left home the going rate for exporting human cargo to the United States from Central America typically ranged between $6,000 and $7,000, with the border crossing alone costing $1,500 to $2,500. He ultimately decided against it, reasoning, "If I give him $6,000 that is a good deal— but only if I make it." He understood the stark economic calculus of smuggling fees. The transaction works only if the migrant crosses the border and repays the loan. Migrants' use-value as labor plummets if they suffer injuries, fall ill, or are apprehended. He explained, "Some people sell their house, get across the border, and then get deported. So what happens? They lose the house and still have to repay the coyote. No, I decide to try myself."

Carlos grew up on a small Salvadoran coffee plantation owned by his father. He began his story by lamenting his lack of education. He was encouraged to study by a mother who "never did school." His father put his young children to work tending coffee plants and harvesting the ripe beans. With no money Carlos had to leave school at the end of his sixth year. "I wanted so much to continue, but I was working three jobs and slept only two hours a night so I got bad grades. I had to go." He too was pragmatic. "Most people pay a coyote, it is more safe that way. But it costs $6,000, and I didn't have that money." At fifteen Carlos embarked on a journey with the equivalent of $10 in his pocket. It would take eighteen months and two attempts before he made it across the border.

I met Corina in person in Grand Rapids, Michigan, on the day she was granted legal status. We had already spoken several times on the phone, and I knew that she came from a family of indigenous Quiché-speaking people in the highlands of Guatemala. She described the hard life she left behind as one of eleven children whose parents worked a meager landholding and could barely feed their children. She left home because she "wanted to be somebody, to go to school, to have a career." She compared her new American life to her mother, who had had twelve pregnancies and was an old woman at sixty, and to her six sisters, all of whom married young. When I asked if that was typical, she replied,

"You see in my family there was all kinds of abuse—sexual, physical, and mental—every abuse that exists in this world. I just couldn't stand what was going on between my father and my sisters. I was the youngest. So I had to leave, but I wasn't sure where to go. I really never thought about coming to the U.S., but I had a brother-in-law in Atlanta who called home once a week and he suggested it."

Unlike the teenage boys, Corina was afraid to set out alone and asked her relatives for money to hire a coyote. When she approached her father, he mocked her, saying that she could not be expected to repay the loan. Her mother, in contrast, mortgaged a parcel of land that she owned, and by combining that money with loans from relatives, Corina was able to hire a coyote her family knew. She remembered buying comfortable shoes for the trip and being petrified but determined. Corina was barely fifteen when she joined a group of migrants from Guatemala and Honduras.

Extending credit to migrants at interest rates of 10 to 20 percent and demanding title to agricultural land and houses as collateral are potentially lucrative ventures for Guatemalans who have minimal household incomes, small holdings, and large families. In Corina's impoverished community, migration is fueled by competition over access to land, inheritance, and education. It is a process that runs on debt. Banks, locals, and relatives lend money to migrants in the hope that the loans will be repaid with interest from the higher wages in the U.S. labor market.[11] Corina's mother and relatives had to decide whether to invest in her migration as a means of securing their own futures. They took a gamble on the potential return by financing Corina's unauthorized journey and steady work in the United States.

In addition to fleeing domestic abuse and the lack of opportunity, young people leave as a matter of mere survival. One teenage boy from Guatemala decided to migrate when his mother's sister, who had sent money for fifteen years, was diagnosed with cancer. "We said to ourselves, if she dies we die too because we will have no food." Another Guatemalan boy, the youngest of six children, was put to work at eight years old in construction or in the fields with his uncle. His mother died when he was twelve. In a frank assessment of the family's prospects, he explained, "I saw the situation. My father was not there. We didn't have a house, we had no food, little clothes, and no shoes. I decided alone. I said to myself, 'How do I get ahead and help them? I come to the U.S.'"

THE JOURNEY

The Cachuco Industry

During the journey to El Norte, young Central Americans encounter the thriving *cachuco* industry in Mexico.[12] This is an intensely violent economic enterprise that generates enormous profits from kidnapping, human smuggling, drug trafficking, extortion, and killings. During journeys that can last weeks or even years, young migrants move through increasingly remote and violent areas in Mexico where survival is a daily gamble. The harsh capitalist forces that push migrants north also dehumanize them. The journeys represent a new phase in the commodification of migrant labor, converting their bodies into objects whose value is set in a parallel transnational economy involving corrupt public officials, smugglers, gangs, and cartels. En route migrants acquire significant use-value and exchange-value as cargo to smuggle, bodies to prostitute, labor to exploit, organs to traffic, and lives to exchange for cash.[13] Migrants may both gain and lose value during their journeys through disappearance, dismemberment, and death.[14]

On Foot and by Bus

Corina, the Guatemalan teenager, began her journey in 2002 in a prearranged smuggling operation that involved handing off migrants to a succession of guides as they traveled north. Her group reached the Mexican border without incident and took rooms in a hotel to wait until nightfall. Many hotels in border towns run a brisk business renting space to migrants, cramming ten or twelve nervous travelers into a single room. At most they stay a day and night and rarely more than two days. The current preoccupation with fortifying the U.S.-Mexico border to stem the flow of illegal crossings has ignored the more porous boundary between Central America and Mexico.[15] Most young people cross the Guatemala-Mexico border by the cover of night, at unguarded checkpoints or by bribing border agents, local police, or bus conductors. In Mexico high levels of impunity in criminal cases and weak law enforcement combine to produce rampant corruption among those seeking to profit from the intertwined markets for human cargo, drugs, and weapons (figure 2).

Corina's group crossed into Mexico in the middle of the night. There the guides split up the group and put them on northbound buses. Central American migrants are alternately feared and demonized in Mexico, blamed for social problems and associated with violent crime.

FIGURE 2. Suchiate River crossing between Tecún Umán and Ciudad Hidalgo along the Mexico-Guatemala border. Photo by Michelle Frankfurter.

Whereas migrant men are linked to drugs and gang violence, young migrant women tend to be viewed in moral terms, as sexual objects. During the bus ride Corina was forced to sit next to the coyote's brother, who pressed his advantage in the dark by molesting her. When they arrived at a hotel near the U.S. border he tried to force her to go with him. When she refused, the coyotes abandoned her, keeping the money she paid them. Her molester took his revenge by calling her mother to say that Corina had cheated everyone. He depicted her as yet another promiscuous girl, claiming that she used her mother's money to live it up with Mexican men. When Corina finally contacted her mother she learned that village gossips had spread the salacious rumor that she was a thief and a whore. Abandoned without any money, she found another guide and renegotiated the terms of her crossing, although she did not say at what cost. The second guide advanced a loan and allowed her to join a group he was leading on foot through the Arizona desert.

In the early 1990s human smuggling was not an armed criminal enterprise. By 2002, when Corina left home, it was becoming a more organized operation dominated by outlaw families and criminal cartels. The old figure of the coyote as a "scruffy punk leading a ragtag group of Guatemalans into San Diego via the bogs and industrial parks of Chula Vista" was disappearing.[16] The buildup of border security that began with the Reagan-era war on drugs and heavy-handed enforcement policies has created increasingly sophisticated, powerful, and ruthless human smuggling operations. More people must now resort to smugglers and pay higher prices for their services.[17] Muscular attempts to stop unauthorized crossings of the U.S.-Mexico border from 2000 to 2012 have upset agreements among Mexican crime families and cartels over smuggling routes, sparking violent competition.[18] Turf wars have broken out among rivals located in American cities and Mexican states, and new hierarchies have emerged based on a loosely coordinated transnational division of labor. The criminal operation that attracted nationwide attention in 2001, luring fourteen migrants into the Arizona desert and then abandoning them to die of hyperthermia, was emblematic of this change.[19]

Corina never knew the identity of her Mexican guides, but it is likely that they resembled the Cercas operation, a family affair working out of Phoenix and the Mexican state of Hidalgo. They had contacts across the United States, in Illinois, Florida, and California, and employed a web of recruiters, lookouts, drivers, and guards to keep the migrants in line and out of sight and guides who did the dangerous work of cutting trails and leading the migrants through the desert. Like any business, that of the Cercas had managers who coordinated the operation and collected the cash. They also used family members to find safe houses, organize pickups and drop-offs, and pay locals.[20]

Five years later, in 2007, Maribel and her cousin left Honduras and reached the U.S.-Mexico border by bus in only fifteen days. Ernesto left home months before Maribel, but his journey took much longer and nearly ended in tragedy. The militarization of the Mexican drug wars that occurred during the Felipe Calderón presidency had the collateral effect of intensifying kidnappings, extortion, and horrific violence against migrants, both mass killings and disappearances. Targeting drug cartels and organized crime became a national priority even as the drug industry employed thousands and poured huge profits into the Mexican economy, further amplifying the phenomenon of "narco corruption."[21]

FIGURE 3. Central American migrants walk along the tracks on the outskirts of Tenosique, a border town in the southern Mexican state of Tabasco. Photo by Michelle Frankfurter.

Ernesto migrated with two friends, hitching rides through Guatemala. Mexican border guards allowed them to pass only after extorting all their money. How did they get through Mexico without money? Did they take la Bestia because it was free? "That train is not free!," Ernesto insisted. "It is too dangerous because people get killed. They go to sleep and fall off." He and his friends used the train tracks as their guide to the north. At stations where migrants had to board or jump from moving trains to escape immigration checks they saw severed fingers, feet, parts of legs, and torsos mangled by the "grinder," the euphemism used for the deadly train wheels. He and his friends walked through Mexico over the next two months, skirting stations to avoid *la migra* (Immigration), begging and working for food or cash at whatever jobs they could find (figure 3).

Not far from the U.S. border Ernesto and his companions were kidnapped by members of one of the most feared criminal cartel syndicates in Mexico, the Zetas, who operate in the Mexican state of Coahuila, a vast desert region south of Laredo, Texas. In 2006 when Ernesto began his journey the Zetas were relatively new arrivals, having worked as enforcers for the Gulf cartel before creating their own operation. The gang's founders, mostly former military, appear to have settled on this area because it is located between the Pacific smuggling routes controlled by the Sinaloa cartel and parts of the east coast controlled by the Gulf cartel. This area had the added advantage of being close to the U.S. border, a location they put to good advantage by using extortion, kidnapping, and migrant trafficking as well as the theft of coal and oil to supplement their drug smuggling income. Since that time they have greatly expanded the territory they control on the east coast and in southern Mexico, as well as in Honduras and Guatemala. They have taken brutality to new levels.[22] Nine of the young people I interviewed— seven boys and two girls—were kidnapped by the Zetas, who planned to extort money from their families or traffick them for sex or to run drugs.

After his capture Ernesto found himself in a warehouse with about forty other people, his hands tied and a gun to his head. Gang members forced him to give them his family's phone number. They intended to call and say that Ernesto needed a "guide" to take him across the border in exchange for a $4,000 fee. Three of the captives who had balked at similar demands were shot dead in front of him. Two teenage girls were dragged out and gang raped in front of the entire group as an ominous warning to the others. The boys were held for five days and repeatedly beaten but kept alive. Captives lose their exchange value if they escape or die before money can be extorted from their relatives in the United States or home countries.

One night a drunken brawl erupted among the guards, and the captives made a run for it. Ernesto described what happened.

> We said we're probably dead anyway, so we broke out of the building and ran in different directions. They chased us, firing at us, but they didn't get me. I don't know what happened to them. I ran so hard that I passed out. I was so weak because I only had crusts of bread and water those days.

Ernesto regained consciousness hours later in a safe house for migrants thanks to the kind heart of a passerby. He learned that the gang had contacted his family, saying that they needed to wire money for him.

His family borrowed the money and sent it. Hearing this, Ernesto knew that he could expect no more help. He weighed the alternatives: "I couldn't borrow more money. So I decided to cross the river. I knew how to swim, but I also knew that the river is strong. It can take you. People die crossing that river. But I see that the U.S. is so close. I have to try."

On the Back of the Beast

One of the most haunting images from Cammisa's film is an interview with Olga and Freddy, nine-year-olds who stop for temporary shelter at the House of Migrants. The House is a privately run shelter located near the train tracks in Coatzacoalcos, Mexico, over a thousand miles from the U.S. border. It is one of approximately fifty private, religiously affiliated Mexican shelters that provide humanitarian aid to migrants. Clustered along the most-traveled migrant routes, the shelters are spaces of respite as well as areas infiltrated by criminal gangs on the lookout for fresh recruits, particularly teenagers, to kidnap for ransom, to enslave for sex, or to coerce into smuggling operations. Local residents keep a wary eye on the constant stream of migrants, recognizing that shelters bring both legal and illegal profits into their midst. They are sympathetic to migrants' plight yet fearful of their impact on the community. They are dependent on migrants' consumption of needed goods and resentful of the scarce resources expended on their behalf (figure 4).[23]

Like the other sojourners, Olga and Freddy had been riding the Beast for three weeks. Olga had set out to find her mother and three sisters in Minnesota. Nothing had happened to her because, she said, "God watched over my journey and blessed it with his blood." In one scene the shelter director undercuts this naive expression of faith with a dire warning to the weary travelers: "That freight train can be your best friend or your worst enemy. It can kill you. The trip to the U.S. is not the passage of Death but Death itself. . . . [O]ut of 100 migrants, 10 to 20 will die. Many of you here will die, you will never see your family again, you will never return to your country." When he asks them how many still want to ride the train, all the hands go up. The next frame shows Olga and Freddy walking, their backs to the camera as they head to the train and an unknown fate.

In 2011 I met a Honduran migrant named Pedro who came north on the Beast. Like Olga, he had left home when he was nine years old. He grew up without a father and was only five years old when his mother

FIGURE 4. Weary and injured migrants rest in a makeshift chapel on the grounds of the Hermanos en El Camino migrant shelter, Ixtepéc, Oaxaca. Photo by Michelle Frankfurter.

succumbed to cancer. She died on Christmas Eve and was buried on "Jesus's birthday." Pedro had a chaotic childhood shuffling between the households of his mother, half sister, and maternal grandmother. Four years later when his grandmother died, he decided to leave. "When I make the decision, I hope my life it change. I do not mind if I die, I was just trying to survive." Pedro hitchhiked and walked through Guatemala, sleeping on the street and begging for food for weeks before he slipped over the Guatemalan border into Tapachulas, a town in the state of Chiapas that is close to the embarkation point for the freight train (figure 5).

Pedro had never been inside a train, much less perched on top of a moving freight car. He was terrified of falling and getting killed. By then he had seen gory newspaper photos and heard the tales of the Beast. He

FIGURE 5. Migrants listen to a sermon by the railroad tracks while waiting for a northbound freight train, Orizaba, Veracruz. Photo by Michelle Frankfurter.

said, "It is a voracious creature who grabs you and pulls you down onto the tracks. If it gets a taste of the foot, it wants the whole leg. If it gets the leg it wants all of you." The first time Pedro tried to jump on the moving train he missed the ladder and fell just inches from the deadly wheels. The second time he got on and watched a group of young men carrying large bags of goods as they moved from car to car. Not recognizing them as a gang, Pedro said to himself, "This is great. They are going to help me." Fellow travelers described them in fearful whispers as "la Mara" (the Mara Salvatrucha). He soon realized that instead of distributing clothes, they were extorting everything of value from the riders and had an arsenal of weapons—machetes, knives, and guns—to press their demands. Pedro had nothing but 10 pesos in cash and a pair

FIGURE 6. Central American migrants board a northbound freight train in the railhead town of Arriaga in the southern Mexican state of Chiapas. Photo by Michelle Frankfurter.

of worn tennis shoes, which they took, leaving him barefoot and broke. Years later Pedro urged his American foster family to watch the film *Sin hombre*, "so they understand my life." A scene in that film shows the Maras brutalizing terrified riders on the Beast. The power to provoke terror through displays of extreme machismo compensates to some degree for the vulnerability and humiliation of being a "social zero" who feels abandoned by both society and the state (figure 6).[24]

Pedro walked barefoot for seven days before finding a pair of discarded sneakers. They were torn and three sizes too big.

> I was always looking for a safe place. It was not safe sleeping outside. I knew nobody, and I was scared that I get bit by a snake or a scorpion and see bad

people. I was walking and asking for food—bread, water, or coffee—and they say, "No, we can't help you." I was so sad and crying a lot, but the third house I came to in Chiapas, they were different. They asked me what I want. They say, "OK, we help you." They give me a pill to get rid of my worms and feed me. I was like a skeleton, so skinny, eyes so deep in my head. They give me soup, and I stay with them three months.

Pedro "devoured food like a beast" and gained weight. He happily chopped wood and worked in their fields harvesting crops and planting corn. Eventually this backbreaking work made him realize that the family's help was tied to his supply of unpaid labor. He figured that the unequal exchange would never end. Despite their professed concern for his welfare, Pedro became restless. He saw a steady stream of migrants headed north to change their lives and "be successful."

All my dreams die when I was cutting mangoes and cleaning the garden. I wanted to go to school. I can't pay for school. I lived without a father and only a mother to help. The family [in Mexico] helped me, but they are not my family. I was working hard all the time, harder than I worked in my own country. I wanna continue my journey. My idea is to go to school and to be somebody.

Three months later Pedro saw boys who had been deported from Mexico to Guatemala and were again headed north. He left with them, and together they caught a freight train. He traveled with different groups of migrants, always remaining "the baby one." "I was a nine-year-old who looked more like he was five," he explained." At one checkpoint everyone jumped and ran from the tracks when shots rang out. A bullet grazed his arm. Pedro realized they were chasing a man in front of him. He ducked into an abandoned building and waited until it was dark and safe to come out. On the next train there was a confrontation involving "bad people with tattooed faces and gold chains," but this time they were solicitous in a way that made the other travelers avert their eyes in fear. They asked Pedro, "Where is your father? You are so young. Don't worry. We will take care of you. You will be better off with us." One eyed his battered shoes and stroked him, saying, "My son, you need shoes! We can fix that." He turned to a boy roughly Pedro's size and said, "This guy will be glad to give you his shoes, right?" When the boy hurriedly removed them, Pedro realized that they were trying to obligate him to join a gang and played along. When the train stopped, he jumped, ran to a car at the front, climbed on, and stayed out of sight. In *Sin hombre,* the Maras adopt a young boy Pedro's age and administer a ritual beating as an initiation into the gang family. To prove his loyalty the nine-year-old recruit must murder a childhood friend who betrayed the Maras by trying to quit. Watching that film years later, when he was in school and had a valid visa, Pedro saw the life that awaited him if he had joined the gang.

A number of young people who rode the Beast were awestruck by the experience. Pedro remembered the wonders he saw heading north. He marveled at the snow-capped peaks etched against a cerulean sky, the pine forests and clear lakes, and then the dry lands with maguey and cacti. The train passed through hundreds of hardscrabble towns with dirt roads and crumbling buildings. It skirted the twisted, rusting hulks of derailed freight cars beside the tracks. Sometimes the train ran for days without stopping, and the boys hooked their belts to the metal railings so they would not tumble off in their sleep. Pedro recalled crossing a bridge and catching the spicy taquitos, containers of water, and sweet oranges that locals threw them from both sides of the tracks. This first trip and the second ended in Pedro's arrest and deportation by Mexican authorities. Desperate to escape another return to Honduras, Pedro jumped from a moving bus filled with deportees by forcing himself through an opening in the door. He eventually made it to the U.S. border (figure 7).

On Carlos's first attempt to cross into the United States he was caught and detained in a Texas shelter for three months and then sent back to El Salvador. On his second journey north he was forced to ride the Beast because he had no money to pay a guide. He was feeling lucky until the Mexican migra stopped the train. People scrambled, jumping off and running in different directions. He escaped the dragnet by hiding in the brush. He remembered the panic of two young women he had befriended, and he searched for them after the raid. One man had seen the officers drag them away and heard them scream.

> I wanted to find them and help them. That man told me, "Don't go back and look for them, you don't want to see things like that." I listened to him, but I always ask myself what happened to them. They have a family and dreams like me.

Like Ernesto, Carlos was kidnapped by the Zetas in Mexico and barely escaped with his life. He broke free and joined a group of six migrants who planned to cross the Rio Grande at night. Like Olga in Cammisa's film, Carlos believed that he was still alive because "God blessed me and my family . . . it was my mission to get here, to work, to

FIGURE 7. Guatemalan migrants ride a northbound freight train, Oaxaca. Photo by Michelle Frankfurter.

help my family, to study, . . . not to die. I was thinking about my mom, and I didn't want her to be more sad." Undocumented migrants crossing through Mexico learned quickly what it meant to lack basic citizenship rights. Divine providence is a way of talking about a quality of justice that cannot be expected from the state, as well as the rationale for the moral compromises that migration often demands. Exposure to chronic violence in Central America and Mexico has provoked victims and perpetrators alike to accept Pentecostal religious beliefs as a justification and shield for the use of violence.[25] Carlos invoked divine forces along with a lucid critique of the forces arrayed against migrants like him.

That train is so dangerous, and another problem is immigration in Mexico. It is a big business with narco traffickers and bad gangs. There is a lot of corruption there. The authority there don't get paid too much. You need to be careful because if they think you have family in the U.S., they use that. They think you can pay a lot of money.

CROSSING THE BORDER

Of the forty young people interviewed, twelve recounted harrowing desert or river crossings in Texas and Arizona, several of which nearly ended in death. Immigrant deaths at the border have risen dramatically because of the enhanced enforcement operations that have pushed migrants into increasingly remote and hazardous desert areas. As a result of the emphasis on deterrence, the number of Border Patrol agents increased fivefold, from 4,208 in 1993 to 21,394 in 2012. In addition to increased manpower, huge resources have been spent on border infrastructure such as double-layer fencing and remote surveillance systems that include towers and trucks mounted with day and night cameras and unmanned drones. In 2002 when Corina crossed, 320 migrants died. By 2012 immigrant deaths had risen by 27 percent to 477 deaths, the second highest total recorded since 1998. And that's counting only those who made it that far. At a time when more children are migrating from Mexico and Central America, it is more dangerous than ever to enter the United States illegally. An immigrant attempting to cross the border in 2013 was eight times more likely to die than a decade ago.[26]

The River

After his escape from the gang Ernesto met three young men who also were desperate to cross the river but had no money for a guide. He surveyed the fast-flowing water and was paralyzed by fear. "I could see the other side, the U.S. I know how to swim. The river was so close! I said, 'I got to try.'" He understood why so many took the chance even when they had only patched inner tubes or pieces of board to keep them afloat. His group crossed, but minutes later they heard the roar of an engine and fearing discovery by la migra they made a run for the river and returned to Mexico. They repeated this scenario twice more. The fourth time they made it to a train line on the U.S. side. Ernesto recalled:

So we said, "It's a train, it's free transportation." It was going to San Antonio. We saw a trailer on the train, two levels with cars, and we thought they [Immigration] would only check the bottom. We split up and I was alone. I got a tool to open the car door. Man, it was nice with cool leather seats. I got in and rode up there until we got close to San Antonio. The train was stopping, and I thought, "I gotta get out," and then I saw that Immigration was on both sides. It was dark, 2 a.m., and I jumped and I ran. I threw away everything I had with me. Somehow, I don't remember how, I broke my left hand when I jumped. I didn't feel pain. My hand was really messed up, but I was so scared and I kept running and I lost them. I waited for another train and I got it.

How did he jump on a moving freight train with a broken hand?

I had to run fast, and I grabbed the ladder with my one good hand. I almost fell because it swing me back, but I didn't release my hand. I held on, but I was only there for thirty minutes and they stopped the train. It was Immigration. This time I said, "I give up." They said, "If you move, we will shoot you." Believe me, I had no plan to run. My American Dream, everything I had suffered, it was gone. So I went with them. They took me to a hospital and fixed my hand.

The Desert

Corina's group departed hastily to cross the Arizona border on foot. They left with inadequate supplies and exhausted most of their water supply in the 110-degree desert heat of the first day. They spent the next day with little water and food before reaching the meeting place where two vans were waiting to pick them up. Corina was one of five hidden in the back of the first van, with three coyotes in the front. Soon after they started out they heard loud voices and a series of pops, and the van abruptly stopped. They saw that the driver had been shot in the stomach and the arm. The surviving coyotes screamed that they had been ambushed and blamed it on rivals who wanted a cut of the smuggling fee. They put the wounded man in the back next to Corina, who was soon soaked in his blood. They continued a wild ride until the tires burst and the van careened to a stop, landing on its side. The coyotes split up the group, taking two of the girls in the second van. They instructed Corina and the others to wait until they came back.

Hours passed, and the coyotes never returned, so Corina and the seven men in her group resumed their desert trek without water, a map, or a compass. Movement on foot under those conditions soon turns deadly. Corina's cheeks, the tips of her ears, and even her eyelids burned; blood dripped from her cracked lips when she tried to form words. From breathing hard in the dry, dusty air her saliva had turned to a sticky paste.

The group stopped at dusk and were overjoyed when one young man found a plastic water jug, probably left by a humanitarian organization to prevent migrant deaths. It had been slashed but was half full of steamy water, and they shared it. Some walkers have died after opening the radiators of abandoned vehicles and gulping the antifreeze, while others have stayed alive by drinking their own urine. Night fell. Corina slept fitfully, dreaming of a lake filled with cool water just beyond her reach. She was tormented by dark visions of relatives mocking her for leaving home. Hours later the sleepers were roused by lights, and Corina saw the others, weakened by dehydration, stagger off in different directions. She was racked by painful muscle cramps, convulsed with nausea, and unable to focus, the symptoms that commonly precede heat stroke. "I couldn't walk, or even move. My legs ached and I kept falling, I was cut and bruised. I was so scared," she said. In the dark no one had realized how close they were to the highway. The lights were from a Border Patrol truck. The driver, "a tall American," stopped, gave them water, and called for backup.

One Who Got Away

Ángel is Mexican and part of a population that is vastly underrepresented in federal custody. In 2012 only 8 percent of the detained children were from Mexico, compared to 34 percent from Guatemala, 27 percent from El Salvador and Honduras, and 2 percent from Ecuador. In 2013 that figure dropped to 3 percent. Mexican youths are the largest group of undocumented border crossers, with increasing numbers coming every year, but the vast majority are quickly returned to Mexico.[27] Legislators intended to close this "revolving door" when they passed the Trafficking Victims Protection and Reauthorization Act (TVPRA) in 2008. The act mandated that CBP officials interview every unaccompanied Mexican child to determine that the child is not a victim of trafficking, does not express a fear of persecution, and is able to voluntarily agree to return to Mexico. The improved screening procedures were intended to identify the threats vulnerable minors face and to prevent their return to unsafe environments.

Unfortunately, the revolving door has continued for Mexican minors. This failure followed the decision of the DHS officials to assign screening duties to CBP, its law enforcement branch. The primary mission of the CBP is to detect and deport undocumented aliens, not to evaluate children's risk of harm. The expected post-TVPRA influx of young Mexicans into custodial care as a result of better screening has never materialized, leaving these children vulnerable to exploitation by criminal enterprises and to harm from repeated border crossings in harsh desert terrain. A 2014 United Nations High Commissioner on Refugees (UNHCR) report based on 404 interviews with migrants ages twelve to seventeen who entered the United States in fall 2011 or later identified a category of harm unique to Mexican children: forcible recruitment into human smuggling operations.[28] These were the very issues that prompted Congress to pass the TVPRA with unanimous support in 2008.[29]

When I met him in 2011 Ángel had a green card and was looking forward to becoming a naturalized U.S. citizen. He was raised in an indigenous area of rural Mexico and left school at fourteen because there was no money for fees and no permanent work. Ángel grew up with a "crazy older brother" who prided himself on finding unique ways to abuse him. He was sixteen when he decided to leave for the United States. He found a coyote who charged $2,500 and agreed to let him pay in installments.[30] Traveling by bus, Ángel made it to the U.S. border and crossed into Arizona. Like the majority of Mexican migrants, he was apprehended within hours and immediately deported. He waited for two days before crossing again, this time joining a group of eighteen in which he was the only minor. They walked five days, running out of water the fourth day. By the time their guide called his U.S. contact and arranged for two vans to pick them up, Ángel was in severe distress. The drivers met them and took them to a remote location, where the guides, on orders from their boss, a Mexican man with legal papers, demanded an additional $300 per head. Ángel wasn't sure who paid or if the migrants negotiated a lower price. He does remember that no one got water until the money was received. Early that afternoon the boss's smartly dressed American wife arrived and took them to a compound with food and "lots of beds." Later they learned that the cost of food was added to the smuggling fees they owed.

This was the beginning of an eight-month ordeal during which Ángel labored at what he described as "different plantations" to repay his debt. He was taken to Florida, where he worked for three months picking watermelons in the fields. He worked in scorching heat seven days a week and paid rent for a cot in a bug-invested trailer "not fit for humans." The laborers slept in shifts and shared one kitchen and two toilets. This was the first of four moves that were organized by the "same boss." Ángel spent a month picking tobacco in North Carolina, then six weeks harvesting corn in Michigan, followed by two weeks each in Illinois and Kentucky. The boss kept part of Ángel's wages to cover his food and rent; Ángel used the remainder to pay installments on his smuggling debt. Then he was apprehended.

After Kentucky, I paid the last of the fee and I am free. I can go where I want and work. I had in my mind New York so I find other people and go with them to pick apples on a big farm. So we crossed the state line and there were eight of us in the truck. It was the middle of the night, about 3 a.m., and the police stopped us. I don't know who it was, the military or the police. They called a different police. They asked for papers. I still couldn't speak English. I had no papers, no license. They looked at me, and one man, who speaks a little Spanish, the white guy, he says, "What are you doin' here, little guy?" Three more cars came and those guys said, "Hey, get out!" I was thinkin', "What are they gonna do?" They hold my hands, and they put on those things, what do you call them? [SJT: Handcuffs?] Yes, I couldn't believe it. I said, "I am done with the American Dream. After all this time, I work and work, I paid my fee, I am free and now they got me."

APPREHENSION

A Vera Institute of Justice analysis of those taken into federal custody between October 1, 2008, and September 30, 2010, estimated that most unaccompanied children are apprehended within hours of entering the United States, at the border or at another port of entry. Approximately 80 percent were apprehended within a week of crossing the border, and 5 percent were caught between eight days and a month. Ángel was among the 2 percent who evade apprehension and live without papers in the country for more than a month.[31]

The process by which children are referred to the federal agency responsible for their custody, the Office of Refugee Resettlement, begins with their apprehension by federal authorities in one of the subsidiary agencies of the DHS. Officers from the Office of Border Patrol, a division of CBP, typically apprehend children crossing the U.S.-Mexico border. Eighty-five percent of unaccompanied children enter the custodial system this way; only 15 percent are apprehended inside the United States.[32] When undocumented migrants are apprehended inside the US as a result of traffic or status violations, law enforcement officers often immediately alert ICE agents. Being Mexican, Ángel was fortunate to be arrested with undocumented adults. The ICE agents who were called to the scene by the New York State Police concluded that he was under-age and a victim of exploitation. They alerted ORR and transferred him to a shelter in New York State.

CBP agents typically screen minors to determine their names, ages, and citizenship. Processing includes searches of federal immigration and criminal databases to determine whether children have entered the country legally, whether they have committed any criminal offenses, and whether they are accompanied or unaccompanied. When CBP agents confirm that the children are undocumented and unaccompanied, they designate them "Unaccompanied Alien Children," or UACs, and process them for immigration violations and transfer to ORR custody. During this time children are locked in secure "hold rooms," cells designed for short-term detention. Under the TVPRA of 2008, CBP's custody of UACs is limited to seventy-two hours unless there are exceptional circumstances. CBP officials are required to notify the district juvenile coordinator for ICE who in turn alerts ORR officials and arranges transport to a federal facility (see chapter 4).

Despite the safeguards put in place, watchdog groups have repeatedly reported on the need for alternatives to holding children in CBP facilities even for short periods. These facilities are secure buildings, guarded and staffed by uniformed and armed agents. Children are placed in locked, windowless cells or cages that are lit twenty-four hours a day and typically kept at frigid temperatures. Migrant children call them *las hieleras* (the iceboxes). Many receive minimal food, bedding, and medical care and are deprived of showers or recreation spaces.

Over the past decade NGOs have reported that CBP agents routinely violate the basic constitutional protections and human rights of immigrants and U.S. citizens along both the northern and southern borders of the United States. In 2008 the NGO No More Deaths published a report documenting hundreds of accounts of abuse by CBP agents. They recommended "clear, enforceable custody standards" with independent oversight to ensure compliance. Their follow-up 2011 report revealed "alarmingly consistent" patterns of mistreatment involving the denial of medical assistance, water, and food, the beatings of children and adults during arrest, the separation of family members, the confiscation of personal property, severe overcrowding in holding cells, deprivation of sleep, and threats of death. Faced with the flat denials of CBP authorities, the authors concluded that "the abuse, neglect, and dehumanization of migrants" was part of "the institutional culture of the Border Patrol," reinforced by an absence of effective accountability measures.[33] The same year four NGOs reported that Border Patrol agents regularly overstepped their authority by conducting enforcement activities outside border regions, making racially motivated arrests, employing coercive interrogation tactics, and imprisoning migrants under inhumane conditions.[34]

In 2010, in response to NGO complaints, the Office of the Inspector General (OIG) investigated the treatment of unaccompanied immigrant children to determine if it was in compliance with government regulations regarding minors, the Flores Settlement Agreement (FSA). After site visits to thirty Border Patrol stations and ports of entry, document reviews, and independent observations, the inspectors concluded that the CBP "was in compliance with the general provisions of the Flores Settlement Agreement." It is significant that the inspectors based this conclusion on a narrow reading of the FSA requirement that children must be held in "safe and sanitary facilities." They focused on the physical infrastructure of Border Patrol stations—the space available to separate and monitor children apart from unrelated adults—and on the conditions in hold rooms—the availability of safe drinking water and adequate food, the proper functioning of sinks and toilets, adequate temperature control, and sufficient medical supplies.

The inspectors did not address CBP compliance with the FSA requirement that minors be notified of their legal rights after arrest, specifically, their right to a judicial review of the government decision to detain them. This critical omission prompted Michelle Brané, director of detention at the Women's Refugee Commission (WRC), to send a written protest to the Office of the Inspector General. Brané explained, "Our agency was furious that the inspectors did not question CBP agents to see if they were notifying children of their rights. The real problem is that we need more NGO monitors in BP [Border Patrol] stations and access to the children while they are in CBP custody. Unfortunately, the CBP has drawn a red line on [on-site] interviews with minors. They won't allow them." She added, "A close reading of that report shows that the CBP was actually out of compliance in a number of areas such as training agents to determine if children needed medical attention[35] or if they had been trafficked or abused. . . . The CBP stations are like a dark cave. Even their top administrators don't realize what is happening to kids in [CBP] custody."[36]

When the number of unaccompanied children in ORR custody nearly doubled in 2012, attorneys from the WRC interviewed 151 children detained in Texas[37] and discovered that many had been treated harshly while in CBP custody.[38] Border Patrol agents had shoved and kicked them, tasered them even when they were compliant, and harassed them with racial slurs and emasculating insults. One child had a gun held to his head to dissuade him from planning an escape, and another was jolted out of a deep sleep when an agent overturned his cot. Border Patrol agents destroyed or disposed of the only possessions of migrants, including their Bibles.

In spring 2014, as unaccompanied children flooded border holding facilities, disturbing reports of the "systematic abuse of unaccompanied children by CBP agents" reemerged. These included body cavity searches, shackling, denial of food and medical services, and verbal, physical, and sexual abuse. On June 11, 2014, civil and human rights groups filed an administrative complaint with the Office for Civil Rights and Civil Liberties and the Office of the Inspector General at the Department of Homeland Security demanding "immediate agency reform."[39] Congress had specifically ordered ORR to write Prison Rape Elimination Act protections in March 2013 to ensure that sexual abuse of children in federal custody was reported, investigated, and punished. They decried the fact that the regulations proposed by ORR remained tied up in executive review.[40] In a break from agency practice, CBP commissioner Gil Kerlikowske announced on June 12, 2014, that he had ordered internal investigators to examine the complaint.[41]

It would be easy to conclude that the mistreatment of minors during the surge that began in 2011 occurred primarily because of the pressures placed on personnel to handle a humanitarian emergency. However, the 2012 WRC report concludes that the rapid influx of minors exacerbated long-standing "structural and procedural problems within HHS [Health and Human Services, parent agency of ORR]" and underscored the need for systemic reform in the care and custody of unaccompanied children.[42] Reports describe the continuous gaps in oversight and the limited access CBP administrators give monitors to tour border stations or to interview detained children.[43] WRC attorneys screened CBP agents and concluded that they lack the necessary training to elicit sensitive information about human trafficking or domestic abuse from children.[44]

"They Treated Me Like a Criminal"

Twenty-four of the young people I interviewed spoke at length about their apprehension and CBP custody. Although these arrests had occurred five to ten years before the recent surge their descriptions are strikingly similar to those collected from 2012 to the present. The youths expressed gratitude for the life-saving interventions of the Border Patrol. However, all but two of them remembered custody as a humiliating and disillusioning experience. They complained about needlessly coercive arrests, intentional neglect, and physical discomfort in CBP stations and reported having been taunted with anti-immigrant remarks. They described agents whose demeanor ranges from indifference—

FIGURE 8. U.S. Border Patrol apprehension of migrants, Rio Grande Valley Sector near McAllen, Texas. Photo by Michelle Frankfurter.

refusal to acknowledge or respond to requests for blankets, food or basic information—to verbal hostility and physical aggression. They were subjected to screaming, shoving, kicking, and threatening or openly mocking comments. The detailed accounts they provided are all the more striking because their stays at Border Patrol stations were so short. All but four of the youths were transferred to ORR custody within seventy-two hours (figure 8).

"Tell 'em You're Nineteen!"

Youths like Maribel were advised by smugglers and other migrants to lie about their age and nationality because the United States detains underage migrants "in jails for years," doesn't allow them to work, and never gives them legal status. Remembering her own time in custody, Mirabel said, "The Mexicans don't stay in the U.S. or the shelters. They get deported. So if you say you are over eighteen and Mexican they send you straight back and you can try [to cross] again." Despite this advice, when apprehended in 2007 she was too terrified to lie.

> So the first day the Border guys caught us. I was so afraid that they would send me back to Honduras. I ask, "Where am I going?" They were questioning me and I was crying and I said, "I can't go back to Honduras." I was so mad. These officers, they put handcuffs on me—like a criminal! It was not right, but I said, "I can't go back. I can't do this anymore." I told the truth. I was so afraid because I was the only underage girl. So they kept us and separated us [she and her male cousin], and I spent the first days in a jail.

Many of the children were terrified when agents drew their guns and ordered them to lie down and, like Maribel, were indignant that "Immigration" handcuffed them "like criminals" or "animals." A number admitted that they had lied about their real age and home country. The repeated lies provoked angry reactions and sometimes retribution from agents. Alberto crossed the border with his undocumented uncle, was arrested in 2009 during an ICE workplace raid in Southern California, and taken to a field office there. Coached by his uncle to say he was Mexican and nineteen, he couldn't answer questions about the national anthem, the flag, or regional foods put to him by an ICE agent who was raised in Mexico. When Alberto stubbornly maintained his lie, the agents ridiculed him, isolated him for long periods, and limited his food for three days, until he finally admitted that he was seventeen and from Guatemala.

Ernesto had heard the same advice, so he told the Border Patrol agents he was nineteen, not sixteen. The agent looked at him in disbelief and shouted, "Do I look stupid? You aren't nineteen! Why are you here? You're just a kid. I will check your teeth to find out your real age, and if you lie we will put you in jail for a long time."

Ernesto figured that "they treat me real bad because I lied and said I was an adult from Mexico." He got his first meal on the second of the six days he spent in the CBP station. When he asked questions he was told to shut up by a paunchy, mean Hispanic man. When advised that he and three other youths would be moved, he asked, "Why are we here? Where are we going?" The agent replied, "Don't ask! What does it matter? You're leaving." Ángel remembered being separated from the adults and held in an ICE facility "while they figured out what to do with me.

One white guy went off at me and screamed, 'Do you know why you are here? You broke the law! You immigrants don't belong here. You are not part of us. We don't need any more immigrants here.'"

"I'm Not a Criminal, but They Put Me in Jail"

Nearly every young migrant described the windowless rooms, metal cots, lack of bedding, and harsh lights in CBP stations. One young man, Felipe, claimed that he couldn't tell if it was day or night. "I wasn't sure if I was even in the U.S.," he said. They remembered the freezing temperatures, the bad food—especially the ubiquitous frozen sandwiches—and the gnawing hunger because most were given just one meal a day. Felipe was held in a CBP facility in Texas for six days before his transfer to ORR and got the "same disgusting ham and cheese sandwich" every day. He added, "To this day I can't smell or even see ham. They treated us worse than dogs because even dogs have rights in your country." Two Salvadorans, Isabela and her younger sister, were made to feel like "trash." They were filthy and hungry and not allowed to lie down for the duration of their thirty-six-hour stay at the CBP station.

Carlos reached his breaking point after he was apprehended the second time and taken to a Texas Border Patrol station. He had arrived in the town of Laredo and joined a group of six migrants, making the dangerous river crossing at night. A pregnant woman in the group was swept away and drowned. The others made it but were surrounded by CBP agents within minutes. Another Salvadoran man traveling with his sister had broken his leg and was doubled over in pain. One of the agents taunted him, "Hey, Chicano, stand up! How come you cross my border and you can't stand up?" Carlos understood "Chicano" as a racial slur for brown people from Central America.[45] After what he had seen on the trains and suffered at the hands of the Zetas, he snapped.

> His sister tried to help him, but he couldn't [stand up], and when the guy started to laugh, I lost it and yelled at him to stop. He came at me and I said, "You can't hit me . . . there are human rights. If you hit this guy with the broken leg I will denounce you and you will go to jail. Push me, not him." They tried to make me to sign the paper saying I agreed to go back to my country. I said, "No way, I am under eighteen." They told me that I didn't know nothing, but then they found me in the computer and they had to send me to a shelter.

Many youths recalled the shame of being handcuffed after arrest and during transfer between CBP stations, ICE offices, and ORR shelters.

Felipe described what happened when he left Arizona with two ICE agents for a flight to California and placement in an ORR shelter.

> One of the guards put handcuffs on me for the plane ride. I said, "Please take them off. I won't escape. I am not a criminal." He was OK. He took them off, but the other guy was a real racist. He kept saying, "Why do they come here, these immigrants? What do we have here that you don't have in your country?"

WHOSE CHILD AM I?

In the documentary *Which Way Home* a U.S. Border Patrol agent describes the dangers child migrants encounter: "Children have been raped and abandoned by their own smugglers. I have seen dead children, kids hiding in trucks, stuffed inside compartments. Parents send their kids with people who get drunk, use drugs, smuggle dope. Their parents shouldn't be surprised if the kid never makes it to the U.S." His moral outrage is expressed as a humanitarian concern, but it is also an indictment of the "bad" parents who left their children behind or hired smugglers who exposed them to life-threatening situations. It denies the children's active agency in the decision to leave home, their resourcefulness in the face of deadly violence, and their resilience in dealing with traumatic experiences. It also throws into bold relief the contradictory impulses engendered by undocumented child migrants: to protect them as extremely vulnerable and to protect the nation from illegal immigration and the Latino threat.[46] As the agency whose primary mission is to secure the nation's borders and to enforce immigration law, the CBP views both undocumented children and their parents—in particular, those who come from Mexico and Central America—as national security risks.

The notion of security has two dimensions. The first relates to children who are themselves seen as risks because they travel alone, work, beg, and live on the street. Like street children, child migrants cause fear and elicit violent reactions from adult authorities when they cannot or will not fulfill their expected roles within the normative realms of family, home, and school.[47] Their very mobility and survival strategies pose a challenge to the consensus on child victims as passive and dependent on adults for their well-being and decision making. It is no accident that some CBP agents became abusive when young migrants tried to pass themselves off as adults when they were obviously underage. It is viewed as an intolerable demonstration of autonomy that children as young as twelve or thirteen try to game the system by getting themselves deported as Mexican adults so they can escape detention and attempt to reenter the United States. That Central American migrants understand and try to benefit from the government's different treatment of Mexican children exposes the inconsistencies in the humanitarian approach to detained children mandated by the Flores Settlement Agreement.

The second dimension of security relates to the racial threat that Latino migrants are said to represent. When CBP agents told migrant children that they "didn't belong" in the United States and angrily demanded to know "why they came," they voiced fears that an uncontrolled influx of impoverished migrants would drain scarce social welfare and educational resources. On a deeper level, they view young immigrants as a threat to the American way of life. The Latino threat narrative depicts immigrants from the south as well as U.S.-born Americans of Latin American descent as an invading force incapable of integrating in the national community. Although Mexicans have historically been seen as the "quintessential illegal aliens," all Latinos bear "the mark of illegality which . . . means that they are illegitimate members of society" undeserving of social benefits from public education to citizenship.[48] When undocumented children are associated with illegal activities such as consuming alcohol, getting high, or breaching the border as drug mules, they cease to be viewed as vulnerable victims and can be recategorized and treated as criminal offenders or terrorist elements.

The demonization of the undocumented has intensified in states like Arizona and California where the wars against crime and immigrants have combined in ways that disproportionately penalize immigrant youth. Proposition 187, also known as the "Save Our State" anti-immigrant initiative; Proposition 184, the "Three Strikes and You're Out" anticrime bill; the Street Terrorism Enforcement Protection Act; and antiloitering laws were precursors to the federal legislation passed in 1996.[49] The 1996 legislation has made it more difficult to become a legal permanent resident. It expanded the criteria mandating deportation even for legal permanent residents and allowed the government to activate "alien terrorist removal procedures" without any due process protections. Harsh anticrime measures implemented in the United States have been exported to Mexico and Central America through multibillion-dollar security agreements. Extravagantly funded drug interdiction and anti–organized crime efforts have increasingly focused on the suppression of illegal immigration as the linchpin of the traffic in weapons, drugs, and human smuggling.[50]

The 2013 proposal to overhaul immigration law shows the complex relationship between humanitarianism and security.[51] In her April 19, 2013, testimony before the Senate Judiciary Committee on Immigration, DHS Secretary Napolitano argued for a humane approach that would give "a pathway to earned citizenship" for 11 million undocumented immigrants. At the same time she emphasized that the primary mission of DHS was "to secure our Nation's borders to prevent the illegal entry of people, drugs, weapons, and contraband" and "to protect public safety."[52]

Nothing better illustrates the contradictions of the Obama administration's approach to immigration reform than the career path of Cecilia Muñoz. The daughter of Bolivian immigrants who grew up in Detroit and studied at the University of Michigan, she earned a nationwide reputation as an immigration rights advocate who denounced border enforcement and unwarranted deportations. Since her 2008 appointment as director of the White House Domestic Policy Council, she has had to defend a formidable deportation machine with little accountability but enormous resources—an annual budget of $18 billion—that had removed nearly 1.9 million people in five and a half years.[53] Although the Obama administration had pledged to focus enforcement on the most dangerous and violent offenders, it has instead arrested and deported thousands of undocumented people who were merely accused, not convicted, of a crime. Deportations continue on an unprecedented scale and have swept up U.S. citizens who have cognitive impairments and mental illness as well as children as young as four.[54]

Young people who leave home undertake a journey across space and time as well as a journey in cognitive, social, and cultural terms. The departure from home, the ordeal of crossing the border, and the humiliation of apprehension remain part of a past that is ever present. A clinician in an ORR program in Phoenix discussed the dilemmas children face in confronting their past as "illegals."

There is a deep sense of humiliation and fear. They say, "We were hiding, we don't feel good, we are not legal." They are afraid, they feel shame, they all start to cry when they are caught. We pretend that they have a voice when they don't. When they describe their experiences, it is important because in this way they create their own understanding.

Through interpretive work young people make astute analyses of gender relations, family ideologies, social mobility, the meaning of security, and the experience of trauma. They bear witness to the horrific and extraordinary experiences that have made them who they are today. Most agreed to share their stories with me because they want the truth to be known. From the moment of their apprehension, a bewildering array of adult authorities speak for and about them: immigration authorities, social workers, clinicians, shelter directors, attorneys, and judges. Telling their own stories allows them to dispel the partial truths that circulate about them in custody, in the press, and in court. It helps them make sense of the suffering they endured, to see themselves in the lives of people in need, and to ease the way for future migrants. Before we continue with their stories we need to examine why the U.S. government got into the business of detaining children and how the detention system has evolved.

3

The Least Restrictive Setting

U.S. Border Patrol officers apprehended Maribel immediately after she crossed the border in 2007. She was designated as unaccompanied and detained in a minimum-security federal facility in Los Fresnos, Texas, that housed 160 minors. Maribel vividly remembered being overwhelmed by feelings of helplessness and anxiety. She never understood why government protection required that she be held for six months in a facility that she was not permitted to leave.

> So they took us to a shelter in Texas. I didn't wanna be there because I was afraid they were going to kick me out. . . . I went there and I saw other girls. It was clean, it had a living room. At first I thought it wasn't like a jail, but then I saw that we couldn't leave. . . . [E]verybody there had depression, and the girls were always crying. . . . Life stopped in there, life was ended. There was no life because all we could see was the fence and the electric cables. You see all that. You see the houses. You can't walk alone. I said, "I am not like a criminal. I feel the difference. I just want to be freed." The shelter was near the main road, and I could see cars going by and I wanted to be in that car. I kept saying, "I wanna be out of here. I wanna see something different."

Maribel's detention occurred ten years after a class action lawsuit against the federal government was settled. That settlement mandated the "least restrictive setting" in detention centers and prompt release for unaccompanied, undocumented children who were in custody pending a removal hearing in immigration court. Was this the vision of federal custody that the plaintiffs had sought?

THE FLORES SETTLEMENT AGREEMENT

In 1985 legal advocates challenged the Immigration and Naturalization Service's (INS's) detention and treatment of unaccompanied children. They brought a class action lawsuit against the federal government on behalf of a fifteen-year-old Salvadoran, Jenny Lisette Flores, who was apprehended in Southern California, handcuffed, strip searched, and held for two months in an INS-contracted juvenile detention facility in Pasadena pending a deportation hearing. After years of litigation, in 1996, the government agreed, for the first time, to establish nationwide standards for the custody and release of the thousands of unaccompanied children who were detained every year. Finalized in 1997, the FSA required that government agencies treat all children in custody "with the dignity, respect and special concern for their vulnerability as minors."[1] Most important, it set forth the principle that a minor "will be placed in the least restrictive setting" appropriate to age and special needs and released "without necessary delay" to family, an adult guardian, or a licensed program willing to ensure the child's well-being and timely appearance in immigration court.[2] It established standards in all federal facilities that specified balanced nutrition, education, psychological counseling, medical services, recreation, and the separation of immigrant youth detained solely for their lack of legal documentation from domestic juvenile or adult offenders. It was an achievement that advocates and scholars heralded as a watershed moment in the troubled history of immigration detention in this country.

The FSA was intended to remain in effect only until the INS passed its own internal regulations. Although the INS issued interim regulations, the government has never adopted permanent regulations and has continued the policy of automatic detention for unaccompanied minors. The unprecedented influx of young migrants crossing the border in 2014 begs important questions. We need to ask how the detention of children became the default policy of the federal government and why government agencies justify institutional custody as the best way to ensure their safety and well-being. How did advocacy efforts come to center on reforming detention rather than ending it? Can a system that uses civil detention as the first response rather than a last resort meet international rights-based norms? Is it possible to conclude, as many scholars and advocates have, that federal facilities are now "modeled more on welfare than corrective regimes"[3] and that a conflict of interest no longer exists between the government's role as a prosecutor arguing for the deportation of undocumented minors and as a protector of their right to humane treatment in custody?

At the heart of the *Flores* litigation and the battles over safe detention conditions for immigrant children are questions central to American democracy: the constitutional right to due process and equal protection regardless of legal status, the right to freedom from unjustified government detention, the state's *parens patriae* (parent of the nation) responsibility for the welfare of the child, and the effectiveness of judicial review of national immigration policy. The divided court opinions in the *Flores* case and subsequent changes to federal custody practices all turn on the unique status of "alien juvenile" plaintiffs. They reveal the tug-of-war between the Constitution's protection of individual rights and the government's interest in border security. They have much to teach us about the justifications for detention, the ability of noncitizens to test the legality of confinement, the best interests of the child, and the right to be held in the least restrictive setting.

LEGAL CHALLENGES TO INS DETENTION

Before 1984 unaccompanied children who were apprehended and placed in removal proceedings by the INS were transferred to the Community Relations Service within the Department of Justice and routinely released on bond to family members or church groups or other community associations provided that a responsible individual or organization promised to bring them to immigration court hearings.[4] In 1984, to "stem the tide" of unaccompanied minors crossing the border from Central America, the INS Western Region adopted a special policy that made detention the norm and release the exception. It limited release to "a parent or lawful guardian" except in "unusual and extraordinary circumstances."[5] The practical result of the new policy was that INS field officers stopped releasing children to anyone but a parent and used the "extraordinary" release exception only for those requiring medical care. Using their broad discretion to detain noncitizens, the INS refused to hold hearings to determine whether detention would be in a child's best interest and declined to establish procedures for the review of detention orders.

On July 11, 1985, attorneys for the National Center for Immigrants' Rights, the National Center for Youth Law, and the American Civil Liberties Union (ACLU) of Southern California filed a class action lawsuit on behalf of four detained teenagers against the INS and two private operators of INS detention facilities in the U.S. District Court for the Central District of California.[6] They challenged "the indefinite detention of juveniles who ... are held solely for the purpose of an administration proceeding to determine whether they should be deported."[7] The first named plaintiff, Jenny Lisette Flores, was fifteen years old in 1985 when she left El Salvador. In 1984, during the Salvadoran civil war, there was large-scale migration of children to the United States. Some came because they had lost family members to the war or were left by parents on the run from political persecution. Others fled forced conscription by the army or pressure to join the guerrillas. Many of those Salvadorans migrated to the Los Angeles area. By the time the *Flores* litigation ended in 1997 Salvadorans in California were seen as a permanent immigrant population and a new minority in U.S. ethnic and racial politics. The wars against crime and immigrants were gaining momentum nationally and in California, combining in ways that had serious consequences for immigrant rights, particularly for youth.[8]

Although Jenny Flores faced no criminal charges and posed no threat or flight risk, her request for release to her mother's relatives, an aunt and uncle with legal status, was denied. The private INS-contracted facility in Pasadena, California, where she was held had no educational programs, health care, or personal counseling; provided few opportunities for recreation; denied reasonable visitation with family or friends; and required some children to share bathrooms and sleeping quarters with unrelated adults of both sexes.[9] To prepare the legal case, Carlos Holguin, one of the lead attorneys for the plaintiffs, explained what child welfare specialists found when they inspected the INS detention facilities: "The kids were held in deplorable conditions by the INS. None of them had acceptable social services for children. Their mindset was that 'We have got them. We should deport them, not release them.'"[10]

The lawsuit challenged the INS's treatment of children, specifically, the routine strip and body cavity searches of juveniles,[11] the lack of a probable cause hearing on deportability, the lack of a proper custody hearing on releasing minors to third party adults, and the absence of an independent review of the detention policy for the sole purpose of ensuring appearance in a court proceeding.[12] The plaintiffs argued that conditions in the facility belied the INS's "professed concern with the welfare of minors."[13] They alleged that the INS's policies "are a thinly veiled device to apprehend the parents of incarcerated juveniles and to punish children in the United States without lawful authority"[14] by violating their constitutional right to the Due Process Clause and the Equal Protection Guarantee of the Fifth Amendment, as well as the right to privacy guaranteed by the First, Fourth, Fifth, and Ninth Amendments.[15]

Although the INS conceded that detention conditions were deplorable, it justified its detention policy by citing the dramatic increase in the number of unaccompanied minors,[16] as well as the need to ensure that the "aliens" would appear for court proceedings. The Western Region commissioner, Harold Ezell, could provide no regulatory justification for the detention policy beyond testifying to a personal epiphany that spurred him to action. Seeing the image of a missing, presumably abducted child on a milk carton at breakfast, he resolved to protect the lone migrants in his care.[17] In court Ezell admitted that the release of the child to a responsible adult was a proven and effective means to secure the child's appearance in court proceedings. He conceded that no juveniles who were released to third parties had been harmed and no lawsuits had been filed against the INS for the improper release of minors.[18] Nonetheless, Ezell linked the more limited release policy to his overriding concern for child welfare, insisting that he could not permit release to "just any adult."[19] In response to criticism that the INS should screen the adults rather than jail the children, he asserted that since "the Service has neither the expertise nor the resources to conduct home studies" of prospective sponsors the minors' interests were better served by remaining in detention.[20]

The U.S. District Court for the Central District of California certified the case as a class action, and Judge Robert J. Kelleher ordered the INS to release Flores on bond and to halt strip searches.[21] The district court, in late 1987, approved a consent decree that settled all claims regarding detention conditions. The decree required all INS detention facilities to provide education, visitation, recreation, and segregation of detained minors from unrelated adults.[22] It left unresolved the constitutional challenges to the INS's release policy. Because the INS agreed to issue new regulations governing release, the district court postponed judgment on the plaintiffs' due process claims. In 1988 the INS issued regulations that codified the Western Region's policy into a nationwide rule.[23] As a result, the district court held that the agency failed to satisfy minimum due process requirements and invalidated the policy of the "blanket detention" of minors.[24] It ruled that an individual hearing before "a neutral and detached official" was necessary to determine if release was warranted and under what conditions. The federal government appealed the district court's ruling to the Ninth Circuit Court of Appeals, and in 1991 a divided eleven-judge en banc court affirmed the district court judgment in "all respects."[25] That decision was in turn appealed to the U.S.

Supreme Court. In 1993 Justice Antonin Scalia wrote for the majority in a 7–2 opinion reversing the judgment of the Ninth Circuit Court of Appeals. The Supreme Court remanded the case to the California district court. Before the new trial could begin, the government reached an accord with the plaintiffs, resulting in the Flores Settlement Agreement.[26]

ALIEN MINORS AND THE RIGHT TO FREEDOM

The divided opinions within the court of appeals and the Supreme Court are instructive in a context where the government's interest in detaining a class of people conflicts with those individuals' rights. Three principal issues were considered by the courts: the first involved the right of aliens to freedom from detention through the habeas corpus guarantee, the second addressed the rights of undocumented children, and the third examined whether a "significant" federal purpose suffices to justify the civil detention of aliens.[27]

The Plaintiffs' Interests as Aliens

Writing for the majority in the Ninth Circuit en banc court, Judge Mary Murphy Schroeder concluded that the INS policy violated the plaintiffs' due process right to personal liberty and to freedom from unwarranted detention.[28] At issue were the rights of aliens.[29] Citing a well-known 1886 Supreme Court decision, *Yick Wo v. Hopkins*, holding that the Equal Protection Guarantee sheltered Chinese nationals from the discriminatory enforcement of a San Francisco statute,[30] Schroeder argued that "any person present in the United States is entitled to equal justice under the law" and that "alienage does not prevent a person from testing the legality of confinement."[31] Similarly, the nature of civil immigration detention did not alter the relevance of the principles of habeas corpus. Schroeder acknowledged the broad discretionary power of the attorney general to detain aliens but noted that such discretion is not unlimited. Citing the individual's strong interest in liberty, she argued that detention was justified "only by clear and convincing evidence" of "an identified and articulable threat to an individual or a community."[32] She further asserted that the constitutional interest at issue "is not the due process right to be released" but the freedom from "unjustified government detention" at the outset.[33]

Writing for four dissenters, Judge John Clifford Wallace contended that juvenile aliens lack any fundamental right to be free from government detention and as a result the majority had mischaracterized the INS regulation as a blanket detention policy. He wrote, "No case has been cited to us . . . in which a court has ever recognized a fundamental *substantive* due process right to physical liberty."[34] Wallace was troubled by the majority's failure to consider the immigration context of the case, noting that the Supreme Court has long recognized that Congress's power to control immigration is plenary and that the INS is entitled to deference in its handling of the undocumented.[35] Citing Supreme Court decisions that authorized the deportation of even legally resident aliens, Wallace argued that the due process rights aliens might have are "extremely limited."[36]

Judge Thomas Tang's spirited Ninth Circuit concurrence took the dissenting judges to task for "standing the Constitution on its head." He argued that the central issue was not, as the dissenting judges contended, the right to be released to unrelated adults but the government's right to detain "children who have committed no offense greater than being *suspected* of being deportable." He noted that freedom from government detention is a constitutional right guaranteed by the due process clause of the Fifth Amendment.[37] Citing almost verbatim the language of the 1886 Supreme Court case noted above,[38] Tang wrote, "Liberty is the norm: arrest, detention and restraint by the state is the exception. To operate otherwise makes a mockery of government of the people and by the people . . . and ignores the very substance of the Bill of Rights."[39] He concluded that the "unproven and overblown apprehensions" and "unsubstantiated speculations" of the INS could not outweigh the children's compelling liberty interest.[40]

The 1993 Supreme Court decision[41] reversed the Ninth Circuit Court of Appeals, sustaining the government's discretion to detain immigrant children and to determine the conditions of release. Writing for the majority, Justice Scalia invoked the plenary power doctrine that gives the political branches of the federal government—Congress and the executive—broad, primary power over immigration and naturalization. The Court accepted the notion of the lesser constitutional guarantees for aliens, noting that Congress "regularly makes rules that would be unacceptable if applied to citizens."[42] It held that the INS had not exceeded its authority because a policy of automatic detention served a lawful purpose.

The Supreme Court majority likewise held that the INS regulation did not deprive respondents of due process. The major issue was not the right to freedom from detention but "the alleged right of a child" with no available parent or guardian to be placed in the custody of a private person rather than a government institution.[43] The Court acknowledged that aliens are entitled to procedural due process of law in deportation proceedings but concluded that due process was satisfied by giving the juvenile the right to a hearing before an immigration judge. Ignoring the particular needs of immigrant youth that compromise due process guarantees, such as the absence of multilingual staff to explain INS detention policies, court-appointed immigration attorneys to inform them of their legal rights, and child advocates to represent their best interests, the Court concluded, "It has not been shown that all of them are too young or too ignorant" to exercise their legal rights or to seek advice from a responsible adult outside the INS.[44]

In Supreme Court Justice John Paul Stevens's dissenting opinion, joined by Justice Harry Blackmun, he interpreted the case as a denial of the right not to be detained in the first place. He criticized this "ill-conceived and ill-considered regulation" on the grounds that it is "belied by years of experience with citizen and alien juveniles"[45] and is neither authorized in current immigration law[46] nor consistent with fundamental notions of due process. Justice Stevens would have held that a rule providing for the wholesale detention of juveniles for an indefinite period without individual hearings was unconstitutional.[47] Equating the rights of alien and citizen juveniles, he argued that Congress had spoken on the detention of juveniles in the Juvenile Justice and Delinquency Prevention Act of 1974 and rejected the "very assumption upon which the INS relies."[48] He echoed Judge Tang in declaring that "it is the government's burden to prove that detention is necessary, not the individual's burden to prove that release is justified," because in U.S. society detention prior to trial or without trial is the carefully limited exception.[49] He concluded that the majority was simply wrong when it asserted that the freedom from physical restraint was not at issue. That was precisely the issue. He insisted that children should not be committed to institutions that the INS and the Supreme Court majority believed were good enough for aliens simply because they conformed to the minimum standards for the incarceration of juvenile delinquents. While waiting for their cases to be heard in immigration court, juveniles had the right to the same equal justice before the law enjoyed by all persons in the United States, citizens and noncitizens alike.

The Plaintiffs' Interest as Children

The Ninth Circuit en banc court decision rejected the INS's contention that the minority status of the aliens changed the nature of their liberty interest, thereby rendering "the detention policy reasonable and appropriate."[50] The court held that the Constitution protects the rights of children—both aliens and citizens—to due process of law. It also ruled that such protections are met only in a hearing before a "neutral and detached" adjudicator.[51] Citing the famous 1967 *Re Gault* ruling on the due process rights of the minor in pretrial detention, the court affirmed that even if the governmental purpose for confinement is "legitimate and substantial" that purpose cannot be pursued when less restrictive means such as foster care are available. Freedom from institutional confinement should be the norm and government detention a last resort; that treatment was necessary to serve the child's best interests.[52]

In his dissent, Judge Wallace conceded that children were legal "persons" under the Constitution who possessed fundamental rights that the state must respect. Nonetheless, their liberty interests were not identical to those of adults. He cited points from a New York ruling that noted that children, unlike adults, are always in some form of custody and naturally under the control of others. He asserted that if parental control falters, the state must play its part as parens patriae.[53]

Responding to the dissenters on this issue, Judge Tang forcefully emphasized the adverse consequences of detaining children and the risk of fundamentally unfair and erroneous decision making recognized by the Constitution when the roles of prosecutor and adjudicator were combined in a single entity, as they were in the INS. Judge Betty Binns Fletcher concurred, describing the case "as among the most disturbing I have confronted in my years at court" and writing that the INS's contention that children's welfare is better served by remaining indefinitely in jail "stretches credulity."[54] Judge William Albert Norris, also concurring, wrote that incarcerating children pending deportation hearings rather than releasing them to responsible adults, whether relatives or not, "not only violates due process but does so flagrantly."[55] Judge Pamela Ann Rymer concurred, based on the fact that no limits had been placed on the length of civil detention and the INS provided no assistance to the children from an attorney, parent, legal guardian, or guardian ad litem.[56]

Writing for the Supreme Court majority, Justice Scalia held that the attorney general had broad discretion to determine the terms of release for an alien awaiting the deportation hearing.[57] Nonetheless, he noted the complications that arise when an arrested juvenile is unaccompanied. Describing the serious problem of dealing with the "thousands of alien juveniles" arrested each year by the INS, 70 percent of whom are unaccompanied, he insisted that "the INS cannot simply send them off into the night on bond or recognizance."[58] However, since there were no findings of fact or a court record showing how the INS interpreted or enforced the regulation, the Court had "only the regulation itself" as a guide.[59] On that basis, the Court dispensed with the plaintiffs' allegation that the conditions of detention were so severe as to impose "an unconstitutional infliction of punishment without trial."[60] Pointing only to the newly promulgated INS regulations, the Court held that "whatever those [detention] conditions might have been when this litigation began," the INS was "presumably now in full compliance."[61] In a rhetorical sleight of hand the Supreme Court majority asserted that "legal custody[,] rather than detention, more accurately describes the reality of the arrangements." It reasoned that since "these are not correctional institutions but facilities that meet state licensing requirements" and are operated "in an open type of setting without a need for extraordinary security measures, it is not punitive."[62] As later lawsuits against the government and congressional testimony would show, Justice Scalia's assumptions about the nature of institutional confinement and the government's compliance with the FSA were incorrect.

The Government Interest in the Civil Detention of Minors

The INS had contended, first, that the child's interests were better served by "detention rather than release to a responsible adult in a living environment that the INS did not have the means to investigate."[63] Second, the INS had argued that the detention policy was necessary to protect the agency from potential liability in the event that a child was harmed after release.[64] The Ninth Circuit Court argued that incarceration served no legitimate purpose since there was no evidence that release would pose a risk to the community or place the child in danger.[65] The majority likewise rejected the INS's claim that it must detain children to avoid lawsuits, noting that federal or state agencies faced greater exposure to liability by keeping children in custody than by releasing them.[66] It recognized the legal incapacity of minors to understand their rights and mandated an individual hearing regardless of whether the child requested it. Both the Ninth Circuit Court of Appeals majority opinion and the concurrences found the government's asserted interests either illegitimate or unsubstantial or both. Without a significant government interest, the court reasoned, the policy impinging on a fundamental right must be struck down.

In his dissenting opinion, Judge Wallace argued that the INS's desire to protect the safety of the detained children and the concern for potential liability were legitimate government ends. The Supreme Court majority agreed, arguing that government custody "in decent and humane conditions" is rationally connected to the government's interest in the welfare of the child. Thus the Court contended that the INS was not required to shorten or end detention.

The Court further rejected the plaintiffs' claims that the child's best interests were better served by release than by INS detention. It asserted that the best interest of the child was neither the legal standard nor the absolute and exclusive criterion that governed the government's custodial responsibilities.[67] So long as institutional custody met minimum standards of child care, the interests of the child could be subordinated to the state's parens patriae interest in preserving the welfare of the child.[68]

In a vigorous dissent, Justice Stevens argued that the INS had failed to provide any evidence of the need for the indefinite incarceration of minor children.[69] In a caustic challenge to the INS commissioner's professed concern for the welfare of minors, he wrote:

> At the time the new policy [limiting release] was adopted, the conditions of confinement were admittedly "deplorable." How a responsible administrator could possibly conclude that the practice of commingling harmless children with adults of the opposite sex in detention centers protected by barbed wire fences, without providing them with education, recreation or visitation, while subjecting them to arbitrary strip searches would be in their best interests is most difficult to comprehend.[70]

Carlos Holguin commented on both the 1993 Supreme Court decision and the Flores Settlement Agreement that followed in 1997.

> I wasn't particularly happy [about the Supreme Court decision] because anytime you get an en banc decision from the 9th Circuit there is only one way to go but down. It is your best chance when the en banc court decides in your favor. You want the litigation to stop because there is no upside to a Supreme Court decision. My interest was in the practical effects on the ground, not in abstract legal arguments. We had nothing else to achieve except to have the decision cut back. The facts were good. In the 1987 consent decree the government agreed to improve the conditions in custody. They insisted that they were doing it to protect the kids. In fact, it was a purely tactical decision by the government to defang the class action lawsuit. . . . Back in 1985–87 it was an illusion to think that we could win this case. We knew all along that there would have to be compromise. Could we end detention? No. Could we get detained kids released to responsible adults? Yes. There was also the

child welfare concern. That was the principal motivation. We didn't want to release kids to a situation of harm but we didn't want to put them in detention with a general population where they would be held with criminals or delinquents. We delude ourselves if we think we have the exclusive ability to control the trajectory of this agreement. It was, and continues to be, a matter of thrusts, moves, and counter moves.[71]

The FSA left unresolved a number of key issues in the treatment of detained children. It did not address the conflict of interest noted by Ninth Circuit Court Judge Tang between the role of the INS as both prosecutor and jailer of undocumented children. Although it permitted children to be released to sponsors other than parents, it gave the government the sole authority to decide where to detain the child as well as the timing and terms of release.[72] The FSA called for "the least restrictive setting according to the age and needs of the child"[73] but permitted children to be held in secure facilities not only when they had been charged or convicted of criminal or delinquent activity but also when they were deemed a flight risk or acted in "unacceptably disruptive ways" in custody.[74] It did not define "disruptive conduct." The FSA also included a significant exception to the least restrictive setting requirement in the event of an emergency. This exception was problematic because the agency defined an emergency very broadly, including national disasters, disease outbreaks, and facility fires. More problematically, it set the threshold level for an emergency influx of child migrants in 1997 numbers, at a time when the capacity of the detention centers was roughly one-tenth its current capacity. Such an influx occurred in summer 2012[75] and continued in 2014 as unprecedented numbers of children were being apprehended and held in Border Patrol stations and military installations in Texas, California, and Oklahoma.

Although the FSA authorized the plaintiffs' attorneys to inspect INS detention facilities for compliance, it did not establish an independent agency to provide monitoring and oversight. In fact, the district court assigned an INS official, the Juvenile Coordinator in the Office of the Assistant Commissioner for Detention and Deportation, to report on his own agency's compliance with the agreement.[76] The FSA outlined general standards for the humane treatment of children in federal custody but did not incorporate the best interest of the child standard, which is the norm in domestic and international law. The agreement required that detained minors be notified of their rights, including the right to legal representation at no expense to the government and the right to have a U.S. district court review the government's decision to detain the minor.[77] Given that undocumented minors had no right to government-funded counsel, no right to an independent child advocate, and only limited means to obtain pro bono counsel, they were advised of rights they had virtually no opportunity to exercise while in detention.

Red Flags on Flores: The Least Restrictive Setting?

In late September 2001, four years after the finalization of the FSA and dismissal of the *Flores* case, the Office of the Inspector General published an alarming report on the INS system of detention for unaccompanied minors. The OIG criticized the INS for weak oversight, overreliance on secure detention, the shackling of "non-delinquent juveniles," improper escorts during the transfer of minors, and gaps in INS records that made it impossible "to demonstrate compliance" with the FSA.[78] Five months later, on February 28, 2002, the Senate Subcommittee on Immigration heard testimony in public hearings on the Unaccompanied Alien Child Protection Act (UACPA), a bill introduced in 2000 by California senator Dianne Feinstein. It sought to address lingering deficiencies in the care of unaccompanied children in federal detention and in the processes used in their removal hearings in the immigration court.[79] Sen. Edward Kennedy of Massachusetts, then subcommittee chair, urged immediate action on the bill because it concerned thousands of immigrant children who were held in custody pending hearings on their immigration status. He began by explaining that the children "enter the country after traumatic experiences, often speak little or no English, and are rarely aware of their rights under U.S. law." Although many were eligible for asylum because they fled human rights abuses or armed conflict, he lamented, they "are not appointed counsel and are left to represent themselves in immigration court against experienced government lawyers." To make matters worse "they are frequently detained and languish for long periods in shelters with no access to translators, telephones, medical care or other vital services." The senator added, "But these are the fortunate ones. . . . [M]ore than 30 percent of the unaccompanied children detained last year were held in juvenile jails, often with dangerous criminals, subject to shackling and strip searches." The proposed legislation was intended to address "extended detention" in prisonlike conditions and to bring the U.S. in line with international norms,"[80] notably by mandating government-funded counsel and child advocates in immigration court proceedings.[81]

In congressional testimony based on visits to eighteen secure facilities and juvenile detention centers run by the INS, Wendy Young, then supervising attorney for the Detention Asylum Project at the Women's Commission for Refugee Women and Children, cited numerous examples of harsh treatment, prolonged detention, and illegal deportations by INS officers. She viewed these "gaps in U.S. policy" as the inevitable outcome of an "irreconcilable conflict of interest" between the competing [INS] responsibilities of prosecuting the children and caring for them. She cited the INS preference for "enforcement goals" and its blatant disregard for the basic needs of detained children.[82] Young brought former detainees with her to the hearing, including Edwin Larios Munoz, who fled violence in his native Honduras. Edwin painted a heartbreaking picture of loss, abandonment at the age of four, and sustained abuse by a cousin. Leaving home alone at thirteen, Edwin worked his way through Central America, finally crossing the U.S.-Mexico border four months later, in August 2000. He was arrested by U.S. Border Patrol agents, shackled like Jenny Flores, and transferred to a juvenile jail for violent offenders. While in detention, he suffered appalling mistreatment.

> I was placed in another cell with a U.S. citizen boy who had serious problems with the law. He was not as bad as the other boys in the jail who were there for murders, having weapons, violence or theft. I spent around 8 months in this jail. I was locked in the cell about 18 hours a day, since we were only allowed out for a few hours for classes. . . . The officers did not know why I or the other children picked by the INS were there. They treated us the same as the others, as criminals. They were mean and aggressive and used a lot of bad words. They hit me with their sticks and shoved me and the other boys when they thought we were not following orders. . . . I lost weight and was usually sick at this jail since I could not eat the food . . . and the jail always smelled like urine. I cried a lot in the cell, wondering why everything was turning out so bad for me here in the United States and wondering if I would ever be free.[83]

Edwin was fortunate: a legal aid team screened him and found a competent pro bono attorney who helped him apply for legal relief. An immigration court judge granted his petition in July 2001, seven months before his Senate testimony. Despite this outcome, Edwin reminded the subcommittee of the lasting effects of his detention:

> It took me a while to feel at home in Michigan. I still have horrible memories over what I went through with INS and at the San Diego jail. I saw many children like me who gave up fighting their immigration cases and accepting deportation because they hated the jail and did not have attorneys.[84]

The 2002 congressional hearing exposed the continuing mistreatment of minors in INS custody despite the FSA. Wendy Young echoed many of the OIG's 2001 conclusions but recounted more egregious abuses.[85] She testified that the INS continued to detain children for long periods, systematically denied their release to family, particularly when their relatives in the United States were undocumented, routinely encouraged children to accept voluntary departure even when they had expressed a fear of returning to their home country, and housed more than a third in secure detention facilities for youth offenders. Citing the example of a fourteen-year-old asylum seeker from Honduras forced to share a cell for four months with a domestic youth adjudicated for assault with a deadly weapon, she insisted that such "commingling was common." Young noted the misuse of the FSA provision that suspended the least restrictive setting requirement in the case of an emergency. She opined, "The exception has overtaken the rule." Young advised the subcommittee that children were still being subjected to handcuffing and shackling, were misidentified as adults and held in adult prisons, and were bereft of the critical assistance they needed from interpreters, attorneys, and child welfare experts.[86] Her on-site investigation was published in a 2002 report by the Women's Commission for Refugee Women and Children.[87] That report took the INS to task on two separate issues: the "wholly inappropriate conditions of confinement" and a "*de facto* denial of access to legal and social services critical to the pursuit of asylum or other forms of relief."[88]

When Stuart Anderson, INS executive associate commissioner, testified at the hearing, he promised reform, insisting that his agency had no vested interest in the status quo.[89] Chief Immigration Judge Michael Creppy was questioned about the number of unaccompanied children appearing without attorneys in deportation hearings. Senator Feinstein cited estimates from the judge's own agency, the Executive Office for Immigration Review (EOIR), that "undocumented children go unrepresented 50%–80% of the time." Judge Creppy insisted that that "those numbers are not accurate" and a "majority of juveniles are represented." When pushed to explain he admitted, "We do not have a system that can accurately give you those kinds of numbers."[90]

FEDERAL CUSTODY, 2002–PRESENT

Federal Legislation

Although Senator Feinstein introduced the UACPA every year between 2000 and 2007, the Congress never passed it.[91] In the face of mounting evidence of continuing and egregious violations of the FSA, the *Flores* plaintiffs' attorneys filed a status report in 2003 with the U.S. District Court for the Central District of California. They cited the excessive use of secure confinement for nondelinquent children and those arrested for petty offenses, the lack of basic services, and the prevalence of harsh disciplinary measures such as solitary confinement and the deprivation of education.[92] Over this period a broad coalition of public and private stakeholders repeatedly demanded reform of the INS detention system.[93]

In 2002, months after the Senate subcommittee hearing, Congress passed the Homeland Security Act (HSA), which dismantled the INS and vested enforcement functions in Customs and Border Protection and Immigration and Customs Enforcement, consolidating them within one federal agency, the newly created Department of Homeland Security.[94] While the passage of the HSA was intended to strengthen U.S. border security and immigration enforcement, the act also addressed the conflict of interest at the INS. It left the detention system intact but transferred responsibility for the custody of unaccompanied children to an agency with a child welfare mandate and long experience in the treatment of refugee minors: the Division of Unaccompanied Children's Services (DUCS) within the Office of Refugee Resettlement.[95]

In addition, in 2008 Congress passed the Trafficking Victims Protection Reauthorization Act (TVPRA). Washington advocates for immigrant children's rights were able to integrate some elements of the failed Unaccompanied Alien Child Protection Act into the trafficking reauthorization bill, including measures that improved protections for children, specifically, those seeking asylum or immigrant juvenile status.[96] The TVPRA included language requiring the prompt placement of unaccompanied minors "in the least restrictive setting that is in the best interests of the child" and provided for the appointment of an independent child advocate for children in immigration proceedings.[97] It also required ICE agents to notify ORR officials after the apprehension of an unaccompanied child and to transfer custody of that child to ORR within seventy-two hours.[98]

Federal Custody under ORR

Following the transfer of jurisdiction from the INS to ORR on March 1, 2003, observers have commended ORR for improving the system. In their 2003 report, the *Flores* plaintiffs' attorneys said they were "guardedly optimistic that ORR will end the pattern and practice of violations."[99] A 2006 report stated that "the importance of this transfer of responsibility to ORR cannot be overstated" because it "presaged a positive and serious change in the U.S. approach" to this population.[100] In a 2012 study of the federal custodial system, the Vera Institute of Justice, an ORR subcontractor that hires legal service providers to screen detained children, declared unequivocally that the conflict of interest was resolved when ORR assumed its role as guardian in early 2003.[101] The Vera Institute's lucrative contract with the federal government should give us pause, however. Could the authors of the report have reached any other conclusion and still maintain their relationship with ORR?

Noteworthy Progress

Operating under the mandate of the FSA, ORR officials have incorporated child welfare principles that consider the safety and rights of the child. Children in custody are screened for potential relief, informed of their legal rights, and required to attend class five days a week. They receive access to social services, psychological counseling, medical care, and recreational time. Although ORR continues to hold the vast majority of children in a system of closed facilities, agency officials have expanded the placement options to include small numbers of group homes and long-term foster care.[102] They have dramatically reduced the use of secure detention facilities. Before 2003 half of all unaccompanied children were in secure facilities.[103] In 2012, of a total of 14,721 placements, only 1,107, or 8 percent, were in secure facilities. In 2013, 25,041 came into custody, but the numbers in secure facilities shrank to 599.[104] ORR has also streamlined the process of release and increased the number of children who are reunified with family members or placed with approved sponsors from 52 percent in 2009 to approximately 65 percent in 2012. That number rose to almost 88 percent by late 2013.[105]

Persistent Problems

Despite the improvements, observers report many of the same problems in the federal custodial system. They describe the system confronting child migrants as "Kafkaesque" because of its "disjointed, labyrinthine character,"[106] noting that many as fifteen federal agencies interact in some way with unaccompanied children. Rather than reduce the number of beds in closed facilities, ORR has instead expanded its capacity and increased the number of federal staff it employs. In the six years since I began this research the total number of federal facilities increased from 39 to 114 in October 2014.[107] The number of unaccompanied children coming into ORR custody reached a new record high in 2014 with 61,340 admissions and is estimated to surpass that number in 2015.[108]

The massive bureaucratization of custody has produced systemic deficits that include a lack of coordination in data collection and tracking, loss or inappropriate sharing of confidential information,[109] unnecessary delays, multiple interviews, and an ad hoc approach to problems that undermines consistency and fairness.[110] In contrast to the protective approach used for at-risk children in the domestic child welfare and juvenile justice fields, an enforcement mind-set still defines the approach to unaccompanied children in immigration proceedings.[111] Most significantly, oversight and overall management of federal interactions rest with an enforcement-oriented agency. ICE remains the gatekeeper with regard to detention, making the initial determination about the child's age and status as accompanied or unaccompanied, as well as the possibility of release to family.

An OIG report published in 2007 noted the conflict between the child welfare model and the enforcement model at the heart of the custodial system.[112] Two years later, in 2009, a Women's Commission for Refugee Women and Children report stated that the treatment of unaccompanied children in federal custody had "greatly improved" but concluded that the 2009 "system of care is in many way a friendlier face superimposed on the old INS model."[113] Wendy Young and Megan McKenna, attorneys now working with the KIND foundation, note that the positive impact of ORR reforms has often been blunted "by conflicting procedural elements and general failures of implementation."[114] For example, the TVPRA of 2008 aligns the least restrictive setting with the best interests of the child, but it is in direct conflict with INS guidelines, still in effect, that preclude the best interest standard from playing any role in the determination of the child's legal status in immigration court.[115]

The custodial system continues to be plagued by problems. These include coercive arrests; inappropriate treatment and inadequate screening of juveniles by CBP and ICE after apprehension; delays in their transfer to ORR custody; lack of a uniform tracking system to follow children from their first to their last contact with immigration authorities; long periods of detention, especially for children with special physical, psychological, and behavioral problems; and a shortage of specialized therapeutic facilities. Young and McKenna criticize the long-standing trend of locating federal shelter facilities in remote border regions "either to reduce costs or to keep children in close proximity to the border and ready for deportation if ordered."[116] Equally problematic are the obstacles children face obtaining direct legal representation while in custody; only 28 percent of detained children had attorneys in 2010.[117]

THE DETENTION MODEL

The ongoing preference for a detention model based on institutional confinement rather than open-setting placement in the home or community is an especially troubling aspect of the treatment of immigrant youths. After the initial screening by ICE, ORR officials evaluate and place the vast majority in a system of closed facilities. Even minimum-security shelters such as the facility where Maribel was held are locked and fenced. It bears reminding that ORR continues to contract for beds in juvenile prisons with barred cells and rigid disciplinary regimens for undocumented youth charged with criminal activity as well as those transferred from less restricted facilities because of their behavior in custody.[118]

A case in point is the NORCOR juvenile detention center located in a rural area ninety miles east of Portland, Oregon. When ORR assumed jurisdiction for unaccompanied minors in 2003, it inherited an existing INS contract with the facility. Under that contract NORCOR received a per diem sum to warehouse minors who were to be held for short periods until their removal from the country. Initially, NORCOR provided no case management, psychological counseling, legal orientation program, or adequate educational services and commingled foreign minors with domestic youths who had been charged with or adjudicated for delinquency. In 2003 ORR managers introduced a "new philosophy governing the custody of minors" and informed the NORCOR director that detention conditions had to meet FSA requirements.[119] When, after eighteen months, the facility failed to comply, ORR canceled the contract. Just three years later, in 2007, ORR managers again subcontracted with NORCOR for secure beds.[120]

ORR-contracted attorneys and child welfare specialists with regular access to the facility during that period commented on the bleak physical plant, the freezing temperatures, the harsh disciplinary measures, and the lack of services.[121] NORCOR continued to commingle unaccompanied minors with pre- and post-adjudicated domestic youths, to shackle youths for court appearances, and to strip-search them after hearings and visits from attorneys.[122] The facility had no full-time case manager until 2008 and never offered the mental health services mandated by the FSA. There was no accredited Spanish-speaking teacher until 2009. As a result, youths spent classroom time studying individually from workbooks. Daily physical exercise took place in an enclosed concrete courtyard covered at the top with a metal grate. Interviews and visitations were held in a "no-contact room" behind a glass partition.

Observers describe the discipline at NORCOR as "super-regimented."[123] Although no corporal punishment or mechanical restraints were permitted, the minors were subjected to a regime of uninterrupted evaluation designed to have them internalize penal rules and supervise themselves. Every day floor staff awarded points in each of four categories: interactions with staff, group behavior, general attitude, and conformity with the rules. Earning fewer points than the required totals meant the loss of privileges and isolation from group activities for seven days, including meals and classes. Youths had to walk on a line in the floor, look straight ahead, stand tall, and avoid physical contact of any kind. They were required to stop, turn, and face the wall before entering individual cells that were six-by-ten-foot rectangles with low ceilings and no natural light. The cells contained only a concrete platform bed with a bedroll and pillow, a stainless steel sink, mirror, and toilet, all visible from the cell window. No personal effects such as photos or letters were permitted, with the exception of a Bible and one book. Those youths who elected not to participate in after-dinner activities, offered only in English, typically remained under lockdown for twelve hours. Nikki Dreyden, the attorney who worked in the Unaccompanied Children's Program at the Vera Institute of Justice, visited NORCOR in late 2009. Although she had toured four of the five secure facilities with ORR contracts, she was so affected by the prisonlike conditions that she sought psychological counseling for vicarious trauma when she returned to New York.[124] Despite these continuing violations of the FSA, ORR did not terminate the contract with NORCOR until September 30, 2010.

CONCLUSION

The late senator from New York, Daniel Patrick Moynihan, said that if he had the choice between a country with the right to vote but no habeas corpus or a country that had habeas corpus but no right to vote, he would always choose the one with habeas corpus. Why? Because if the government had the power to detain people without having to provide justification in court, as habeas corpus required, then all other rights were meaningless.[125] As a result of the *Reno v. Flores* case, the right of the federal government to detain immigrant children who are charged only with immigration violations is now firmly established. That ruling settled the question of a legitimate government interest in the civil detention of noncitizens. The automatic confinement of the majority of unaccompanied minors in closed facilities rather than open settings for unspecified and sometimes prolonged periods of time puts the United States at odds with international conventions on children's rights that urge states to end the "inappropriate and widespread use of detention" except as a "last resort."[126] Wendy Young, current director of KIND, agrees: "Most of these kids have done nothing wrong. Their sole 'crime' is to cross the border without documents. Often it was not their sole decision. Detention is a punitive measure. There is nothing to punish."[127] To insist, as the Supreme Court justices did in the 1993 majority opinion, that these detention facilities are not "correctional institutions" or to describe detention even in low-security shelters as simply "legal custody" is to practice Orwellian doublespeak. A custodial system that works in tandem with immigration courts that violate minors' rights to due process protections and ignore the best interest standard also stands in sharp contrast to the treatment of U.S. citizen children in child welfare systems as well as in family, dependency, and juvenile courts. Even children held in pretrial custody because of serious criminal offenses are afforded protections in the form of legal representation and guardians ad litem.[128]

Fifteen years on, the weakness of the original Flores Settlement Agreement is demonstrated by the fact that its major provisions mandating prompt release or the least restrictive setting have not been fully implemented. Complaints about the treatment of children in federal detention continue. The *Houston Chronicle* investigated the compliance of ORR shelters and foster care programs with state licensing regulations in Texas. Over the past decade, state child care licensing investigators documented more than one hundred serious incidents involving staff who violated regulations governing the care and supervision of children in federal facilities.[129]

Congress has acknowledged reports of abuse in ORR-contracted detention facilities in appropriation bills since 2005 and has directed DHS to use alternatives to detention. Although the federal government has closed facilities in Texas, Indiana, and Oregon following internal complaints from ORR staff or legal action by NGOs, federal officials have repeatedly failed to hold abusers accountable and have been slow to enact procedures to prevent, report, and punish abuse. DHS retains wide discretion to open any detention facility for unaccompanied children and families, to screen children first after apprehension, and to set the conditions for custody.

One of the most problematic features of the original FSA is the absence of a mechanism to review the government's compliance with its own provisions. Since then Congress has repeatedly failed to codify the FSA by legislating minimum detention standards and by mandating independent oversight to track compliance. Thus a voluminous provisional set of regulations, based on an outdated agreement without enforcement mechanisms or a congressional mandate, is what guides daily operations in federal facilities.[130] A system that in the past prolonged detention to the point where young people "self-deport" even when they have an avenue to legal status cannot be termed protective.[131] A similar conclusion can be drawn about the overloaded system in 2014 that detains and releases exploding numbers of children without proper screening or follow-up services.

ORR relies on both protection and enforcement rationales to justify supervised custody. The enforcement agenda has had priority in the treatment of undocumented children who were brought to the United States in early childhood, raised in this country, and referred to immigration authorities by police, probation officers, juvenile judges, or child welfare agencies.[132] Undocumented children who suffer abuse or neglect or run afoul of the law are often trapped within competing state and federal systems that function at cross purposes. ICE enforcement priorities frequently trump the protections afforded to youths in state welfare and juvenile justice systems.[133] They run the risk of being treated as aliens first and as children second.

The litigation that produced the FSA coincides with a deportation experiment whose history extends back to the Alien and Sedition Acts of the 1790s.[134] In the post-9/11 period the federal government has used detention and deportation as harsh tools of social control against discrete, marginalized groups in our society. Mechanisms originally envisioned as appropriate only at the border and at points of entry have extended a border control regime deep into the interior of the nation. Post-entry laws have made the immigration system less discretionary and more arbitrary by imposing harsh penalties for criminal or political conduct that can be applied retroactively and are subject to minimal judicial review.[135] Harsh immigration laws have built on a domestic war on crime dominated by racial profiling and draconian policies such as mandatory minimum sentences, three-strikes laws, truth in sentencing, and wide disparities in penalties for drug possession.

In the next chapter I follow Mirabel, Corina, Ernesto and Modesto into a federal custodial system shaped by this new context.

4

Placement in Federal Custody

Ernesto was completely disoriented after his transfer to an ORR shelter.

> You don't know what's going to happen. On the second day in that [Border Patrol] station I still didn't know anything and I asked, "Why do they send me here?" The [Border Patrol] guy said, "What difference does it make? You're leaving." Later they brought in three more kids, and we asked them again, "Where are we going?" They said, "Don't ask!" We were so afraid. Were they going to take us somewhere and kill us? Then they took us to a shelter in Nixon, Texas. That was in 2006. I had to stand in a line with alotta new kids. Still we didn't know anything. I thought, "Where am I now? Why are these kids here?"

Maribel too had vivid memories of her arrival at a large facility in Los Fresnos near the Texas border in 2007.

> So they took us to a shelter and gave us new clothes and food. They didn't ask too many questions. They gave us a toothbrush and sent me to the blue house. All the houses had different colors. I asked myself, "What was the meaning of this? Was it for criminal people?" I thought, "I don't know why I'm here—just like a criminal."

Orlando, a youth who had lived in the United States since the age of nine, felt a sense of betrayal when ICE agents said that he was being transferred from the Adobe Mountain School, a juvenile facility in Arizona where he had spent a year, to federal detention in Virginia. He was outraged that the secure ORR facility was far more restrictive than the Arizona detention center.

> I couldn't believe that I got sent here. I did my time and when the parole board released me I thought that was it. But they said, "No, ICE is gonna pick you up." Instead of going home I came here.

DHS AS GATEKEEPER

ICE officials are the gatekeepers for evaluating the security threat posed by undocumented youth.[1] They make the initial determination about a child's age, the possibility of release to family members, and his or her status as accompanied or unaccompanied. Under the Homeland Security Act of 2002, an Unaccompanied Alien Child (UAC) is defined as one who is younger than eighteen, does not have lawful immigration status, and is without a parent or legal guardian in the United States available to provide care and physical custody.[2] This UAC label is both the legal term and the default shorthand used by most public and private stakeholders throughout the system. If the child claims to be over eighteen, as Ernesto did, or there is doubt about age, DHS can request a dental or skeletal radiograph to determine age—a procedure that medical experts have deemed scientifically unreliable because its estimates of age are so imprecise, having a range of eighteen months.[3] In the past ICE and ORR tended to interpret bone or dental scans differently. If a scan revealed a child to be between seventeen and eighteen and a half years old, ORR typically recorded the child's age as seventeen, whereas ICE recorded it as eighteen and a half, thereby disqualifying him as a minor.[4]

CBP or ICE agents conduct the initial screening interview and open an immigration file that follows the child throughout custody. Time pressures mount at this stage because under the TVPRA of 2008 unaccompanied children must be transferred within seventy-two hours to the custody of the Division of Children's Services within the Office of Refugee Resettlement. Those who are deemed unaccompanied are referred rapidly to a national juvenile coordinator at ICE who notifies an intake team at ORR headquarters in Washington, DC.

The designation of minors as "unaccompanied" and "accompanied" is often arbitrary. It is frequently based on incomplete, misleading, or incorrect information. It obscures the existence of family relationships, mischaracterizes the child's background, and has markedly different effects on placement in custody and eligibility for legal status. "Unaccompanied Alien Child" describes not one but three populations: children who have no relatives in the United States; those who are merely separated from parents or family members already in the United States; and those who live in the United States and come to the attention of immigration authorities after running afoul of the law or after referral to child protective services. At apprehension many children are afraid to disclose the existence and location of undocumented relatives and refuse to do so. This is a legitimate fear because the Bush administration ended the "catch and release" immigration policy that governed apprehensions until 2002. In some cases ICE officials have classified minors as unaccompanied and transferred them to ORR custody even when they were advised that parents or relatives were available and willing to care for them. In others ICE agents have classified children with family members in the United States as accompanied even if they refused to release the child. In both instances ICE decisions turn children who have families into unaccompanied minors subject to federal detention.[5] In contrast, children who were apprehended with relatives were typically designated as accompanied and detained together pending a hearing in immigration court. If children from Mexico or Canada were categorized as accompanied by a parent or guardian, the group was quickly deported. The imperative to evaluate and move children quickly out of temporary detention in CBP stations can lead to initial placements that are ill suited to their needs and background.

What follows is a description of the placement process up to the massive surge that began in spring 2012. Since then it has become very difficult for NGOs, legal advocates, or academics to get up-to-date statistics or gain access to government shelters and programs.

THE INITIAL PLACEMENT: SHELTER, STAFF SECURE, OR SECURE?

Using information gathered by ICE on the child's nationality, medical and psychological condition, prior juvenile delinquency or criminal history, and gang involvement, the ORR team first determined the level of risk the child poses to himself, to others in detention, and to the immigration court system. The risk assessment was the primary basis for placing the child within a tiered system of closed facilities organized by three security levels: (1) low-security shelters, (2) medium-level staff-secure facilities and therapeutic treatment centers, and (3) high-security juvenile detention centers.[6] Available bed space, age, gender, geographic location at apprehension, and evidence of psychological trauma were important but secondary considerations in the placement decision.

The Placement Tool

The vast majority of children admitted into custody between 2008 and 2012 were initially placed in low-security shelters. This placement trend represented a marked departure from the punitive model employed by the INS. As we saw, the FSA required the least restrictive setting but permitted DHS and ORR to consider prior adjudications or charges when deciding on initial placement. Unfortunately, ORR often received incomplete background information from the initial DHS screening, particularly for children entering the immigration system by way of state child welfare, juvenile, and criminal justice systems. Incomplete data about the nature and extent of the child's involvement in state systems were a significant problem because some ORR-contracted shelters were prohibited by state licensing requirements from admitting youths with any delinquent or criminal history. Conversely, juvenile detention centers in some states stipulated that only minors with serious criminal charges could be admitted to their most secure facilities. For that reason, state regulations at juvenile jails such as the NORCOR facility in Oregon permitted the use of strip searches and mechanical restraints such as shackling and handcuffs.

In 2008 ORR partnered with the Vera Institute of Justice to improve the initial placement process by developing more objective measures of risk. They designed a standardized in-house questionnaire that quantified the threat level with a numerical score and matched it to the appropriate level of custody.[7]

SECURITY FIRST

The security focus in the placement questionnaire is evident in the scoring instructions. The questionnaire assigns numerical weights to prior arrests, charges, and adjudications within the U.S. juvenile or criminal justice system, to suspected gang involvement, and to the probability of flight risk. The fear of suspected or confirmed gang membership is pronounced throughout the ORR system. The separate score for gang involvement identifies youths who admitted to or were suspected of being gang affiliated. The questionnaire also flags minors who have a history in government custody and are deemed to pose the threat of disruptive behavior. The questionnaire ranks offenses on a scale from nonviolent to violent and assigns scores that increase with the gravity of the act and the number of incidents. It considers dismissed charges as active charges and scores serious threats of violence or flight the same as actual incidents. The sum of the highest risk scores determines the initial place-ment score. Initial intake scores of 0–5 indicate placement in a low security shelter, 6–12 in a medium-level staff-secure facility, and scores of 13 or above in a high-security facility.[8] For example, a youth with one or more nonviolent petty offenses such as disorderly conduct or shoplifting receives a score of 2 and a recommendation for placement in a minimum-security shelter. A youth with more than one serious, non-violent offense such as car theft, alien smuggling, or prostitution is given a borderline score of 6. If that youth has previously been in government custody and has documented behavior problems, one point is added, for a total score of 7 and placement in a medium-secure facility. If a youth has been arrested for an assault with a class one weapon such as brass knuckles and gang involvement is alleged, the score is raised to 13.

ORR supervisory staff members were permitted to exercise individual discretion and override the placement score upward or downward. Those I interviewed between 2009 and 2012 indicated that supervisory staff frequently exercised their discretion to request more restrictive place-ments for youths with a history of offending, whether or not there were formal charges or court adjudications, particularly when drugs or gangs were involved. This practice may have been more pronounced between 2003 and 2008, when many children were placed in secure facilities in part because beds in less restrictive settings were unavailable.[9]

A third section in the placement tool focuses on the child's psycho-logical profile. In contrast to detailed scoring values given for offenses or escape, questions on "the child's mental or therapeutic needs" carry no numerical value. Instructions say that intake staff may "take into account all available information" and consider the possible link between past offenses and "a therapeutic need." If mental health issues are identified the team is advised to consult with in-house ORR professionals on the need for a specialized therapeutic placement. If not, the instructions direct staff to submit only "the most serious and highest scoring value" per question. Judging from the few available therapeutic beds—only 88 of 2,927 in 2012—mental health was a secondary consideration.[10]

A 2012 Vera Institute publication depicts the placement tool as a fail-safe mechanism that makes placement decisions more uniform, transparent, and objective.[11] In fact, interviews with federal staff and immigration attorneys showed that placement remained a complicated and subjective process that was too often compromised by missing information. Many interviewees did not view the numerical score as more accurate, objective, or helpful, citing instead difficult compromises and fraught negotiations over placement in custody, particularly for youth who were deemed medium- or high-security risks.

TRANSFER TO ORR

Once the placement decision was made, the ORR team typically checked for an available bed at a subcontracted facility within a national network of private service providers.[12] ICE officers transported the child to the designated facility. Soon after arrival, legal aid attorneys under contract to the government came to the facility to screen children for legal relief, explain detention and removal proceedings, and advise them of their rights. Current law does not permit the appointment of government-funded counsel for unaccompanied minors but mandates that they receive the contact information of free legal service providers. Unfortunately that information was not regularly updated and children's access to phones was restricted. NGO monitors discovered that ORR provided information only about legal service providers under contract to the government through the Vera Institute of Justice instead of the more comprehensive and legally mandated list of free or low-cost attorneys approved by the attorney general.[13]

Once in custody the children were issued a Notice to Appear in an immigration court near the detention facility. They were taken for an initial appearance in removal proceedings where they faced government attorneys from the Department of Homeland Security and immigration judges without the benefit of direct legal representation (see chapter 7).

APPREHENSION AT THE BORDER: A LOW-SECURITY SHELTER PLACEMENT

After their apprehension Maribel and her cousin were held at a Border Patrol station where agents questioned them separately. Maribel was a first-time border crosser, had no parents or guardian in the United States to provide care, and readily admitted to being under eighteen. A background check for both a delinquency and criminal history yielded nothing. They designated her as a UAC and referred her to ORR. Because of this low-risk assessment and an open bed close at hand, the ORR intake team placed her at a large shelter in Los Fresnos, Texas, close to the border. In 2007 Maribel entered a custodial system that had total annual referrals of 7,399. The facility was coeducational and housed 160 unaccompanied children, a much larger capacity than in 2010 when the total bed space was reduced to 120.[14] In 2007 half of the children were boys and half were girls. There were five houses in the girls' section with two groups of eight girls and two shelter workers per house. In 2010 it was a minimum-security coeducational shelter, but girls made up four-fifths of the population.

THE PHILOSOPHY OF CARE

By 2007 legal reforms had introduced some due process rights and child welfare protections for detained children by limiting placements in high-security facilities, reducing the average length of stay, and expediting the family reunification process. Based on the FSA requirements, the ORR Provisional Policy and Procedures Manual mandated that UACs be placed within a "non-institutional home-like atmosphere of care in the least restrictive setting"[15] and that program services be administered in a "child-friendly environment."[16]

The ORR philosophy of care signaled a shift from the enforcement-oriented approach of the INS to an approach that was more child-protection oriented. The FSA stipulates that custody must comply with state child welfare laws, and the HSA requires that the child's "interests" be considered in the decisions relating to confinement.[17] Informed by a Western developmental paradigm, this philosophy views the child as an innocent and dependent being in need of adult protection and close supervision. In this paradigm child development is a progression of cognitive and psychosocial factors that evolve in a linear fashion, with the transition to adulthood determined by the bright line of age: eighteen.[18] The individual child has the right to be treated differently than adults and to be protected from exploitation, abuse, and discrimination. Staff members are required to use appropriate interviewing and observational techniques in order to identify victims of trafficking and to assess serious risks to the health and safety of UACs. The manual instructs staff to provide the rules "in a language the child understands" and to include a description of the actions that result in "disciplinary sanctions."[19] Recognizing the child's right to privacy, the ORR regulations stipulate that all personal and medical information remain confidential except in cases of suspected child abuse or when the need for services demands limited disclosure.[20] In accordance with state licensing requirements federal staff are required to establish and maintain professional boundaries when interacting with children.

The philosophy of care is also informed by a paradigm that views children as autonomous, rights-bearing individuals with the capacity to make rational decisions and to be held accountable for their actions.[21] It reflects the increasingly porous boundary between the child, the adolescent, and the adult and the tendency to treat younger and younger individuals as adults. In accordance with this conception, ORR staff informed UACs of their right to receive timely information on their case, to attend a legal rights presentation and be screened for legal relief, to file grievances, to express their views on daily programs and recreational activities, and to benefit from the confidentiality guarantee of attorney-client privilege.[22] Soon after their arrival, children had to sign paperwork indicating that they had received a copy of the facility regulations and approved the individualized service plan created by the facility case manager. They were likewise informed of their right to participate in formulating a plan for release from custody.

The director of the Division of Unaccompanied Children's Services at ORR[23] was the most visible and powerful communicator of this philosophy at staff training meetings, major conferences, and public talks. The director communicated her deep commitment to reunify vulnerable children with family members or responsible sponsors and to protect them from people who might victimize or otherwise hurt them. The director focused on the safeguards taken to ensure their special care and safe release. She used specific cases to illustrate the exceptional compassion shown to undocumented children in ORR care. One such case in late 2006 involved a seventeen-year-old Honduran boy who suffered from an advanced stage of heart disease and became gravely ill while in custody. ORR covered the cost of the heart transplant needed to save his life and provided him with the best available medical care. The agency also flew his mother from Honduras to be with him during the postoperative phase of his care. The director vividly recounted "making the decision to do everything possible for the boy," repeating the story in a voice choked with emotion at trainings and national meetings of ORR staff.[24] Between 2006 and 2012 there were equally extraordinary examples of American largesse extended to the detained children. A youngster I met in 2009 at a Miami shelter had lost a leg to cancer and received a state-of-the-art prosthesis. Another child underwent successful open-heart surgery and was recovering in an Arizona shelter I visited in early 2010. These cases illustrate the exceptional value placed on an individual life as well as the extraordinary efforts of U.S. authorities to protect the child's best interests, despite the legal challenges they faced as unaccompanied undocumented children.

In 2010 I attended a meeting at a Texas shelter in Harlingen where facility staff and the ORR regional manager—known as a federal field specialist (FFS)—reviewed the status of the children in their custody.[25] The FFS made a point to explain the ORR philosophy, emphasizing the dramatic improvement of care since the INS days. She referred to the enhanced training facility staff received in order to recognize and manage the various effects of childhood trauma.[26] New proactive methods were being used to handle a traumatized population. They involved taking the child seriously as a person, training staff to elicit positive reactions, and using a firm but consistent approach. The FFS expressed a widely shared view by both staff and attorneys when she discussed the emotional fragility and natural distrust of kids who "have seen so much and been so traumatized."

> We have to build trust with these kids. We tell staff to just praise the kids, don't focus on the negative. We include a lot of downtime for play. We do simple games, for example, "If you were a tree, what would you do?" "At five in the afternoon what do you do in your home country?" This is the way to build relationships. If you show concern they will respond to you. We try to sell the program, but to do it you have got to believe, you have got to be genuine. It has to mean something. Some kids look at us at a big brother, uncle, or aunt. Now, we are NOT taking the parent's place, but it is OK if they see you like that because trust takes time to build.[27]

The director of a Phoenix shelter used the metaphor of a boulder in rapids to describe the benefit of "custodial care."

> The kids are exhausted and lost when they get here. We give them a place to rest, time to reflect on which direction to go. We encourage them to express their desires. We want them to reunify with family and to feel safe. We attend to their daily needs—hygiene, clothing, and medicine. We test them and get them into school at the level that corresponds to their skills. We are sensitive to their feelings. We understand that many came to work so the family back home can have clean water and food.[28]

What went unsaid were the challenges of providing not only individualized case management but also recruiting and training of qualified staff as the number of children in detention increased rapidly. At the annual ORR training conference in 2010, ORR managers addressed the repeated complaints from the field staff regarding excessive paperwork, duplication of efforts, and "a cookie cutter approach" that failed to consider the child's individual needs and goals. In a revealing acknowledgment, ORR administrators promised to enhance "the quality of case management" by introducing holistic individual service plans tailored to "the best interests of the child." They pledged to coordinate criminal background and child welfare checks to improve risk assessments and to avoid "placement breakdowns" for children suffering from trauma and abuse. Significantly, they proposed to "streamline transfers," improve institutional efficiency, and "enhance federal oversight" of all cases.[29] ORR administrators repeated these same promises nearly verbatim to government, academic, and NGO stakeholders at an interagency meeting on December 12, 2013, convened in the midst of the surge of undocumented children crossing the U.S.-Mexico border.

"We are not Immigration," was one of the first messages children heard repeatedly during their first days in custody. This message signaled a departure from the harsh conditions many had encountered in Border Patrol stations. After arrival children were examined by medical personnel, given immunization shots, and provided with clothes and hygiene products. They were offered a hot meal and showers and assigned a bed in a residential unit. Their personal property was removed, cataloged, and held in storage. They were assigned a facility case manager and clinician and introduced to youth care workers who alternated day and night shifts to provide direct supervision. They met weekly with a social worker or district field coordinator (DFC) from the SAFE Haven program (managed by the NGO Lutheran Immigration and Refugee Services [LIRS], an ORR contractor for family reunification screening until September 30, 2010) and with attorneys from local service providers. Case managers, DFCs, and attorneys conducted intake interviews that centered on their lives at home, their migration experience, their family history, and the whereabouts of close kin.

Children attended a Know Your Rights (KYR) presentation during this period, a cornerstone of the mandatory orientation for new arrivals. In 2005 ORR launched a pilot project, the Unaccompanied Children Program, to create a pro bono model of legal representation for youths in ORR custody. The model relied on a network of legal service providers to locate pro bono counsel—either staff at NGOs with nonpublic sources of funding or private volunteer attorneys—to represent minors who are eligible for legal relief.[30] Administered by the Vera Institute of Justice and funded by ORR, this program recruited legal service providers across the country to screen detained children for possible legal relief and to educate them about their rights. These were short programs usually given in Spanish to introduce unfamiliar legal concepts and terminology. I attended a Know Your Rights presentation at Maribel's shelter in 2010 that was similar in structure and content to the four others I observed in shelters in Arizona, California, New York, and Texas from December 2009 to July 2010.

KNOW YOUR RIGHTS

A charismatic Honduran educator who worked for Pro Bar, the local ORR-contracted legal service provider, gave the legal orientations at five shelters in the Harlingen-Brownsville area. On the day I observed she spoke to the nine new arrivals—three from Guatemala, three from El Salvador, two from Honduras, and one from Colombia. These numbers mirrored the proportion of nationalities in the 2013 custodial system. She explained the different roles of the many adults who interacted regularly with detained children. First, there was the shelter staff: the director, case managers, clinicians, youth care workers, teachers, and cooks. Second, there were the DFCs who evaluated the children for family reunification and came weekly to work on the release process. At the top of hierarchy were the federal field specialists who monitored a number of facilities and made the final decisions on release.

She listed the names of the legal aid attorneys at Pro Bar. Looking at the kids, she emphasized the big difference between the shelter staff and the attorneys: "People in the shelter all work for the government, but attorneys don't. We do not work for the shelter. We do not work for Immigration. We do not work for the court. This is important because if you tell us something we must keep it confidential. This means we cannot share it with your case manager, your counselor, or even your parents." Did they have rights? Absolutely.

No one has the right to hurt or abuse you—not the director, not the staff. You have the right to a balanced diet, to see a doctor, and to go to school. It is all free. New kids ask me if they have the right to watch TV. To listen to music. To play sports. Yes! If you can't sleep or you are depressed you have the right to see a counselor. You will have a case manager who will follow your case. You will have a social worker, a DFC, who helps you to reunify with family members in the U.S. or to find a sponsor. Remember that social workers are very important, but they are not attorneys! Only attorneys can answer legal questions and represent you in court. You have rights while you are here, but you also have obligations. In the shelter you must show respect for others and follow the rules. This means that you can't insult or humiliate other youth or the staff. Respect for others means sexual respect. There can be no sexual propositions or relations between boys and girls. You must take care of property, yours and the shelter's.

She drew a map of Central America and asked the children to locate their home countries in relation to the southern Texas border and to major U.S. cities. How would they describe their journey? Five children had crossed the Rio Grande and called out "Danger," "Cold," "Fear." One child said "Crocodile," prompting peals of laughter. It was no accident that the educator began by defining terms like "ICE," "Border Patrol," "immigration court," "immigration law," and "alien numbers." The children had already experienced these abstract concepts as concrete actions that highlighted their status as "without papers" (*sin papeles*) and prompted their detention. She contrasted legal residents who had the right to live and work in the United States to those who came without permission and broke the law. When one child asked if you need a passport to be legal, she responded that having a passport meant you were a citizen, adding, "You could also be a legal resident with a green card or a work visa. If you came without papers you don't have the right to work. You can leave, but you need permission to return. If you come back again without it that is a crime and you can be deported back to your home country." One youth asked, "Can they deport you because you are poor?" She dodged this question and went on. Those who came without permission still had the right to see an attorney and to get a hearing in court. She listed the options for legal relief.

Asylum: If you are afraid that you will be tortured or killed in your home country because of your faith, your sexual identity, your politics, or the group you belong to you can ask for asylum.

Special Immigrant Juvenile Visa: If you have not had the love or protections a child deserves from his family, if your parents are dead, if they abandoned you and you lived on the street, if they neglected you by not giving you food and clothing, or if they beat you, then you can ask for a Special Immigrant Juvenile Visa. If the judge approves this, you can't return to the mother or father who hurt you.

U Visa: If you are the victim of a crime and you agree to help the police solve the crime, you can get permission to stay in the country.

T Visa: If you were brought here and forced to work for someone against your will, you can ask for this visa.

A LOW-SECURITY SHELTER PLACEMENT

Maribel's memories of her first days at the shelter were colored by her painful separation from her cousin. He was housed in the boys' side of the shelter, and the staff made no exceptions to the rule of segregating males and females. "We couldn't see them except at birthday celebrations, and we couldn't talk to them. If we did and the supervisors found out it was bad. One of the workers got fired because she was passing letters between the boys and girls." The intake interview was awful. There were endless questions about her and her family. "I was afraid that they would send me back to Honduras! If not Honduras, would it be another place?"

The rules governing behavior were very strict, especially with regard to food. If they gave it to you, you had to eat it. Maribel read "all the stuff the staff passed out" on what you do if you are sick or sad or have a problem. What really counted was the informal knowledge passed on to the new arrivals by the girls in her house. The youth care workers provided around-the-clock supervision in the houses and were required to report all behavioral issues to their superiors. Although they were at the bottom of the staff hierarchy, they had the most direct effect on the girls. "The other girls told us that the only things that those workers really cared about were appearances—if you cleaned your room and made your bed, if you got up on time, didn't talk too loud, stayed in bed after lights out at 9:00, if you cleaned your plate, if you didn't lose anything that belongs to the shelter."

The youth care workers were very different from one another. Some, like Rosa, acted like big sisters and overlooked the stringent regulations requiring professional boundaries between the staff and the girls. They passed love notes from the girls to the boys, let their favorites use cell phones, shared stories of their own romances, and cradled them when they cried for their mothers. Others, like Carolina, inspired dread when they came on duty. They were "like prison guards," always on the lookout for bad behavior, reveling in their power to punish. If one girl broke the rules they made the whole house suffer. "If you talked after lights out, shared your food, looked at the boys, or made nasty comments about a worker, you got a bad mark. Three bad marks and you got put on one-on-one. That meant staying alone with a staff member. I never wanted to be on one-on-one. I even had nightmares about that." The girls were told that they had the right to complain, but they knew not to abuse that privilege.

Maribel's recollections can be compared to the results of the investigations conducted over the past decade by Texas child care licensing personnel. Investigators documented over one hundred serious incidents that occurred in ORR shelters.[31] Eighty-eight of those incidents involved youth care staff or their shift supervisors who demonstrated a "lack of prudent judgment" in discharging their duties. Investigators cited inappropriate behavior, unprofessional relationships, inadequate supervision, maltreatment, and sexual, physical and verbal abuses.[32] Their constant presence and physical propinquity to young girls and boys must certainly have contributed to confusion over their roles. Were they disciplinarians holding the line on an unstable population? Immigrant role models who had stable jobs and normal lives? Empathetic counselors who shared a common culture and language? Substitute parents who provided intimacy for emotionally bruised teenagers? Poorly trained and low-paid staff members who abused the power they had?

In her first week Maribel attended the Know Your Rights presentation and spoke individually with an attorney from the local legal services provider. Trust was a big issue. So was the shame of revealing the abuse that she had endured.

> In the beginning you don't want to say what happened. It is not for them to know. I said at first, "I won't say it out loud to the lawyer. I won't say that my dad is crazy and that he wanted to kill me." But it is their job to convince you. They are there to help you get a good case.

After his apprehension in Texas, Ernesto was also sent to a minimum-security shelter. He noticed the cordial greetings between the ICE officers who transported him and the shelter worker who signed his paperwork. Despite the staff insistence that "this is not Immigration" he concluded that all adults who worked for Border Patrol, ICE, the immigration court, and ORR were part of the same enforcement system. He wondered if the shelter would offer a refuge from the turbulence of his journey and deliver on the promise of his dream. Instead it was the beginning of a painful ordeal, this time at the hands of federal-contracted U.S. staff.

> We were scared, and then we heard the presentation by the lawyers and the social workers and how it was supposed to be in there. There were problems and a lotta rules, but they didn't apply to the workers. One lady abused kids. She took advantage of them. She came to me and said, "If you have sex with me I will give you rings, jewelry, and money." She did that with other kids.

I didn't want to, but I had no choice. After it happened I didn't tell nobody, not the attorney who came to talk to me, not the social worker. The other workers knew what was happening, but they didn't say anything.[33] So the attorney said I didn't have a case. He said it would be best to accept deportation. I didn't want to. I suffered so much. And when I went to court, they said if I get deported I can't come back here for ten years. I didn't want that, but I thought I had no case. So the next time all the kids went to court the judge asked who wanted to go back [take voluntary departure] to raise our hands. So I did and it was arranged. I called my mom and told her to pick me up at the airport. I was so happy because I was going to see my family. The night before I was supposed to leave the FBI came and asked me about that worker. They said, "Don't be afraid to tell the truth." I said, "Don't worry about it, forget it." They said, "No, this woman broke the law. We saw it on camera. You need to tell the truth." I thought I could make a deal, so I said, "If I tell you the truth will you let me leave?' They said, "No, we can't let you leave until the case is closed. We have a machine that shows if you are telling the truth." So they closed that place [Nixon], and we were all sent to other places. I went to another shelter in Corpus Christi, Texas. I was so mad, I had to tell the truth for their case but I didn't have the right to leave? I had to stay in Texas for fourteen months because of what happened.[34]

PLACEMENT IN A STAFF-SECURE FACILITY AFTER APPREHENSION IN THE UNITED STATES

I met Antonio in late 2009 shortly after he was transferred to an ORR facility with both shelter and staff-secure beds. I had traveled to the New York State facility with two attorneys from Catholic Charities, an ORR-contracted legal service provider in New York City. Antonio was then a seventeen-year-old. He had been brought to the United States at the age of three and lived in a mixed-status family that included U.S. citizen siblings and an undocumented mother. He had spent his childhood in New York City and attended school there. He had no memory of his country of birth, Mexico, and spoke only broken Spanish. He had opened the doors between the cars of a moving subway train, was arrested by transit police, transferred to a police station, and ultimately jailed at Riker's Island juvenile detention facility. In 2009 ICE agents were routinely stationed in jails at New York's Riker's Island where they questioned youths about their immigration status. When questioned about his family, Antonio insisted that he had none. He had learned from an early age to keep his mother's undocumented status a closely guarded secret. Even though his mother had no papers, he believed that growing up in the United States made him a legal resident. As a result of his arrest, Antonio learned for the first time that he was "illegal." The ICE agent classified him as unaccompanied and contacted the ICE juvenile coordinator, who notified ORR. Instead of enjoying the due process protections afforded to U.S. citizen minors after arrest—getting both appointed counsel and a guardian ad litem and having local law enforcement officials decide on his eligibility for release to family members—Antonio was held at Riker's Island and transferred to ICE custody.

ICE received information on unaccompanied children through formal agreements with law enforcement and informal mechanisms whereby state police, probation officers, juvenile court personnel, and child welfare agencies voluntarily contacted Immigration authorities. Historically, the Immigration and Nationality Act permitted state and local police to enforce the criminal provisions of immigration law but not the civil provisions of the law that deal with visa violations and unlawful presence. That changed in 1996 when Congress passed the Illegal Immigration Reform and Immigrant Responsibility Act (IIRIRA).[35] Section 287g of the act empowered state and local police officers to collaborate with ICE to enforce federal immigration laws.[36] It was largely ignored until after 9/11, when it garnered new attention as a tool to identify undocumented immigrants who were deemed criminal or terrorist threats.[37]

ICE has claimed that it focused internal apprehension efforts on "serious criminal aliens," an assertion explicitly laid out in the now-famous memo issued by John Morton on June 30, 2010.[38] In practice under the Obama administration, immigration enforcement has targeted any noncitizen who has had contact with law enforcement, including youths arrested for nonviolent, petty offenses. A detailed catalog of such offenses in ORR's initial placement tool is a testament to this trend. Offenses include "disorderly conduct, disturbing the peace, drug possession, DUI, false ID, public intoxication, resisting arrest, shoplifting, technical probation violation, and vandalism."[39] Antonio told the attorneys, "[At Riker's Island] a guy in normal clothes who didn't act like a cop asked me where I was born. Then he wanted to know how long I lived here." His attorneys surmised, based on their experience with agents who used deception to obtain information on the immigration status of minors after arrest, that "the guy" was with ICE. ICE agents were known to enter juvenile detention centers in plainclothes, not uniforms, and to lure minors into answering questions.

Once the ICE agents determined that Antonio was undocumented and potentially removable from the United States, they issued an ICE hold or detainer on him. In theory these detainers are requests that state and local officials notify ICE when a minor is ready for release. In practice it means that local authorities enforce ICE detainers by holding noncitizen children in jail until their custody can be transferred to immigration authorities. Thus, at a point where a U.S. citizen youth would be released from custody to family "because the youth was never charged, faces only minor charges, is not a flight risk, poses no threat to the community, paid a bond or served a sentence, was found not guilty or had the charges dropped," undocumented teenagers deemed security risks were sent to immigration detention.[40]

In light of the arrest, the ORR intake team evaluated Antonio as a medium-security risk and placed him in the staff-secure wing of the New York facility. Antonio was fortunate that his apprehension occurred in December, when overall admissions were down and one of the fourteen beds in the facility was available. Bed space during peak admissions in the spring and summer was a constant problem, and ORR staff struggled to place unaccompanied children within seventy-two hours of their apprehension. If there were no available beds at the appropriate security level, children could be sent to facilities out of state. Antonio could have been placed in a staff-secure facility in Texas, Oregon, Virginia, or Washington or in a minimum-security shelter.

Attorneys who worked in a San Antonio legal service office reported that they had numerous cases of teenagers sent to large-capacity Texas shelters from Riker's Island after an arrest for a petty offense.[41] In peak admission periods some children were held in ICE custody for longer periods or sent to more restricted facilities where they were commingled with minors who had been charged with or adjudicated for violent offenses. A case manager in a staff-secure facility in Portland, Oregon, remembered an incident that had occurred in July 2010.

> We got a fourteen-year-old boy who was waiting to be placed because there were absolutely no beds. He was held in a hotel room in LA for three days with ICE officers. He was kept chained to a bed and unchained to eat and to go to the bathroom. He ate ramen noodles and watched television for three days straight.[42]

Antonio had arrived exhausted and disoriented at the facility along with three other "internal apprehensions." Three of the four had been in the United States at least five years and remembered little about their "home countries." They lived in mixed-status families. The fourth, a sixteen-year-old who had fled gang violence in El Salvador, had lived with a group of adults before he was arrested during a routine traffic stop. Although those who lived for longer periods in the United States knew they lacked U.S. citizenship, Antonio and another boy thought they had legal status because of their long-term residence, school attendance, and community ties. Since three of the four considered their first language English, the attorneys conducted the presentation in English.

The attorneys first outlined the types of legal relief available to undocumented minors. Then, anticipating the difficulty youths typically had grasping the different rules that applied to federal custody and immigration proceedings, one attorney drew a double black line down the center of the board. Writing FAMILY REUNIFICATION on one side and IMMIGRATION COURTS on the other, she described them "as entirely separate systems." She emphasized the different goals and the separate decision-making processes of each.

> The goal of federal custody is first to release the youth to approved sponsors. That means family, close friends, or foster families as soon as possible or to return the youth to ICE for removal. The decision about family reunification is made by the facility. The decision to grant legal status or to issue a removal order is made by the immigration judge.

In the question-and-answer period, Antonio and the other teenagers confused the immigration court with the criminal court. They did not understand that the processes of release and family reunification were disconnected from the question of legal relief.

Antonio: When you get a sponsor does that sponsor need to have papers, a green card?

Attorney: That is a really good question. No, not necessarily, but when a person has no status in this country, it is risky. It is hard for that person to come and pick you up [at an ORR facility]. It can be a long way to travel, and along the way there may be checkpoints and problems [with Immigration].

Antonio: If your sponsor is your mom can you be released to her custody? Can she pick you up here?

Managing attorney: That is a really good question, but it is a family reunification question and we can't answer it. We deal with legal questions. You need to talk to the person here at the shelter who handles family reunification decisions.

The second minor, Alberto, had lived in the United States for ten years with a grandparent who had legal status. He interjected, "What I want to know is that even if you have no family back in the [home] country, can you still get deported?"

> *Attorney:* That is a very good question as well. Sometimes in court you get a bad result. That can happen. It is true that the [immigration] judge is not concerned with where your family is, only with your individual legal case.

> *Antonio:* They said [at Riker's] they would detain me. They put me in [juvenile] detention and then Immigration picked me up. They said they could send me anywhere in the U.S. I been here since I was a baby. I learned to read and write here. Will that change the judge's mind?

The attorney drew a picture of the federal courtroom with an immigration judge, a government attorney, and the minor respondent. All the teenagers were confused. The third minor, Marco, who had fled gang violence in El Salvador and had lived in the United States for a year, asked, "Where is the jury?"

> *Attorney:* There is no jury because this is not a criminal case. The immigration court handles civil matters.

> *Antonio:* Where is the police? The parents?

> *Attorney:* This court hearing is for you. Your parents don't need to be there.

> *Antonio:* My mom doesn't know how to get here. If they reunificate us, will it help me to get papers?

> *Attorney:* Remember it is a separate process. The reunification decision will have no effect on your immigration case.

At this point, the pace of anxious questions increased, with boys shouting over one another.

> *Antonio:* If they drop the case, if you beat the case, it depends on the judge, right? [Pause] Why do they treat us like immigrants? When did I become an immigrant? Will they allow us to stay? What happens if they [parents] didn't come over [to the United States] with a visa?

> *Alberto:* So, say your father was a resident of this country, but he went to prison. You didn't know him, they took his papers away and deported him. If you get abused, you get a visa, right?

> *Marco:* If I go back to my country, I'll be killed. Anyone on my street back there can be killed [by the gang].

Placement was more complicated for youths with any type of juvenile or criminal history, but it was especially complicated for those with more serious offenses. When I toured a large Texas facility, the staff pointed out a distraught teenager who had just arrived from New

York.[43] He had served a nine-month sentence in a juvenile detention center, but instead of being released he was held on an ICE detainer and transferred to Texas, where he faced a second period of detention, this time far from his family and with no set endpoint. Attorneys noted the obstacles that such youths faced when they came to the attention of immigration authorities. Undocumented teenagers were subject to zero-tolerance policies and diversion into the adult criminal justice system. They also experienced police misconduct in problem neighborhoods, as well as the rancor of overworked probation officers whose hands were full with troubled domestic youths. Those charged with an aggravated felony or multiple misdemeanors that constituted crimes of moral turpitude under immigration law would be automatically barred from obtaining legal relief. Similarly, those who were advised to plead guilty of certain offenses in return for a lighter sentence by public defenders with no background in immigration law could find themselves ineligible for relief. Sometimes serious charges that were listed as active had been reduced or dismissed but the records sent to the ORR intake team were not updated or were incorrect, creating the perception of a dangerous youth who needed a more restrictive placement.

Facility directors and case managers working in facilities at all security levels complained about the inadequate screening conducted by CBP and ICE and the paucity of reliable information they received from ORR prior to a medium- or high-security placement. They indicated that initial placement scores were often based on charges listed, without any explanation. The director of an Oregon staff-secure facility remarked, "We would get a report with a list of scary charges, and I would think, 'What are they sending us?'"[44] A staff-secure facility director in Chicago complained that the numerical score assigned by the intake team "was so subjective. They routinely send us kids who don't belong here at both ends of the spectrum."[45] One case manager at NORCOR in Oregon expressed a common complaint: "We didn't know the backstory behind the arrest. Did the kids have family in the U.S.? Did they grow up here? Was there a history of abuse?"[46] Two case managers in a Virginia facility with both staff-secure and secure wings described their frustration dealing with a sixteen-year-old boy who was detained after being arrested and charged with the sexual assault of an underage girl.

> This was potentially very serious, but we couldn't get any information—not the delinquency record, not the police report. The juvenile records are sealed tight. We have to gather information in order to know what to expect

behavior-wise and to work on family reunification. We call probation officers, the defense attorneys, caseworkers, the DA [district attorney], child protective services, juvenile jails, juvenile courts. We need records. We tell them that the kid is with us. ORR is the legal guardian! Sometimes it makes a difference, sometimes it doesn't.[47]

Case managers in staff-secure and secure facilities had to conduct their own time- and labor-intensive investigations in order to be ready for the mandatory thirty-day review. A common problem was the lack of information exchanged between state and juvenile courts and the federal government regarding unaccompanied minors. One case manager described the difficulty he had gathering information on an assault charge filed against an undocumented fifteen-year-old from Orange County, California. After numerous false starts he finally connected with the probation officer. When he explained that the teenager was in government custody and the goal was to reunify him with his family, the probation officer was aghast. "That kid is no good and we don't want him back in this community," he said. The deputy district attorney on the case described the alleged incident as a "brawl with twenty illegals in a vacant lot." The case manager explained:

> The DA said that our kid had cut a guy up with a broken beer bottle. I asked about evidence, and he said that he had no witnesses and the victim wasn't talking, but he was sure that the kid did it. He only dropped the charges because he was told that the kid would get deported. What choice did that leave me? I couldn't recommend the kid's release back to a place where he faced jail time and a $3,000 fine. He really was at risk because his only family was a brother who was homeless. He was not a bad kid. We managed to step him down to a less secure facility, but his long-term prospects were not good.[48]

Shelter directors were hesitant to accept teenagers who were being transferred or "stepped down" from staff-secure facilities just as some directors of staff-secure facilities balked at taking those from a secure facility. The need to handle kids with suspected criminal issues, gang affiliations, conduct disorders, and histories of trauma posed thorny dilemmas for staff whose mandate was to reduce disruptive incidents that suggested a lack of control, to decrease the length of stay, and to facilitate a rapid release to approved families and sponsors. The ORR commitment to help vulnerable children fleeing violence and abuse conflicted with the need to manage problem youths who were labeled high risk because of their criminal record or bad behavior in federal custody. These conflicting pressures often began with disagreements regarding the initial placement.

In the facility where Antonio was detained the supervising attorney asked to discuss just such a placement with the shelter director. I followed the attorney to the central office, where sixteen monitors tracked movement in and out of common areas, including the entrance, stairwells, halls, kitchen, dining area, and recreation rooms. The attorney asked about Miguel, a youth she had already screened. The director indicated that Miguel's initial placement in the minimum-security shelter was "wrong" and she wanted to "step him up" from the shelter to the more restricted therapeutic staff-secure unit. She turned to me and explained, "You are in the shelter now. Staff-secure kids need close monitoring so we don't mix the two populations. They can't be in the same room at the same time." The attorney asked what Miguel had done.

> *Director:* He threatened the staff—three staff members to be exact—and he also threatened to beat up one resident. The first week we had an incident on the soccer field. We had a game between the boys and staff, like we do, and it was getting dark so we gave them the fifteen-minute warning. They need exercise, and we use it as an incentive. Well, after the time was up, we asked them to return to the house. Miguel made a scene and threw a tantrum. We never use hands on the kids. We don't touch them. So they brought him back inside and he refused to do anything, to participate in anything. He just sat down and completely dissociated from everyone. He is very isolated. The root cause is his anger. He called us "racist" and "liars" and said we favored some kids over others.

> *Attorney:* But things were going pretty well when I saw him last time, right?

> *Director:* Actually, no. Things were going downhill. He is from Guatemala and used the expression—excuse my language—*"mi vieja"* [my bitch] to call one of the kids. He used an obscene gesture with another kid. Then we got the psych evaluation. [To me:] They are reassessed after two weeks in the system and the recommendation was transfer to staff secure or a therapeutic residential facility. We use a point system here to incentivize kids. It's good because if the kids are responsible they earn certain privileges, like they can use an MP3 player or watch a movie. Miguel can no longer stay in the shelter. I just don't feel safe.

> *Attorney:* Do you mean that he can never return to the shelter?

> *Director:* No, he cannot return to the shelter. He will go to staff-secure or therapeutic care.[49] There are serious behavioral and mental health issues here. He refuses to take his medicine.

> *Attorney:* Will he be eligible for foster care?

> *Director:* He is no longer eligible [to stay in the shelter] because of his behavior. I spent time with him. But he saw our exchanges as fighting. He gestured like a fighter. He needs to have one-on-one staff supervision to

make sure there is no fighting. He lost his privileges and had restrictions for outings on weekends. Our goal is a therapeutic setting.

SJT: Could you explain the difference between the shelter and staff secure?

Director: The staff-secure kids all have charges . . . they are criminals.

During a 2010 visit to a Texas facility with both shelter and staff-secure beds, I observed a disagreement over the placement of José, a teenager with a complicated history.[50] A tense negotiation ensued between the case manager, the DFC, and the FFS. A policeman had stopped José after he spotted a broken taillight on his car. When he could produce no ID or vehicle registration, José was arrested. A check of integrated FBI and DHS databases confirmed his undocumented status and showed prior arrests for drug possession, burglary, possession of a stolen car, and driving without a license. José had been apprehended, detained, and released from ORR custody once before. Based on his prior charges the ORR intake team assigned a borderline score that indicated placement in a staff-secure facility. Nonetheless, the social worker and case manager argued for the shelter side of the facility saying that the charges were old and involved nonviolent offenses. They also considered mitigating personal circumstances. José lived with his mother, pregnant girlfriend, and stepson. His willingness to settle down and accept responsibility suggested different life choices. The director and the federal field specialist agreed, and he was placed in the less restricted shelter side of the facility with the goal of rapid family reunification.

PLACEMENT IN A SECURE FACILITY

I met Orlando in a secure facility. He had turned sixteen during a twelve-month detention in the Adobe Mountain School in Arizona. On the day he was scheduled for release his mother and stepfather were waiting to bring him home. Instead, local ICE officials issued a hold, reapprehended him, and designated him as unaccompanied, although they knew that he had family in Phoenix. They transferred him to a juvenile prison under contract to ORR in Virginia. Three days later he called his mother from across the country to say he was back in jail. The ORR intake team received very little paperwork from the Arizona facility and recommended a secure placement based on his adjudication and detention for the assault. According to his clinician, Judith Reifsteck, "When he got here, he was one angry kid who wanted out."

Before I met Orlando, Jason Skeens, the deputy director of the Virginia facility, gave me a tour. He had worked there for the past ten years, beginning as a floor officer and working his way up to an administrative position. The facility encompassed two separate areas, a secure wing with thirty-eight beds and a staff-secure wing with twenty beds. The secure wing housed both "federals" from ORR and "domestics" from local counties. That day the facility was at 45 percent capacity, with fifteen individuals held in the secure facility and nine in staff-secure. Boys made up all those in secure detention and six of the nine in staff-secure. The facility was new and had only served unaccompanied minors since 2009, when it was awarded the ORR contract. Facility directors had partnered with the Vera Institute and the Annie E. Casey Foundation to design a "short-term, secure, and residential placement" for children ages ten to seventeen. According to the facility's promotional literature the goal was "to hold juveniles accountable for their actions while fostering growth and minimizing the damaging effects of detention."

The tour began when we passed from the open administration offices through a metal door into the locked detention center. We stopped at the "heart of the facility," the central control room, which was equipped with cameras to provide constant monitoring of all hallways, common areas, and entry and exit points. We viewed a large multipurpose room that served as a library, a group therapy room, or an alternative classroom for art, music, and ESL instruction. We visited the large gym where a full-time teacher supervised a commingled group of eleven "domestics and federals" working out on treadmills and shooting hoops. We passed on to what the deputy director described as a full education department with state-of-the-art classrooms equipped with smart boards, TV screens, and computers. The classrooms were all empty and dark because the secure wing had been on lockdown for four days "following threats and fights between two groups of boys." Instead of attending school, the boys were confined to their "pods," or residential living units. Each horseshoe-shaped pod had ten individual locked cells. The cell doors opened into the center and faced a control desk located at the open end.

A Troubled Kid

Judith Reifsteck, a Ph.D. in child psychology who taught at a nearby university, conducted Orlando's initial intake interview, listening for any indication of abuse, abandonment, or neglect at home. She explained the rules and the behavioral management system and Orlando's rights. She had received only a one-paragraph report from the Arizona psychologist, which stated, "Orlando is a very angry kid who needs help because he has serious mental health issues and substance abuse needs." She read from her intake notes: "He exhibited an oppositional attitude, is arrogant, and in full adolescent bloom . . . sees himself as victim. He blames his stepfather for his situation and insists that he got here by accident . . . he claims that he was incarcerated because he is poor and undocumented." She remembered that soon after his placement he picked a fight with another minor. His belligerence stood out because "he didn't even try to fake good behavior or to pretend he was sorry for the things he had done."[51]

To prepare for the mandatory thirty-day review of Orlando's placement in the secure facility, his clinician and case manager faced the challenge of gathering the necessary information on Orlando's family background and criminal history. The deputy director explained:

> The big issue for us is the availability of information because we don't decide initially, DC [i.e., ORR] does. The issue is criminal charges. How serious are they? Is the kid on meds? Is there a history of mental health issues or of absconding? We know DC is working under the gun because they only have three days to place the UACs. But there is a real danger of misinformation or inadequate information for the boys and especially for the girls who are placed here. We have very few true delinquent girls. They mostly tag along and get involved with boys who do stupid things.[52]

They contacted the Arizona detention facility, obtained the probation officer's report, and interviewed his counselors, teachers, and social workers, including staff from Phoenix child protective services who had a file on the family. They discovered that Orlando's mother gave birth to him when she was thirteen. When Orlando's mother decided to leave Mexico to find work in the United States, she left her son with his grandmother. His father dropped out of his life when he was only four years old. In 2004, when his mother was twenty-two, she arranged for nine-year-old Orlando to come and live with her. She had married a young undocumented Mexican and had two children with him. Orlando knew no English when he arrived and had a very difficult year in school and at home. According to his clinician:

> By the time he was ten, he was skipping school. At twelve he stole condoms, at thirteen he stole cars. He was abusing alcohol and drugs and had criminal charges in the eighth grade. His stepfather tried to parent him, but he was very young too, and Orlando broke all the house rules. His probation officer suspected that he became involved in a local gang as a substitute for family.

Things came to a head when he ran away from home and was found high on the street three days later. His stepfather confronted him and there was a fight. His stepfather broke a board over his legs, and Orlando retaliated by stabbing him with a screwdriver. The police were called, Orlando was arrested and, ultimately, ordered to be confined at the Arizona detention center for a year.[53]

Orlando's clinician and case manager developed an individual service plan that involved weekly group and individual counseling sessions. Dr. Reifsteck used exercises to help him manage his anger, express his feelings, and enhance his self-image. The facility contracted with an outside psychiatrist, who diagnosed Orlando with attention deficit disorder and impulsive conduct disorder. The biomedical intervention included prescriptions for mood-enhancing drugs to manage his anger. When these made him lethargic and unable to focus in school, his medicine was changed. This made him less irritable and more talkative. His behavior and performance in facility classes improved significantly.

When the team reviewed Orlando's placement they faced a conundrum. The psychiatrist had recommended a residential treatment facility because of his behavioral issues. The FFS who monitored facility operations and managed the FAST review rejected this plan. First, there was a shortage of residential treatment beds; in 2010 only 36 youths of a total of 8,446 admissions were sent to residential treatment centers. He argued that since Orlando was not traumatized and had no serious mental illnesses, the three options were a return home, a transfer to the staff-secure wing of the facility, or a step down to a shelter in Arizona or Texas. Given his troubled past and continuing behavioral problems, the FFS thought it very likely that if Orlando were released he would "reoffend and be back in ORR care or get deported." There was also the matter of his mother. The clinician depicted her as a "problem" parent: "She only spoke Spanish, was very aggressive, and felt entitled." She had refused to cooperate in developing a postrelease plan with the team, and, worse, one of her other children, a fourteen-year-old, had been removed from the home by child protective services. ORR would probably not approve Orlando's mother as a sponsor for her son.

Two case managers at the Virginia facility spoke at length about the problem of releasing undocumented teenagers like Orlando who had criminal histories and substance abuse problems. There were two different populations in secure detention. First, there were the kids who had been in the country only a short time before their apprehension. A quarter of that population had no options for legal relief. In those cases the attorneys generally recommended that they take voluntary departure and return home. One case manager added, "But it depends on how desperate they are to get out or what will happen if they go back." He mentioned a teenager who had been kidnapped by a gang and forced to carry drugs across the U.S.-Mexico border. He had been caught and deported thirty-four times. On his last run, gang members had accused him of stealing $50,000 from them, and he overheard their plans to kill him. He fled, crossed into the United States, and turned himself in to ICE. He had been at the Virginia facility for four months.[54]

The second population in secure detention consisted of teenagers who had lived in the United States since early childhood and had police records. The same case manager mentioned the pitfalls of family reunification in such cases: "We have had kids with felony charges here, so if they get released and reunify with their families they will be tried as adults in the criminal justice system." He hesitated, then continued, "When I think about it the common denominator for criminal history and serious charges is the background. The less family and support they have, the less established they are here, the less English they know, the greater the chance that they get serious charges after an arrest."[55]

Later that day Orlando came to his clinician's office and spoke openly about his anger. He insisted that he needed to be released and reunified with his family. I learned for the first time that he had a baby with his teenage girlfriend. He remembered his first weeks "as very difficult." He complained that as a foreign kid who was poor and had a record, he had few rights and faced discrimination. Juvenile detention in Arizona was empty, wasted time, when the only thing he learned to do was cook in the facility kitchen. It was a place where there was little direction, no rehabilitation, and limited counseling. When ICE reapprehended him he was not allowed to call home as the juvenile justice authorities had promised. ICE imposed a "total blackout" on contact. He couldn't call his parents for four days. By then he was in "another jail," one that had locked cells and was all the way across the country. He was "really mad" and lashed out at everybody because of his "anger issues." His clinician asked him how he compared the Abode Mountain School and the ORR facility. He replied:

> That other place was more open than here. There were no locks on the doors and we could hang out with other guys. But it was a really violent place and we didn't get a lotta attention. Not like the staff here who is real strict. Over there [in Arizona] we had nothing, no books, no activities, and we had to buy our own hygiene stuff. I was real mad over there. Like now, I am the strongest I ever been. I learned about drugs, why they are bad, why we

shouldn't do them. Here we have a case plan and we memorize it. We go to school—a different kind of school—but we learn. One kid has been here for four months and he gets real aggravated, but we learn to cope . . . I am like a different person here. I don't get high. I'm happy, and I don't need drugs. They were messin' me up. It helps a lot to talk about things. My next step is home or a shelter.

After he left I asked Dr. Reifsteck if Orlando could be stepped down or released, as he hoped. What chance did he have to lead a normal life— to kick his drug habit for good, build a relationship with his mother and stepfather, and be a father to his child? She replied:

Well, if he is not stabbed or shot there is maybe a chance. What I see is that the past behavior is predictive of future performance. In this job we have to focus on the present moment, so the rest is not in my hands. Some of these kids will respond to the seeds that we are planting. Will he kick his [drug] habit? Will he conquer his demons? I have had kids who have lost more and seen more. This experience [in custody] is a brief oasis of clean and sober time. It is crisis stabilization. Two weeks ago if you had asked the same question, I would have said voluntary departure was the best option, but now I don't know.[56]

CONCLUSION

ORR's commitment to deliver services that purport to incorporate best practices in child welfare conflicts with placement procedures that rely heavily on screenings by immigration enforcement personnel and on an assessment tool that prioritizes the threat of criminal and delinquent behavior. Once in custody undocumented children interact with numerous state and federal agencies and government contractors that use different procedures, have competing mandates, and operate at cross-purposes. They face the likely possibility of being moved between facilities and programs with little notice or explanation. They have to navigate a disjointed and confusing labyrinth without the help of appointed counsel or independent child advocates. Maribel and Ernesto both spoke of the jarring disconnect between the appearance of a home setting and the reality of involuntary confinement. Orlando decried the injustice of serving one sentence imposed by the juvenile judge and a second, indefinite period of detention in a prison with locked cells and "more strict rules" than the Adobe Mountain School.

Federal staff in the facilities as well as subcontracted personnel from legal and social service providers repeatedly reminded children that they were "not immigration authorities" and "not the court." This was a tactic that was intended to separate custodial care from the enforcement tactics that landed children in detention. Nonetheless, the young people I interviewed understood their custody as a continuum that stretched from apprehension to release. None of them differentiated the adult authorities who worked directly for "the government" from those who claimed to be independent, such as the attorneys and child welfare specialists under contract to ORR. Most kids shared Ernesto's suspicion that the immigration authorities from CBP and ICE and the ORR staff all worked for the same system.

Despite the creation and implementation of a numerical assessment designed to make initial placements more uniform and objective, federal staff frequently exercised their discretion to request more or less restrictive placements depending on the information they received and the backgrounds of the young people who had been in custody. Facility directors were reluctant to admit youths who had a purported history of offending, particularly involving drugs or gangs, or who had a record of misconduct in federal custody. While some staff members were happy to have an assessment instrument that reduced the guesswork, others viewed the placement process as inconsistent. The focus on security exposed ongoing conflicts of interest between the immigration enforcement goal to prosecute Unaccompanied Alien Children for violating the law and child welfare principles to provide care and rehabilitation until they could be safely reunified with families.

A number of case managers, clinicians, and immigration attorneys believed that the placement tool revealed the true goals of detention. One attorney, who worked for an ORR-contracted legal service provider before going into private practice, voiced the views of many others when she claimed that the system "was not about benefiting kids but rather about getting them into immigration court and deporting them."[57] Many of those I interviewed were troubled by the mounting numbers of "internal apprehensions"—undocumented teens like Antonio—who had lived in the country since early childhood as well as by the apprehension of border crossers as young as four who were detained and placed in removal proceedings.[58] I do not know what happened to Antonio, Miguel, José, or Orlando. Given Miguel's and Orlando's records as high-risk detainees, it is likely that they were returned to their countries of origin. It is supremely ironic that Orlando received more effective counseling and expert rehabilitation in immigration detention than he did in a domestic facility. Release was likely to undo the physical and psychological progress he had made because the costly therapeutic services would end. More important, the proof of his rehabilitation would have no effect on his immigration case. Orlando's status as an undocumented youth trumped his status as an at-risk minor in need of follow-up services. The individualized plan designed for him by his clinician and case manager focused only on his needs as a troubled adolescent and ignored the fact that he was a young father with responsibilities to his U.S. citizen child.

It is equally likely that Antonio and José were reunified with their families. Despite their deep ties in the United States, neither was eligible for legal relief. I wondered if Antonio graduated from high school and stayed in New York with his family. Did José continue to work and support his girlfriend and child? Did the young men stay out of trouble and appear for their hearings in immigration court? If they were granted the benefit of voluntary departure to a country they didn't remember, did they take it? Or did they skip the removal proceedings in immigration court, get a deportation order in absentia, and disappear into the shadows? After the 2012 executive order offering temporary relief from deportation proceedings and work authorization, known as DACA, I wondered if Antonio was able to get "dacamented." It is impossible to answer any of these questions since ORR does not track undocumented youths after their release.

There have been many cases of young people like Antonio and José who have lived in the United States from early childhood, have been arrested for nonviolent offenses and labeled as unaccompanied, and have been detained, sometimes for long periods. Those kept in detention for longer than three months frequently exhibited behavioral problems. Some grew despondent and showed signs of depression; others became angry and acted out. Some eventually gave up and accepted voluntary departure to "home countries," unfamiliar places that held no memories and distant family ties. Others were stepped up to secure facilities, a move one ORR clinician termed "the last stop before deportation."

5

In Custody

Soon after a child's arrival in custody, case managers in the ORR facility and the district field coordinators affiliated with Lutheran Immigration and Refugee Services in Baltimore, Maryland, conducted intake interviews to gather information on his or her family, migration, and medical histories.[1] DFCs also gave orientation presentations to new arrivals. At a Texas shelter orientation in March 2010, the DFC explained that he was there to assist with safety, food, and health concerns but, most of all, to organize family reunification. "I am not an attorney," he said, "and so I cannot give you any legal advice. I don't work for the shelter. I am from a private agency, outside the shelter. We are independent." He wrote CONFIDENTIALITY on the board. Two of the fifteen kids were in federal custody for a second time. When he asked what "confidentiality" meant, one of them called out, "That's stuff we tell you that you can't share." Pleased, the DFC replied, "Correct. What you tell me stays with me. If one of the boys tells me something, I can't tell anyone." Turning to the subject of family reunification, he said, "Before we can release you, we have to check the home to see if everything is OK. Safety is our first concern. Every situation is different. We can only do this with your permission. We are empowering you to be part of the decision!"

Emphasizing his empathy for their suffering during their journey, he urged them not to be angry or to fight but to act like brothers, to follow the rules, and to take advantage of what the shelter offers and make something of their lives. They would have medicine if they were sick, glasses if they had poor eyesight, classes in school, and help with their problems. Did they have any questions? One of the new boys raised his hand and asked who decided on release: "Is it you?" "No," he replied, "I can only recommend it. The FFS must approve it." This was an adult figure many of them would never meet.

When young people remembered their first days in custody, most described the hot meals, warm showers, and kind attention of facility staff. Because of their anxiety, many could not recall any information on legal rights or suitable sponsors, much less admonishments to behave. Only later did they realize how critical and difficult it was to follow "all those rules." Establishing a record of good behavior was imperative for rapid release to biological families, foster care, or group homes, whereas problem behaviors could trigger prolonged periods of detention through a transfer, or step up, to a higher-security facility, making release to an open setting more difficult if not impossible.

Detained children were subjected to constant monitoring and rigid behavioral prescriptions. ORR staff members used intensive, panoptical systems of behavior management drawn from social work, medicine, psychology, and psychiatry.[2] Administered by social professionals— youth care workers, case managers, clinicians, facility directors, psychologists, psychiatrists, DFCs, and FFS's—custodial care was designed to create a stable environment for a short-term stay. Under pressure to release detainees to sponsors "without unnecessary delay" and to turn over facility beds rapidly, the staff were urged to accelerate the flow of clients through the system. To do this they had to work rapidly to identify risk factors and neutralize problems. ORR policy procedures explicitly excluded "laying hands on the kids" as a means to correct unwanted behavior. Instead, the staff used incentives and restrictions so that clients adapted quickly to the highly regulated institutional setting, internalized behavioral norms, and, ultimately, came to correct themselves. As one facility director put it, "We now use a psycho-educational model. We don't touch the kids. If they act out we verbally redirect them. We manage behavior by putting the responsibility on them. We give them choices and freedom so that they think they have control."[3]

The standards that govern daily life in federal facilities are a legacy of the FSA and specify child welfare principles that were absent under the INS system. UACs are required to have six hours of daily academic and vocational instruction by competent teachers, to have dedicated time for "large muscle exercise outdoors," and to engage in daily leisure activities. They are to be housed in a "non-institutional home-like atmosphere of care in the least restrictive setting" and to receive services that are "developmentally appropriate" and promote "positive development, self-esteem, and nurturing."[4] The UAC must be made to "feel valued, safe and comfortable."[5]

"THIS IS NOT DETENTION!"

I first visited an ORR shelter in Florida in September 2009.[6] At first glance, the building was a spacious, well-maintained suburban home in a middle-class neighborhood. A closer look revealed metal fencing, locks, and mounted surveillance cameras. The shelter director and the FFS explained that all facilities in the system, even low-security shelters such as this one, were closed and operated with controlled entry and exit as well as supervised movement within the shelter. On site visits, I always asked what was the best word to describe the ORR system: care or detention? Why were closed facilities deemed the best way to handle this population?

Most supervisory personnel—facility directors and FFS's—objected to my use of the words *detention* and *detainees,* referring instead to the "custodial care" they provided to "clients." The director of a staff-secure facility in Chicago glared at me, insisting, "This is NOT detention." Staff emphasized the benefits that children gleaned from education, counseling, and comfortable housing, as well as socialization and a safe environment. They highlighted the new experiences and opportunities for play that produced "smiles on the faces of kids" whose extreme poverty and traumatic journey required them to go from "diapers to adulthood" and to skip the normal developmental stages of childhood. The FFS in Miami asserted, "Fences work both ways. They don't only keep children in, but keep out inappropriate sponsors, abusive family [members], and smugglers."[7] An FFS in Houston, Texas, insisted, "The fences keep them safe." Referring to a staff-secure facility outside Houston that he monitored, he declared, "When it is time for release, these kids don't want to leave!"[8] An FFS in Harlingen, Texas, who had worked with unaccompanied children before ORR operated the facilities, contrasted the "guardlike mentality" that had prevailed under INS custody with the genuine care shown to kids in 2010.[9] A shelter director in Arizona echoed this view, emphasizing the "deinstitutionalized setting" of his shelter. He insisted, "There are no fences, no guns, no guards, no physical abuse here."[10] The director of the Miami shelter admonished me to remember the reasons that "they cross [the border] and risk it all. They have given up hope and risk it all. We have to care, we have to do better by them."[11] Commenting on the cases under review the day of my visit, one staff member in Harlingen remarked, "How many times have they been lied to and disappointed? Some misbehave and detach from others. It is a shield they use to protect themselves. I say that there is no such thing as a big kid! There are only kids!"[12]

The supervisory staff emphasized the homey surroundings in ORR-contracted facilities and the careful attention given to vulnerable children. One of the refrains I heard was their commitment to the "best interest of the child." During my visits program directors and case managers proudly displayed tidy sleeping areas, modern bathrooms, clean and well-appointed classrooms, kitchens, dining areas, common areas with comfortable furniture, televisions, and electronic games, and outside recreational areas. Staff pointed to the many benefits the kids enjoyed. They played soccer, learned how to play basketball, saw American musical theater, enjoyed bowling parties, and developed vocational skills. They attended classes with dedicated teachers, cooked meals together, watched TV, and learned to use computers, and some had the opportunity to earn GEDs. In one of the San Diego shelters the children raised chickens and designed a water filtration system for breeding freshwater fish. In an Oregon staff-secure facility the staff implemented an innovative mural project and vegetable garden initiative that had achieved excellent results for boys with "anger management issues."

"They are in the U.S. now!"

Recognizing that many of the Central American and Mexican children in detention were poor, had minimal or no schooling, and were forced to fend for themselves even at very young ages, at home and during their journey, ORR policies called for specific programs to "acculturate the UAC to the U.S. in healthy ways."[13] The socialization of foreign children began with a general orientation to American culture through English-language instruction and organized activities, an introduction to medical and dental care services, and instruction on personal hygiene that was often new to children from underdeveloped rural areas where homes had no indoor plumbing or electricity. One facility director explained, "This is a new world for them. We have to show them everything, how to use toothpaste and to wash daily. They need to learn basics like opening a milk carton."[14]

Structured meals at appointed times and balanced nutrition based on USDA guidelines were essential aspects of this acculturation. "Showing kids how to eat properly" was also important. A facility director noted, "We work hard on table manners. We have to teach them to respect the structure of mealtime. We have to show them how to pass the food, how to serve themselves, how everyone gets a first helping before taking seconds."[15]

Children who came from corn-based cultures where protein was derived mainly from beans and foods were highly seasoned typically disliked the bland American diet and had difficulty digesting dairy products. Carlos, the youth who survived his ordeal on the Beast and with the Zetas, hated having to drink milk. He was bewildered when the youth care workers laughed at him when he asked for coffee with his breakfast.

Shelter staff had clear expectations for socializing the foreign minors into middle-class understandings of mental and physical health and of childhood as a protected period with well-defined spaces, stages, and activities. Children who had been without proper parental guidance, sometimes for years, needed "to hit the reset button and become kids again" so they could learn the basic values that they missed and make the right choices to improve their lives. The organization of the shelter day reflected American notions of a healthy middle-class childhood by alternating formal schooling with free play, regular exercise in structured team and individual sports, activities that were modeled on high schools such as weekly dances, and organized outings on weekends such as bowling or swimming. The facility rules, posted prominently in most of the shelters I visited, emphasized social norms such as punctuality, cooperation, participation, and respect for the opinions of others, along with individual moral prescriptions such as honesty, trustworthiness, and self-control.

Acculturation involved learning class-based rules and social codes such as initiating proper greetings, making introductions, respecting the personal space of others, and participating in team activities. Social presentation included the choice of appropriate dress, hairstyles, and "nice language," as well as attention to body language and the management of social space. These conveyed important messages about the worth of the individual immigrant. During one visit I commented on the social presence of the teenager who gave me a tour of his residential unit. He shook my hand, was careful to look at me directly when we exchanged greetings, and used carefully rehearsed English. The facility director explained:

> This is important. If their behavior is inappropriate in the shelter they lose privileges like outings because we can't take the chance that they will act out in the community. What will they think of immigrants? We must show them good manners and who the kids really are. We allow no baggy jeans that hang low and expose underwear. We respect their individual teenage culture, but we have to guide them. We show them how to tie neckties and wear nice shirts. When they dress like that they are so impressed with themselves.[16]

Socialization into American culture meant getting lessons in civics and self-governance. According to one facility director, "We teach them how to keep order, manage their affairs, conduct a community meeting, and express opinions. These concepts are completely new to them."[17] A number of shelters viewed their role as schooling clients in basic citizenship rights such as voicing grievances, requesting a meeting with an attorney or case manager, and participating in free elections to choose the leader of a residential unit or the representative to a shelter student council. In several shelters the director created a structure to meet weekly with elected representatives or to receive anonymous complaints. One facility director created the office of shelter "president" and was delighted with the election campaigns run by the eleven candidates. The winning candidate promised to negotiate better privileges such as "more leisure activities" and more "time outside."[18]

The organized activities revealed the importance placed on individual identity and personality development in mainstream American culture. Classroom exercises were designed to enhance language skills and to draw children out by asking them to write poems or stories about who they are and where they come from. One teacher had distributed outlines of an outstretched hand and had the pupils write personal attributes on each finger. One ten-year-old girl described herself as *"divertida," "amable," "responsible,"* and *"amorosa"* (amusing, nice, responsible, and loving).[19]

Teachers encouraged clients to embrace the possibilities for social mobility in a nation they depicted as guaranteeing equality of opportunity for all. A number of classroom bulletin boards displayed writing assignments on the themes "My Dreams" and "If I Were President." Despite these edifying messages facility staff faced enormous challenges in providing the required instruction in math, science, and English for a short-term population that included, at one extreme, illiterate street

with no schooling and, at the other, undocumented teenagers
merican public high schools. A display in a Chicago staff-secure
exemplified these divergent needs. A large poster of the periodic
in chemistry on one wall faced a display of the primary colors
labeled in English and Spanish.

A common complaint from the Central American and Mexican kids
involved the language instruction. Ángel, Corina, and Maribel described
being taught to read and write English by doing workbook exercises
and memorizing word lists. They did not have enough opportunity to
learn colloquial expressions and to develop functional speaking proficiency. Other kids, like Ernesto, were too anxious to focus on school
while they were in custody. Those who had completed primary school
at home, like Ernesto and Maribel, felt that they learned nothing new.
A third population from indigenous areas in Guatemala, like Modesto,
could speak only their native dialects when they arrived and faced the
challenge of learning Spanish before they could begin to learn English.

"We value culture"

An important component of custody involved both awareness of and
respect for the unique cultural identities of UACs. Staff members organized activities to honor the cultural traditions of the Central American
children who were the majority in detention. As one staff member
explained, "We cannot impose mainstream [American] culture on them."
From my observations and interviews, the staff tended to view culture in
two ways. It was seen first as a collective heritage of practices and symbols that were shared by all, handed down through time, and worthy of
commemoration. Thus they cooked authentic ethnic dishes, organized
heritage festivals, broadcast national sports competitions, encouraged
Independence Day celebrations, and displayed national flags.

Staff members recognized that culture was linked to resonant social
spaces back home. In some facilities children were encouraged to draw
pictures of their houses and local communities. Most of the art I saw
displayed on classroom walls in shelters across the country depicted
bucolic verdant landscapes with high mountains, rivers or oceans teem-
ing with fish, and brightly colored houses bathed in brilliant sunshine.
There were also impressively drawn self-portraits and a profusion of
national flags. In a staff-secure facility in Chicago I was brought up
short by an arresting picture on the wall. Drawn by a teenager in custody, it depicted the chaos in a town under attack. A helicopter gunship

hovered over the rooftops raining deadly firepower on terrified civilians in the streets below. My guide noticed my reaction and remarked, "It is alarming, isn't it? This is the reality of their lives back home."[20]

This image highlights the second view of culture prevalent among attorneys, NGOs, and federal staff members as a culture of poverty and intergenerational instability born of economic deprivation, political corruption, social breakdown, and rampant lawlessness. In the weekly meetings held to review individual cases staff members were exposed to a bruising litany of pathologies. They heard horrific stories of wife beating, child abuse, incest, neglect, alcoholism, drug addiction, and sexual assaults within families. In one meeting alone, the staff discussed cases involving a mother who had trafficked her daughter for sex, a father who had punished his son for missing church by forcing him to kneel on rocks for two hours, a child who had lived in the street after being abused and abandoned by his mother, and a fourteen-year-old Guatemalan girl who was raped by her father's brother. When facility staff confronted sexually aggressive teenage boys, the explanation was the culture of machismo imported from Central America. When they dealt with rape victims who suffered from low self-esteem or girls who followed boyfriends into gangs, the problem was "the culture in Central America" where there was a double standard regarding sexual reputations and girls were socialized to be "doormats." When children denied that they had been abused but described routine beatings as normal, it was evidence of culturally deficient value systems that tolerated high rates of domestic violence, child abuse, and femicide. When teenage boys insisted that they needed to work so their families could have clean water and food or to repay loans made to coyotes, staff frequently blamed it on a "different culture of childhood" that ignored the developmental needs of children, not structural violence. One staff member told me, "They grow up too fast. They don't have childhoods. We need to make them understand that they are endangered if they work at fourteen! They need to be in school!"[21]

Migration itself was often considered a form of pathology because it destroyed normative family structures by separating parents from children for years at a time. It exposed children to drug cartels, criminal gangs, and human traffickers who waged campaigns of terror through kidnappings, extortion, and murder. Migration created new categories of transnational parents, mixed-status families, and large blended households composed of biological kin, step relations, and unrelated adults. Presenters at a 2012 conference on unaccompanied children emphasized the negative effects of separation within transnational families and the links between migration and psychosis. Migration constituted "a catastrophic change" that could provoke "an outbreak of madness or a slow, inexorable descent into mental illness."[22] Broken attachments and intergenerational conflicts made each case of family reunification a Gordian knot for staff to unravel; it disrupted their normative placement standards and expectations based on two-parent, nuclear families.

To make sense of the problem behaviors children displayed in custody many staff members conflated social norms and structural factors as explanations for a range of pathologies. Children who became orphans, lived on the street, or were raised by grandparents, siblings, or distant relations were understood as developmentally unfinished or psychologically damaged. Their cases were viewed through the lens of trauma, and most children were deemed at risk or suffering from psychiatric disorders. Intake interviews invariably plumbed family histories in order to uncover incidents of abuse, neglect, and self-harm. The director of a foster care program explained:

> Ten years ago the greatest needs were language training and family placement. Now we see much more trauma. From their earliest childhood their development is compromised. They come from places where there are no child welfare laws or formal protection from abusive home environments with domestic violence and substance abuse. The children are made to watch the rape of their mothers; they are beaten and suffer gross neglect. They have little opportunity for education. They are put to work at five or six, are on their own at six or seven. They cannot form normal emotional bonds. Most suffer from reactive attachment disorder.[23]

SAFETY AND SECURITY STANDARDS: THE MANAGEMENT OF DAILY LIFE

A Penal Model

Although federal personnel emphasized the homelike atmosphere, committed staff, and educational opportunities in ORR facilities, life in federal custody was anything but normal. All those in custody had to conform to the same communal living standards. Children were required to wake up and eat early and had set time limits for personal hygiene and bathroom use before going to class. They ate meals in a common room, attended school in the facility, played supervised sports within fenced areas, and participated in approved group or individual activities until lights were turned off, generally no later than 9:30 p.m. They left the facility only for court appearances, special medical or psychiatric treatment, and supervised community outings.

Commenting on the importance of "a structured environment," the director of a shelter for boys explained, "Some have trouble accepting the rules, accepting authority. A recurring problem is that the boys want to move outside the structure whenever they want. Control is a big issue."[24] Several DFCs agreed: "They were left on their own, walked through the desert, took care of themselves. They get into custody, and they can't deal with the structures. They say, 'What! You want me to stand in line to get lunch?' or 'You have to ask to go to the bathroom?' We have to constantly remind them that the rules are for their own safety."[25]

All of the closed facilities I visited, including minimum-security shelters, were organized on a penal or psychiatric model: locked or monitored entry and exit and controlled movement inside, even in the absence of high fences, and barred windows or gated entrances. Facilities used internal surveillance systems as well as twenty-four-hour "awake" supervision to ensure that the clients were never left unattended. ORR procedures required a daytime staff-to-client ratio, generally one staff member to six minors in shelters during the day, and higher ratios in more restricted facilities or when clients went on community outings.

There were line-of-sight checks at intervals determined by the security level of the facility: thirty-minute intervals in shelters, fifteen minutes in staff-secure facilities, and constant checks in secure facilities. One Texas minimum-security shelter used visual checks to identify heightened risk and to modify problem behaviors. I attended a meeting in which the staff reviewed the twenty-seven cases listed on the weekly census report. Fifteen of the twenty-seven clients were marked "code red," a condition that required five-minute line-of-sight checks. Code red was routinely used to monitor high flight risks, such as clients during the first fourteen days of custody and those who had accepted voluntary departure, received deportation orders, or were about to turn eighteen. Staff also deemed it an efficient mechanism to control "noncompliant" kids. "Code reds" were not permitted to participate in organized outings and had every word and action recorded by youth care workers. The shelter director explained:

> The staff use codes for each activity. There is one for eating, one for meeting with the attorney, going to class, for personal care. They come off red if their behavior improves and there are no violations for a full seventy-two hours or after fourteen days. They are evaluated every Thursday, and their new

status shows up on the Friday census. [Laughing] They live for the five-minute check system because it provides proof of their good behavior![26]

Staff Monitoring

Detailed rules governed clients' behavior in custody, at court hearings, or on outings. Children interacted with a wide array of adult authorities with enormous power to facilitate or hinder their movement through the system. A hierarchy of staff composed of three or four levels continuously monitored children's behavior and psychological state. At the lowest level were youth care workers, who were always present in residential houses, common areas, and shelter classrooms. They kept daily records on food intake, attitude, sleep patterns, verbal interactions, and classroom participation and controlled access to the phone. They paid special attention to the relations among peers, noting alliances and friendships. Being a loner was as problematic as becoming too attached. If clients "acted out" by deviating from prescribed rules and facility norms, youth care workers reported to case managers, who in turn directed children to medical coordinators and/or clinicians. Clinicians reported to staff psychiatrists.

Fernanda, who spent six months in a Texas shelter, remembered the rules.

> We had to keep an arm's length from another person and to maintain this distance without touching. We couldn't play rough, talk loud, run around, touch the windows, or send messages to other kids. We had about fifteen minutes to pee and brush our teeth in the morning, and the same time to take a bath at night. There were always two workers in each house. They were watching us all the time. If you sleep a certain way at night and then turn over, they write it down. If you wake up in the middle of the night, they write it down. Some girls tried to hurt themselves, so they wouldn't let us have scissors or spiral notebooks. If you broke the rules they put your name in a black book and it would go in your record. They told us the [immigration] judge sees that record.

Maribel described the uncertainty, boredom, and importance of small distractions.

> There were five houses, eight in a group, two groups with two youth care workers. We didn't fight, and we didn't break the law. But everybody there had depression and the girls were always crying. They were sad because they haven't talked to their mom. One said, "I was raped," and she was telling her story. I heard that some kids tried suicide. I don't know if it happened, but everybody was affected. The workers had to be there for us. We had to

not think about life outside. They had to keep us busy. We did crafts a lot. We wait all day for the craft. If we lost the needle, the worker freaked out and said, 'No more craft! Back to your room.' They think it was a little thing, but it wasn't. Life is too beautiful to be there. I would say, "Why am I here—just like a criminal." Life stopped in there, life was ended.

Ernesto spent four months in a shelter in Corpus Christi and remembered the regimented routine there: "When we got moved to Corpus Christi they put all of the boys from Nixon into one of the four houses. We were in a house for bad kids."

SJT: How did you know that it was the house for bad kids?

Ernesto: I know because of what the other kids said. After a few weeks, one kid said, "You're not a bad kid, why did they put you in that house?" Also I knew from the way the guards treated us. They were nasty, and sometimes we got shoved against the wall. I said [to myself], "OK, you got to accept this, it is not so different from what I had in my country." Then one day, an important guy, a big guy who spoke Spanish, came to talk to the boys from Nixon. He gave us his card and told us we had rights. We had the right to go live with a foster family, to go to school, and that we would all get our papers [legal status] when we got there. We were all so happy. We said, "We are lucky!" Then another guy, this time a white guy, came and asked us questions and said when we got released the documents would be waiting for us. I thought this is the only thing that matters. Not the abuse but getting the papers.

Ernesto understood that those who earned good marks for their behavior stood a chance of being released to an open setting, whereas those who accumulated "incident reports" were labeled as potentially dangerous and subjected to more restrictions.

Other children who left behind desperately poor families suffered abuse or neglect, and had no relatives in the United States were happy to accept the exchange involved in federal custody. In return for abundant food, decent housing, English instruction, and the hope of legal relief, they voluntarily surrendered their freedom and played by the rules even when they didn't understand or like them. Confinement ended their need to stay on the move, fend for themselves, take dangerous risks, and make adult choices with few resources.

Corina, the teenager who nearly died in the desert, explained, "I appreciated everything at the shelter. I got a case worker who explained all the rules. I said, 'Rules? What is that? I never had rules at home.' So I said, 'OK, if that is what they want I will do it.' But they never explained why we had to follow those rules." Guadaloupe, a young Guatemalan woman who spent eleven months in custody and won legal relief, exclaimed, "It [the shelter] was really good! I get to live like a little girl again. My family is really poor and my dad treated us bad. They gave us all this food and I was taking classes. When I get frustrated and sad, I talk to the case managers. They are giving me words to feel better." Modesto, a young man from a Quiché indigenous group in Guatemala, explained:

> When they got me I said, "Why should I run away? Where would I go?" I was happy at the shelter. They said they would help me with the paperwork to stay in the U.S. and get an education. I was able to call my family and talk for five minutes. We weren't locked up. Why would you want to leave? You have everything right there. I have been on my own since I was seven or eight. My mother died when I was two, and my father was never around. For the first time I had people watching over me.

Even the model kids had behavioral episodes the longer their confinement lasted. After six months Corina began to act out.

> I was the best girl in the house, I was never in trouble. But I was getting desperate and everything started to bother me and I got into an argument and slapped a girl. They made me stay alone [with a youth care worker] in my room. One of the staff asked what was going on because I was not that kind of person. I think when you get to that point you don't care about the punishment. I challenged him and said I wouldn't do my homework. He said, "Then you will spend another week in here." So I did it. I stayed four more months in that place.

Information Control

Information on individual cases was channeled vertically up and down the chain, from the individual facility director through the FFS who monitors facilities in specific regions to the ORR management team at Washington, DC, headquarters. Despite the stated commitment to empower clients by including them in the processes that governed their lives in and after custody, case managers, clinicians, and directors tightly controlled the information they gave to detained children.[27] They monitored all calls to preapproved contacts, denied access to the Internet, including email, and provided incomplete information on family reunification options and limited or delayed updates on the "case," such as the results of a home study on a prospective sponsor, the possibility of a foster care placement, or the timing of release. In the interests of "security, safety, and protection," staff members withheld advance notification of removal from the United States or a child's transfer to more restrictive facilities. Children were often told of those decisions just hours before their departure. ORR staff also used elements from case files that had been disclosed in confidence to case managers and clinicians to deny transfer to less restricted settings such as a group home or a foster family, especially if children reported involvement of any kind with gangs, smugglers, or drug dealers.

Staff controlled the announcement of good news such as the completion of required paperwork for family reunification, the approval of a sponsor, or the date of release. Their justification was to protect the minor's confidentiality and to reduce the anxieties caused by the delays and inefficiencies of bureaucratized care. One case manager explained, "We just can't get their hopes up until we know for certain if their sponsor is approved or if we have a foster family."[28] Another case manager cynically labeled restrictions on information as a "cover your ass" strategy that governed the entire custodial system.[29]

ORR policies clearly stated that "all UAC records including case management, medical and mental health files, papers, emails, letters, reports correspondence, photographs, forms and other UAC specific documentary materials are the property of ORR" and cannot be released to anyone, including the child's attorney, without prior authorization.[30] ORR made exceptions for information to be released to network service providers and DFCs as well as to local law enforcement and child protective services in the event of reported abuse. Despite mandating that UAC information "be held in strict confidence," ORR staff shared case files with ICE containing information that children had disclosed in confidence regarding family history, criminal activity, and substance abuse. This practice violated standard child welfare and mental health practices, which hold that files must remain strictly confidential except in crisis circumstances.[31]

Attorneys reported the adverse effect such information sharing had on a child's legal case. ICE trial attorneys used information from case files in removal proceedings to challenge a child's credibility and argue against legal relief.[32] As a result of the misuse of information in court proceedings, some case managers and attorneys warned children against disclosing sensitive information while in custody. Staff who received sensitive information sometimes elected to write case histories that lacked documentation and specifics.[33] This tactic could compromise a legal case. It also affected the placement of children with federal foster care families after their release from custody. It exposed the ongoing conflict of interest in the role of DHS as legal guardian and federal prosecutor.

BEHAVIOR MODIFICATION: REWARDS AND PUNISHMENT

In custody children were subjected to a comprehensive step-by-step "behavioral plan" that centered on the identification, classification, and modification of problem behaviors. As outlined in the ORR regulations, the plan was based on a safe and humane "system of discipline." It precluded the use of physical restraints, relying instead on "conflict resolution," "verbal de-escalation," "clear rules," "immediate feedback," and "positive coping skills." The goal was to foster "personal growth and development, decision-making skills, a sense of accountability and self-control." The behavioral plan was intended to condition children to replace "inappropriate behaviors" with "appropriate" ones based on a nonpunitive "system of privileges" and consequences.[34] In this light, the government's professed concern for fostering personal growth and positive coping skills can be understood as part of a larger disciplinary project. This project encouraged behavioral conformity with insignificant monetary rewards—typically earning $1 a day—whereas repeated violations were punished with tightened restrictions.

Although supervisory personnel in different facilities emphasized the unique approaches they developed, in fact, there were only superficial differences in the behavior modification programs I observed. Most facilities used a system of levels and awarded points based on behavior that correlated with certain privileges. One shelter director described her point system.

> When the kids arrive we establish a behavior contract. We go step by step. We teach to behaviors, but we don't discipline. Instead, we show them how to solve problems, how to talk to peers, how to interact with authority figures. They earn points if they follow the rules. They learn that negative behaviors, such as arguing, talking back, fighting, damaging property, have consequences like losing outings and being put on one-on-one supervision. They can earn back points for good behavior and then use those points to go shopping. They could get an MP3 player, a phone card, or hair gel—a really hot item! In the weekly house meeting every client gets a sheet with the problem behaviors listed, such as "refuses to take feedback," "won't accept responsibility for actions." They have to rate themselves and discuss the results in the group. They then elect a house leader by secret ballot based on who carries his weight and who doesn't. Of course, we can override the vote for student leader if necessary.[35]

Other facilities dispensed with levels and points in favor of "strength-based" incentives designed to focus on "adaptive behaviors." The director of a staff-secure facility in Oregon instituted monetary incentives and immediate, short-term punishments rather than movement among levels: "If you lose a level you lose a lot and you are punished for longer periods of time. We punish bad behaviors right away. Then it is over and the kids get a clean slate. We give them the chance to process what has happened by writing letters to peers and staff members." His lead case manager agreed: "Our kids come from secure facilities or juvenile detention. They are being punished a second time because they are undocumented. Why should we treat them as prisoners?"[36]

The director of a ninety-eight-bed Arizona facility with sixty-four floor staff, six case managers, and four clinicians described the smooth operation he ran: "They feel safe here. It's the structure that keeps them here. The skills the kids learn more than compensate for their stay. All the kids are treated humanely here. Our goal is to give them back a childhood. It is hard for them to become kids again."[37]

When I asked him to describe the shelter rules, he proudly shared "the book of consequences" the staff had developed with input from "clients" (in custody) who were student council representatives. It defined inappropriate behavior "as a response to needs that a person is not always aware of." Staff had "to talk with the client about motivation" and use consistent responses that emphasized understanding and education as well as consequences and repair.

The comprehensive thirteen-page manual organized inappropriate behavior by categories related to personal demeanor, management of social space, respect for individual boundaries, and interactions among clients and between them and staff. Like the ORR placement tool, misbehaviors were ranked from the least to the most severe and paired with immediate feedback and corrective responses. Minor infractions involved refusal to participate in activities, wearing hats or sunglasses indoors, sleeping or speaking out in class, failure to follow staff instructions or to respect the personal space of peers, and eating outside the dining area. More serious infractions included wearing pants that exposed undergarments, sharing personal items, refusing to clean up, insulting staff, inappropriate intimate contact with or intimidation of peers, unauthorized entry into restricted areas, spitting, swearing, and aggressive play.

The most serious incidents were changes in personal appearance, for example, tattoos or piercings that suggested gang affiliation, stealing, intentionally lying to staff, sexual advances or threats, and physical aggression. After an incident staff used "words" to educate the client and impose consequences based on the number of occurrences and the degree of inappropriateness. For example, wearing sunglasses indoors prompted a discussion on "socially acceptable and respectful behavior" and resulted in a loss of their use for one day. Yelling at or insulting staff members demanded temporary separation of the staff member and the minor and an immediate time out. Serious instances such as physical aggression toward a staff member required an incident report and one-on-one supervision or resulted in transfer to a more secure facility.

To repair the infraction the minor had to complete a specified number of community service projects, such as writing a "forgiveness" letter or providing unpaid labor by cleaning bathrooms, mopping floors, or washing dishes. The stated objective was to repair misbehavior and restore the client's place in the community through "useful work." In a residential treatment center I visited outside Chicago "useful" labor was an integral component of mental health therapy for youths with serious mental illness.

One could also argue that performing menial tasks had as much to do with keeping order and enforcing docility as it did with rehabilitation or therapy. Boys who broke the rules were expected to suppress bad attitudes, correct their behavior, and project at least an outward respect for authority. Accepting responsibility for their own actions put the burden squarely on them, not the facility, for choosing the right behavior and getting the best outcome. These service projects undercut the inspirational classroom messages on equal opportunity and the American Dream. Swabbing a dirty toilet or scrubbing pots was the kind of low-wage, low-status work typically performed by unskilled, undocumented immigrant labor. These were the only jobs that those released without papers would likely get.

ACTING OUT

Children who acted out could be transferred, or stepped up, to more restrictive facilities and held for longer periods. Patterns of misbehavior were linked to abnormal family structures, a culture of violence, and migratory trauma but were framed as mental disorders that posed different levels of risk. Drawing on Western psychological and psychiatric diagnostic models, staff identified a range of trauma-related problems that required treatment, from mild anxiety to conduct disorders to PTSD to suicidal ideation. Because mental health services were limited in ORR facilities and many case managers and clinicians lacked the skills or time to provide intensive talk therapy, staff focused on controlling the symptoms, rather than addressing the causes, of behavior problems through medication.

Facility staff and immigration attorneys alike reported high percentages of children on psychiatric medications, particularly when the period of custody exceeded two months.[38] For example, one case manager in an Arizona shelter shared case notes for the sixteen clients she managed. Of that number, nine youths had been at the shelter for at least two months and seven had been detained for more than six months. Their average length of stay was 184 days. Of the nine, all but two received medication for "panic attacks," "mood disorders," "depression/PTSD," and "suicidal ideation." Those with mood disorders, depression, and/or PTSD were given Celexa, Trazadone, or Depakote in combination with Seroquel. A seventeen-year-old girl who had been at the shelter for ten months was deemed a suicide risk and given a prescription for Clonazepan after she suffered a panic attack that triggered a call to 911. Whereas most staff members viewed the use of psychiatric medication as a necessary and pragmatic response to the complex mental health needs of traumatized children, others expressed concern than the children were overly medicated. Attorneys I interviewed tended to view the biomedical approach as a way to control a challenging teenage population whose behavioral issues worsened with prolonged periods of custody.

STEP UP

ORR policies required that staff rank and record all non-normative incidents that occurred in custody. This procedure was conceived as a monitoring tool to ensure that facilities complied with federal policies and procedures. Originally the FFS's intended role was to provide additional oversight and to prevent violations of custodial regulations. By 2009 the oversight function of the FFS had been largely co-opted by security concerns.[39] The documentation and tracking of all incidents were used less to monitor facility staff than to identify, isolate, and remove problem kids whose behavior disrupted the normal functioning of the facility. An accumulation of serious incidents could, and did, result in a request to step up the child to a more restrictive facility.

Significant Incident Reports

Carlita left home in El Salvador at thirteen with her boyfriend, was kidnapped by a criminal gang in Mexico, trafficked for sex, and forced to transport drugs for two years before she escaped and crossed into the United States. Because she had been drugged and starved for much of her captivity, she admitted to not "being good in the head" after her transfer to a large ORR shelter in Texas. Her erratic behavior and emotional outbursts attracted attention and resulted in "many incident reports." She described the conditions at the shelter.

> They would punish us a lot. We would cry because they only allowed us to talk [on the phone] to our family for ten minutes. That would frustrate us and we would talk back to the staff. We didn't have the right to talk back, to use bad language. We had to eat everything on our plate because if we didn't they said it meant we were trying to harm ourselves. They would punish us by putting us on one-on-one [supervision] when we broke the rules. I got three days of that once. It meant that you had to stay alone in your room, to eat there, not to go to school, and to have a staff lady with you. They would write a report about us that said we had bad behavior, but they never told us what they wrote. Then the supervisors would call us into the office and talk to us, but our word didn't count, only the word of the staff.[40]

Carlita was involved in a physical altercation that resulted in her step up to the staff-secure wing of the facility in Virginia where Orlando was detained. In contrast to her experience in the Texas shelter, she received in-depth, effective counseling, in addition to psychiatric medications, and established an exemplary behavioral record. She was stepped down and released to a foster family she came to love.[41]

Minor incident reports were generated and circulated internally among floor staff, case managers, and clinicians in the facility and differed from significant incidents, which required submission of a report with "all pertinent facts and follow-up actions and recommendations" within twenty-four hours to ORR. The notification chain included the ORR/DUCS hotline, the DFC, the FFS in the region, and project officers at ORR headquarters.[42] Significant incident reports (SIRs) were required in the case of alleged violations of ORR regulations by staff.[43]

SIRs were generated in the case of injuries, accidents, fights, threats, escapes, disclosure of domestic abuse, or child trafficking, as well as medical problems and psychological conditions such as oppositional defiant disorder or suicidal ideation.[44] In the hierarchy of serious incidents, an escape represented one of the most serious breaches of security and mandated the involvement of local law enforcement and the local ICE juvenile coordinator. All SIRs were recorded in the child's file. Once a SIR was reported to all the necessary parties, it could be corrected and updated but remained part of the minor's permanent file. The case file was the official government memory of a particular childhood history and its encounters with the many agencies in the custodial system. Constructed by immigration authorities and federal staff, it favored the authoritative voices of experts under contract to the government over those of children, family members, and attorneys.

What factors prompted a step up to a more secure facility or a lateral transfer to a facility at the same security level? What was the most serious kind of infraction? Was it easier to step up or step down? The case managers, DFCs, and facility directors I interviewed all agreed that a step up could be justified if a youth threatened or attempted to escape, initiated a physical altercation whether or not it resulted in an injury, engaged in inappropriate sexual behaviors, or displayed a pattern of insubordinate or disruptive behaviors that showed, in the words of one case manager, that "they needed less freedom and more intensive scrutiny."[45]

The majority of facility directors I interviewed insisted that they didn't like "step ups" and rarely resorted to them, emphasizing their proactive interventions to prevent transfers. However, case managers, clinicians, and DFCs agreed that it was easier to get ORR authorization for more restrictions than for less. The question of step ups generated considerable debate among federal staff. Some defended a step up as essential because patterns of misbehavior posed a risk to the safety of kids "who followed the rules." One case manager in Houston explained, "We need to monitor these boys. Escapes are very serious because some of these boys are coyotes or drug mules and they need to be under special scrutiny."[46]

In contrast, a DFC of Puerto Rican ancestry with an MA in counseling and a BA in criminal justice criticized "the legal and carceral model" governing the treatment of detained kids and their interactions with staff.[47] Many federal staff members and immigration attorneys believed that structural features of the system such as the aversion to risk and the emphasis on security led to step ups. They saw inflexible rules, inconsistent consequences, long stays, and no set endpoint of detention as the very reasons that clients acted out and accumulated SIRs.

A DFC who was promoted to the position of ORR FFS shortly after our 2010 interview explained the difficulty of obtaining step downs: "Placement in staff-secure or secure facilities is a stigma. When shelters see the history of a kid from staff-secure they see a rough population, write-ups for fighting, evidence of bad influences like gang tattoos, and they are afraid to take them. So I have had some success by providing lots of supporting documentation to the facility director, who has the power to decide what is appropriate. I include a letter from the clinician and I shift the language from describing clinical problems to listing positive results. I document what has worked, not what has gone wrong."[48]

ORR policies stated that UACs should not be sent to a more restrictive setting without first making a best effort to keep them in the current placement.[49] In order of priority, the factors to be considered included the child's individual needs, potential for family reunification, status of immigration case, protection from smugglers, and behavioral issues. In interviews facility staff emphasized that the decision to transfer a client from a shelter to a staff-secure, therapeutic staff-secure, or secure facility[50] took into account many factors. One case worker listed the questions to consider.

> Did the misbehaviors constitute a pattern that posed a safety risk to the staff, their peers, and to themselves? Were they linked to a personal history that included arrests, criminal or delinquency charges, gang affiliations, and court supervision? Were there underlying clinical disorders that required intensified counseling in combination with psychiatric medications?[51]

Another DFC also noted:

> We have to see what the facility director's threshold tolerance level for difficult cases is. Are they willing to work with kids who were marked as difficult and in need of special help?[52]

Most staff insisted that there was no direct correlation between the number of SIRs and a step up. Nonetheless, when they described specific cases the typical rationale for the transfer included the number and type of SIRs.

The decision to transfer a particular youth was made by facility directors in collaboration with staff, DFCs, and ORR FFSs. Like the information on individual cases, each transfer request was sent to the FFS and project directors at the Division of Children's Services at ORR headquarters. Disagreements were referred to the director, who made the final decision. There was no formal mechanism to appeal the decisions made at ORR headquarters.

The decision to grant or deny a step up gave considerable discretion to upper-level management and could lead to unwarranted transfers. Many facility staff members expressed frustration with the structure of decision making and the priority given to security considerations. They cited examples of kids "who shouldn't be here [staff-secure or secure facilities] because they aren't criminals" or "because that's how teenage boys act." One local administrator related the story of a seven-year-old boy held in a Chicago shelter who received an SIR for "assaulting" a youth care worker in a shelter. He was outraged that the staff recorded the boy's "violent, aggressive, and unsafe behavior" in the file and requested his transfer to a staff-secure facility: "He kicked a staff member in the shin! He is seven! Not everything is evidence of an underlying pathology."[53] Another case manager complained about unilateral decisions, describing a teenager who was stepped up from a staff-secure facility to the NORCOR juvenile detention center. After the boy's involvement in a fight the facility director requested the transfer based on a prior adjudication for a minor crime. This request posed the risk that his application for release and reunification with family in the United States would be denied. Those who turned eighteen while in custody were immediately taken to adult immigration detention.[54]

Many attorneys also complained about the flawed process governing transfers. One attorney opined, "ORR regularly transfers kids for minor infractions. The step-up process is arbitrary and capricious, and it depends on a one-sided exchange of information. The facilities have staffing meetings without attorneys present and yet expect attorneys to share everything in their file. In the past confidential documents we sent ended up in the ORR file and got shared with ICE."[55]

The DFCs had similar complaints. They were hired to monitor the kids' treatment and to make recommendations on family reunification but had no say in the final decision. In their view many of the shelter staff were not trained to deal with the behavioral challenges posed by detention or to identify underlying symptoms of trauma. One DFC explained, "The shelter staff tend to focus on the kids who act out. They don't understand the different manifestations of trauma. Some kids internalize the harm and appear to cope well. This can look like good behavior—especially when the kid is in a 120-bed facility—when, in fact, it isn't."[56] Facility staff were under pressure to limit costly services and to maintain order, not to prioritize therapeutic interventions. DFCs saw their function and goals as different from those of facility staff and FFSs. They saw themselves as "the child welfare specialists" who were "the eyes and the ears of the detained child" tasked with an independent monitoring role.[57]

A Serious Flight Risk

To maintain control over the flow of clients into and out of their facilities, facility staff used clinical assessments and incident reports strategically to build a case for eliminating problem cases or refusing to admit new ones. I visited a Miami shelter known for its excellent educational services and enrichment activities thanks to the director's impressive community outreach efforts and organizational skills. This exemplary record relied in part on constant monitoring and inflexible regulations that ensured smooth operation and eliminated potential disruptions. DFCs reported that clients who committed even the most minor infractions were transferred out. They gave the example of a teenage boy who left the facility with a staff member for a doctor's appointment. En route, he saw his cousin on the street. Although the boy knew he was not permitted to approach anyone while outside, he tested the rules, telling his escort, "I could just go over there and talk to him. What could you do?" Although he did nothing, the staff member reported the incident to the facility director, who filed an SIR identifying the boy as a serious flight risk and requesting a transfer. Because his behavior in the shelter was excellent, the director made the case "by looking back to his record, citing an arrest for public intoxication, his tattoos, and the substance abuse issues he had had in the past."[58] The DFC negotiated a lateral transfer for the boy to a shelter where "the director was willing to give him a chance." She added, "That experience taught us not to try to keep a kid in a facility where he is not wanted. The staff will maneuver to get rid of him. They will issue SIRs for even little violations. We don't want those kinds of records in the kid's file. Facilities have a common goal set by ORR, but each has its own agenda."[59]

Carlos's Step Up

We met Carlos in chapter 2 during his journey north, his escape from the Zetas, and his apprehension at the border. He was screened, deemed eligible for legal relief, and initially placed in a shelter in Washington State. He explained:

> They sent me to a shelter. I said, "Who are these people?" An officer signed me in, and a nice lady took my information and asked me all kinds of questions. Then they gave me food. It was so good and I was so hungry because I went without eating for a whole day. When they told me the rules, I thought, "This is not a jail!" They gave me clothes, took me on trips, and we took turns cleaning the bathrooms and the kitchen. They explained the point levels. There was level 1, 2, and 3. You start at one level, and if you behave OK you stay there. But if you say bad words, if you don't go to your room when they tell you, if you touch a friend on the arm, on the head, anywhere, they lower your level and they can kick you out. One day I was sitting next

to a guy and the staff came up to him and said, "OK, it's time to go. You are leaving us." I didn't understand what was happening at first. Later I knew. At that time I was at level 3, the best level. I was doing well in school, I was learning English, I had twenty-three stars [for good behavior]. I got extra food—two hamburgers and ice cream. I was happy because I behaved well and they said I could be reunified with a [foster] family. Then some guys in the house started to bother me. One day it was my turn to use the computer in class. I went to sit down and another Guatemalan got there first and elbowed me hard. He broke my nose. I was bleeding, crying, and I ended up in the hospital. I went back to the shelter, and two days later I hit him. I was mad because they didn't punish him for what he did. A few days after that I was sleeping and one of the staff woke me up and said I had to sign papers and be taken to a different place [a staff-secure facility]. What did I do? I punched him . . . but not hard. He wasn't hurt. It wasn't fair. It was a step up, and it was so different in the next place. I was locked up all the time. They had levels too, but you couldn't go up a level in less than a week. The best level had TV, CD, and radio, but the level I started on had nothing, no movies on Friday nights, no radio. The rooms for my level were the oldest and the dirtiest. It was bad and I was there for four months. I couldn't qualify for a foster care family because I got stepped up. Then I turned eighteen and they sent me to the adult detention center. I really suffered there.[60]

Carlos's attorney explained that he was represented as "a peer challenge" and an "instigator" by the shelter staff, who used the "minor altercation" to request his step up. The attorney worked with the local ICE office to obtain Carlos's release from adult detention and helped him to obtain a visa based on the severe abuse he had suffered at home. She expressed her frustration: "The justification for the step up did not involve anything serious. So if the kid poses absolutely no danger to anyone, why do they need to detain him in the first place? Why did he need to go to a staff-secure? That put him on a path to adult detention."[61]

Hanadi's Transfer

In July 2010 I attended a case review meeting in a shelter in Southern California with the facility director, the clinician, case managers, and the DFC. Hanadi's case had assumed special urgency. Attorneys at a local legal aid organization had determined she was a credible candidate for asylum and were preparing her legal case. As political chaos had engulfed her native Somalia, Hanadi's father was killed by a local militia and her brother narrowly escaped being burned alive by members of the Somali Islamist group Al Shabab before he too disappeared. She fled the country and spent time in a Kenyan refugee camp before leaving Africa with a smuggler. Her journey to seek refuge in the United States was interrupted when she was detained in Panama for six months. After release, she crossed the U.S. border, was apprehended, and was transferred to ORR custody.

Hanadi had been detained for seven months at the time of the case review. She wanted to reunify with a male cousin in the Midwest. They had not been in contact for years, and the shelter case manager had no luck locating him. Even if they had been able to contact him they would have had to collect extensive documentation on his background, finances, home life, and employment status, as well as verification of their family connection. Given the years of separation, it is likely that the DFC would have recommended a home study or suitability assessment before approving Hanadi's cousin as a sponsor. Home studies usually took two to three months to complete. When there were no family members in the United States able or willing to provide care, children could be released to long-term foster care. This process was also complicated and labor-intensive due to the dearth of foster care beds. Of 2,927 funded beds, only 181 were with foster care families.[62] At seventeen and a half Hanadi was too old to be considered for a foster care placement.

Her attorney, the shelter staff, and the DFC had all observed signs of Hanadi's mental deterioration. The clinician and case manager had repeatedly urged her to take psychiatric medication and were recommending a transfer to a residential treatment facility before she could be released to an open setting. They reported her adamant refusal and ardent desire "to be free." Hanadi's behavior had precipitated a crisis. One night in the main room she had suddenly screamed that she wanted to die, covered her face with her hijab, and wrapped a computer cord around her neck. She was sent to the local hospital and discharged to the shelter after a psychological screening revealed that she posed no threat to herself or others. Her shelter file included numerous internal reports on disruptive behavior, but the suicide threat triggered an automatic SIR to ORR headquarters. Her case dominated the review meeting.

> *Director:* She had a psychiatric evaluation last week and a counseling session. The doctor strongly recommended that she get medicated, but she refused. She said, "I will feel better now and I don't want it [medicine] to make me sick. I will change now."
>
> *DFC:* She has never had any [comparable] incidents before this, right?
>
> *Clinician:* Not true! She has tantrums, throws her shoes at the staff, and pounds the wall.

Case manager: That's right, she hits the table with her hand, storms out to her room. She peed on herself once.

Clinician: We have never seen a suicidal gesture before. The psychiatrist recommends a blood pressure medication to lower the level of arousal. I am not a physician, but my professional opinion regarding her symptomology is that she suffers from PTSD and depression. She is unstable and really needs medication and more intensive therapy. We really can't provide for her needs here.

The shelter staff argued strongly for Hanadi's immediate transfer to a residential treatment facility so "she could get help for her PTSD" and "begin to build coping skills." The problem that soon emerged was the lack of bed space in such shelters during the high summer season. There was also the timing of a transfer out of state given the upcoming interview at the local asylum office.

DFC: If Hanadi stabilizes and we can't get her cousin approved as a sponsor, then we have to push the foster care option. That is the goal here. Does she really need residential treatment?

Clinician: Absolutely, or if not, then a lateral move to another shelter [several hours away with specialized psychological therapy]. If she stays here she will just burn through the staff.

Later the DFC met with Hanadi, who began to sob.

Hanadi: I don't like. When I was coming here, had no English, food, and religion was different, difficult to be here. I don't want group home. I want freedom. Not fair. Two years. I have no life. In Somalia good life. Now not better life. Said what I wanted. Said I don't want to be here. They say, "Be patient." Why? They think if send me to another house, then OK. NOT OK.

DFC: They have your story on paper, and they know you want more freedom, but they need to make sure that you are OK, that you feel ready.

Hanadi: It is Ramadan, I have to go to mosque, Muslims have to pray, I don't want group home. I'm not crazy. I just want freedom. I go with cousin if foster care don't want me. I want that, but now they say stay, more time in group home. I wait too long. Please help me get out of this house.

When Hanadi left the room, the staff reconvened. They agreed that reunification with Hanadi's cousin was impossible. The DFC suggested that the problem was not acute psychosis but severe stress caused by long-term detention. What she needed was a less restrictive setting. The case manager strongly disagreed.

Case manager: She is too unpredictable. Why not a residential treatment center? She doesn't want to be detained. She feels that we treat her differently because she is black. You know just last week we made a banquet of her favorite [Somali] foods. We really went all out. She didn't even acknowledge it. We really expected a different reaction.

DFC: She is culturally isolated from the Somali community. She sees a residential treatment center as another group home. Would it provide any therapeutic benefit?

The clinician held up a thick stack of incident reports from Hanadi's file, saying, "She has worn the staff out. She is not getting better here. She is deteriorating and the staff is not trained in her set of issues. She does not have the tools to deal with this. We all face disappointment and frustration. Is she a danger to herself? No. The issue is how she communicates her distress. Will these behaviors be repeated? Absolutely, if she stays here. What really concerns me is the impact on the others. They also have trauma. It shouldn't be stressing them. She needs a change, more supportive services as a transition to long-term foster care."

The case manager added, "We have a long history with her. She talks back, is disrespectful, storms around. Once she hit the table and sent food flying. She says threatening things like, "If you don't make my phone call, I can do something." When the DFC asked if Hanadi had any other incidents of suicidal ideation or had been physically aggressive, the clinician said no but began to read from dated entries in her file: "On July 4 she claimed that the staff threatened to deport her." "On June 28, she swore at a male client, saying, 'Get out of here you fucking Hindi.'"

Listening to Hanadi's case review, I thought back to a residential treatment center that I had visited outside Chicago earlier that same summer. That facility was heavily secured, had a staff to client ratio of 1 to 3, and provided intensive therapy for clients who were all managed with psychiatric and psychotropic medications. They had received a range of diagnoses, including severe depression, physical aggression, sexual acting out, mood disorders, and schizophrenia. One client heard voices, and another sat in the stairwell clenching his fists and banging his head against the wall. The clinician explained that stays in the treatment center were typically six months. Hanadi's rapid decline in the shelter setting begged the question of how she would fare in such a place.

The DFC put Hanadi's case in a broader context: "In any detention setting there is a disconnect between the field and headquarters. You need oversight and child advocacy. ORR is the legal guardian. The shelter staff and the FFS have the entire responsibility and must shoulder the burden of liability. We need to prioritize best interest determinations by asking what clinical and educational services they need and assessing the family situation."[63]

In follow-up interviews, Hanadi's clinician described the acute mental health needs of "[detained] kids who all have trauma with a capital *T*. The kids are in a foreign culture and away from family. They need safety, security, and a sense that somebody understands their feelings."[64] He expressed concern about "the lack of psychological sophistication and misreading of mental health issues" that was typical of shelter staff. He criticized case managers who challenged the credibility of kids when they recounted horrific incidents like it was "a TV show they had seen the day before." Such deadpan narratives, he insisted, "didn't mean that what they experienced wasn't traumatizing. It absolutely was." He criticized the judgmental comments of youth care workers about "bad" kids and the defensiveness of the case manager who took children's complaints personally. Although he acknowledged that Hanadi's prolonged detention was certainly a factor in her behavior, he saw the trauma she had suffered in her long journey from Somalia to the United States as the primary cause of her mental health problems. He viewed her refusal to take medication as a symptom of mental illness rather than as a legitimate right to express her opinion on medical treatment. His rationale for her transfer was based as much on her repeated tantrums, peer conflicts, and disrespect for the staff as it was on her therapeutic needs. Although the staff justified their request for her transfer by citing angry outbursts and the use of profanity, the real issue may have been, at least in part, her attack on their integrity when she accused them of racism and anti-Muslim bias. They viewed such allegations as unwarranted and unfair given their "all-out" effort to honor her Somali ethnic traditions.

I asked another clinician within the ORR system about mental health services for detained children. She responded:

We collect all this information about their emotional and psychological needs, but we should ask ourselves if the counseling works and if it is necessary. The FSA stipulates that we provide regular counseling sessions. At the beginning, yes, it is a good idea but not necessarily once a week. Some of the kids don't want or need it, frankly. Aren't we violating their right to refuse it? Doesn't it violate the ethics of mental health services if we mandate it? Are we doing more harm than good?[65]

I met Hanadi a week later, this time in the hallway of a shelter in another part of the state where she had been transferred for more intensive therapy.

CONCLUSION

The increasing numbers of undocumented migrants, both adults and children, entering the United States have produced a shift in the mechanisms of containment and control at the nation's borders and within the interior. In the wake of annual admissions that have multiplied since 2000, federal authorities were more attentive to the security risks posed by unaccompanied children, whether they were apprehended after crossing the border or within the interior after long periods of residence in the country. In the custodial system, U.S. immigration authorities and federal personnel under contract to the government took on the role of evaluating the children deemed suitable for release as well as those who were willing to sponsor them. Federal custody is a process that separated the "good" clients from the "bad." Staff prioritized a protective environment such as family reunification or federal foster care for the former and a more restrictive setting or removal for the latter. Good migrants understood the need to accept behavioral restrictions that many found both arbitrary and unfair. They were rewarded with extra food or recreation, stepped down to low-security shelters, and fast tracked for release to open settings. Problem youths challenged authority, created disruptions, and received sanctions. At best they were labeled as psychologically unstable, diagnosed with personality disorders, and managed with psychiatric medication. At worst they were categorized as security, terroristic, or criminal threats, transferred to more restrictive facilities, and detained for longer periods, making release to an open setting or a foster family more difficult if not impossible.

The system of care for unaccompanied children has developed within a framework based on middle-class Western ideals of childhood as a time of dependency and innocence when children are socialized by adults and slowly become independent social actors. It is assumed that economic responsibilities are the province of adults so that children can be freed from the pressures of work. This framework views the treatment of children in terms that transcend political and class divides, assumes a universal model of childhood development, and supposes a consensus on what policies represent the best interest of the child, in particular, emphasizing a therapeutic model of service provision.[66]

Movement through the custodial system is often depicted as a game that combines the luck of the draw, knowledge of arbitrary rules, and strategic moves. Border Patrol agents refer to the daily hunt for undocumented immigrants who cross the remote stretches of the U.S.-Mexican border as "the game."[67] Many immigration attorneys who screen detained children for legal status and have to choose the cases they are likely to win also see it this way. At a 2012 children's conference in Washington, DC, Shalyn Fluharty, an immigration attorney with Catholic Charities in New York, and two game designers from the New School for Social Research, Lien Tran and William Jin, presented a board game they had created for use by undocumented youth in U.S. detention. The goal of the game is to manage the unpredictable obstacles that can prolong detention or hasten release, such as gaining access to case managers, talking to clinicians, meeting with attorneys, or following the terms of probation if there is a criminal history. The game introduces circumstances beyond the individual's control that delay release, such as a foster family placement that falls through or a sponsor who has not submitted the fingerprints of all adult household members. It also replicates the competition that pits detained children against their peers for limited resources such as pro bono legal representation and foster family placements. Let us turn now to how the game played out for young people who were released from detention.

6

Release

In early 2010 I attended the orientation on family reunification given by DFCs to eleven new arrivals at a large shelter in Phoenix. They were part of a larger group of forty teenagers who had been apprehended near the Arizona border between December 22 and January 10, 2010. That day there were four girls and seven boys in the group, all sixteen or seventeen years old. Six came from Guatemala, two from El Salvador, and three from Mexico, figures that matched the nationalities already at the shelter. All but one claimed that this was their first time in the United States. That Mexican boy had been deported several times but kept crossing the border because, he said, "I have no family."

The DFC explained to the group:

> After your release you have rights, but you also have responsibilities. You have to follow the rules, attend school, go to [immigration] court, and live only with the approved family after release. We will need to fill out a big packet with documentation of everything. All of that paperwork must be completed before you can leave here. We need to verify your age. Any sponsor needs to explain how they know you. Are they family members? Do they have papers to prove this? If they are not immediate family they have to show how they are related. Are they your cousins? Uncles? Friends? In some places your sponsor must have legal documents. For example, a family friend without papers is not a good sponsor. The same thing goes for release to a boyfriend or girlfriend. It will not be approved. Say your mom or dad is working in the U.S. without papers. Could they be a sponsor? It's possible but not a sure thing. Could their boss be a sponsor? That is not a good idea

because the boss could take advantage of an irregular situation. Any sponsor with a criminal history, even it was years ago, even if it is a parent, is not the best choice either. When the packet is complete, someone on the outside goes to the sponsor's house to check it out and report back to us. If we have questions or worries we might have to make another visit. It can take twenty to thirty days.

The preparation for release began just days after the child's detention and was termed family reunification, even if the child was not approved to join family members in the United States or had not previously lived with the sponsor. Family reunification—defined broadly as blood relations or surrogate family—is the ostensible goal of the custodial system and the primary means by which undocumented children are permitted to stay in the United States. Federal staff typically portrayed family reunification as a social good that was bracketed from the chaotic market forces and enforcement policies associated with immigration.[1] For example, at a November 3, 2009, stakeholder meeting held at ORR headquarters in Washington, DC, the director of the Division of Children's Services announced that 58 percent of those referred to ORR by immigration authorities in 2009 had been released from custody and reunified with family in the United States. Adding that 24,000 children had been released to family since 2003, the director explained that the process of reunification was modeled entirely on "national child welfare standards." The primary concern was to verify the child's relationship with family and to identify risk factors that threatened a safe release, such as domestic violence, substance abuse, or financial insecurity. The director made no mention of immigration proceedings because family reunification decisions are intended to be separate from the issue of legal status. Her superior, the new director of ORR, insisted that his goal was to make custodial care a "life changing experience" that goes "beyond the legal requirements of Flores [Settlement Agreement]" and takes seriously the best interest of the child.

Although framed in terms of the ethical imperatives that govern the child's best interest, the process of reunification functioned as a system of control closely tied to immigration enforcement, global labor flows, and economic conditions. Decisions about suitable sponsors were determined as much by security considerations—criminal history and legal status—and financial solvency as by emotional bonds and family connections. The DFCs tacitly acknowledged this when they laid out the unwritten rules for reunification. Being undocumented and having a criminal record could trump even the closest blood relationship. So could being poor and living in overcrowded housing conditions. Reunification priorities based on American middle-class standards of household composition and family structures collided with the economic constraints, social needs, and cultural values of would-be immigrant sponsors. The intrusive scrutiny by ORR of prospective sponsors before release—including parents and close relatives—condensed powerful anxieties about national culture, race, and ethnicity in the nation of the future.

FINDING A SPONSOR

The FSA stipulated an order of preference when releasing a child to a sponsor, prioritizing a biological parent or legal guardian, followed by an adult relative, then an individual designated by the parent or legal guardian, and ending with a licensed program or adult approved by ORR.[2] In 2008 ORR issued stricter rules for the release of a child to a sponsor designated by the parents or legal guardians. These regulations were intended to thwart smugglers, traffickers, and unscrupulous bosses who might masquerade as benefactors. As a result, all sponsors—including parents and guardians—were required to complete a detailed family reunification packet that verified their relationship to the child and to undergo a thorough background check to investigate any criminal history or record of child abuse. Sponsors had to provide accurate information on employment, financial status, household composition, and immigration status. A facility case manager interviewed the child and the potential sponsor and prepared the family reunification packet along with a recommendation for or against release. Upon completion, the packet was submitted to the DFC for an additional layer of review and a recommendation on release. If there were concerns about release to the proposed sponsor, the DFC could recommend a home study and/or follow-up services. As the local-level ORR representative in contracted facilities throughout the country, the FFS made the final decision if, to whom, and under what conditions a minor would be released from custody.[3]

ORR reported data for children released to sponsors from October 1, 2008, through September 30, 2010. Over that period 32 percent of the sponsors they screened were the children's parents, 27 percent were family friends, 19 percent were aunts or uncles, 9 percent were siblings, 5 percent were cousins, and 3 percent were grandparents.[4] Children who had no viable family reunification options in the United States could be released to long-term foster care, as Maribel, Carlita, Corina, and Ernesto were, or to therapeutic foster care. Such youths were eligible to stay in foster care programs only until they reached the age of majority (eighteen), when the ORR mandate to provide funded care ended. An additional protective provision of the TVPRA of 2008 provided for the transfer of minors with an approved Special Immigrant Juvenile Status (SIJS) classification to existing Unaccompanied Refugee Minor (URM) programs administered by ORR. By law and in accordance with most states' foster care licensing regulations, the URM programs could only accept children before their eighteenth birthdays. Once they were admitted, they received the same funded services as refugee minors until the age of twenty-one. Another release option involved transfer to an extended care group home or a transitional independent living center. Younger children as well as those deemed too vulnerable to hold in a shelter, such as pregnant or physically disabled teens, could be admitted to a transitional short-term foster care program while staff identified family reunification options. Finally, children who had no sponsors and little likelihood of obtaining legal status could request voluntary departure and return to their countries of origin. Those like the Mexican boy who reentered the country after taking voluntary departure one or more times would be deported.

A Case Review Meeting

After the orientation session I attended a case review meeting with the two DFCs, the FFS, four of the eight case managers, and one of the four clinicians who worked at the Arizona shelter.[5] With input by the DFCs, the case managers provided updates on prospective sponsors for the 81 minors in custody that day, 59 of whom were seventeen or older, 15, sixteen or older; 2, fifteen, one, fourteen; and 4, eleven or younger. Over half of the detained minors were from Guatemala, and 49 had been at the shelter one month or less. Given the large numbers of new arrivals seventeen or older, the goal was to expedite the process of release by identifying and quickly approving suitable sponsors. The updates centered on what paperwork had been submitted for the reunification packets and what was missing. More than once the FFS reminded the staff, "I need thirty beds!"

As the review proceeded myriad complications emerged. There was the aunt who agreed to be a sponsor but lost her job and couldn't commit, as well as the case of a male cousin who was undocumented and fearful to step forward. In another case, a teenage girl with "abandonment issues" changed her mind about having her parents as sponsors, requesting a foster family instead. This was a problem given the shortage of foster care beds and the thirty-day referral window allowed by ORR. Only six of the 178 minors then in ORR custody in the Phoenix area were in foster care. DFCs maintained a long waiting list for foster care placements, adjusting the minors' place in line depending on their birthday, date of arrival, and length of time in custody.[6]

One case manager reported that five of her fourteen cases were considering a return to the home country because a family member—a father, sister, aunt, cousin, or brother-in-law—could not be a sponsor and "there was no case [for legal relief]." Then there was the sixteen-year old Mexican girl who was living with her twenty-two-year-old boyfriend. Her brother had come forward as a sponsor but then changed his mind. The case manager viewed the girl's undocumented father as the best bet.

One case that had appeared to be ready for approval was falling apart. The client's uncle had proposed his wife as the sponsor for their seventeen-year old nephew. Staff had received most of the required documentation, including proof of the family relationship and the consent form from the boy's parents in Honduras. Suddenly the "wife" had backed out, proposing her younger sister who was a U.S. citizen. If this were true, wondered the case manager, why had the sister refused to provide her birth certificate? And it was a household with ten people that included unrelated adults. They were all required to undergo a background check, and none had done so. Some needed to have their fingerprints taken but were too afraid to have it done at the local police station because they were all undocumented. The house was small and had only two bedrooms. Where would the teenager sleep? There was also the issue of income. Several adults didn't have paycheck stubs because their employers paid them in cash. Could they get a notarized letter from their employers to prove their income? All these issues needed to be resolved, and time was passing. The boy had already been in custody a month.

Another case involved a sixteen-year-old Guatemalan youth who fled an abusive father and sought to reunify with his undocumented mother in the United States. Although she had a stable job and was eager to sponsor her son, she had a troubled past, which the staff discussed at length. Five years earlier her live-in boyfriend had assaulted her. They were concerned about domestic violence in the home and wanted clarification of the police charges brought against him. Pending criminal charges raised red flags. Was the boyfriend still in the picture? Was the mother getting counseling? Given her personal issues, how would she handle a son whom she had not seen in years? How would her son respond to this home situation given his general mistrust of adults? The case manager wondered if they could recommend a "straight release" without a home study. The DFC responded with a qualified yes, adding, "The mother must provide a letter indicating that her son would have psychological counseling." A home study involved an investigation by an outside caseworker. It was a labor-intensive and costly process that could extend the custody of children by two to four months. Many staff members and advocates did not favor its use except when required under the provisions of the TVPRA of 2008.[7]

The conflicts regarding professional codes of ethics and confidentiality standards emerged in the gathering of information required for family reunification. A best practice manual for the background investigation prepared by the LIRS SAFE Haven program mandated that social workers respect clients' right to privacy, protect the confidentiality of all information, including clients' written and electronic records, and inform clients about the disclosure of confidential information.[8] Recognizing the potential conflict between the security interests of the government and the protective mandate of the social service provider, Lutheran Immigrant and Refugee Services, the manual admonished DFCs to remember that the child was their "primary client" and "the client's voice should be heard."[9] Nonetheless, in the information-gathering process sensitive details regarding criminal history, mental health needs, and living situation were shared among ORR staff but not with the child or the sponsor. In cases where questions arose, when an attorney sought information on a home study for presentation to the immigration judge or when a social worker discovered new information with a bearing on the legal case, ORR became the arbiter of what information to release and to whom.

PREPARING FOR RELEASE

Reunification with Family

The first hurdle in preparing a release was filling out the family reunification packet—a procedure most case managers described as very complicated and overwhelming even for an English-speaking person. Once the packet was complete, there were three options. ORR could deny release to a sponsor and keep the child in custody because of an inappropriate living situation or a sponsor's criminal history. Conversely ORR could approve a "straight release" for children who came from a low-security shelter, presented no behavioral issues, and had parents, relatives, or designated guardians with a clean criminal record and the economic means to provide suitable care and housing. Finally, ORR could release teenagers who had been referred for a home study with a recommendation for follow-up services such as mental health counseling.

Seeking Foster Care or a Group Home

Once the ORR staff agreed to release a minor without family sponsors in the United States, they prepared a referral and contacted an NGO provider of foster care or a group home to seek approval for a placement. When NGO staff evaluated a referral they had to determine if the requested placement was "appropriate." When I asked them to define an appropriate placement, they explained that safety was their first concern. Would the youth stay in the community and be safe with the other children in the program? Would he respect the rules, accept the restrictions on travel, meet with his social worker, and receive regular counseling? Would he be able to handle public school classes in English? To find answers, staff plumbed ORR reports on behavior in custody, age at apprehension, family background, psychological profile, and aptitude for acculturation. Children who needed more personalized care were referred to short-term or therapeutic foster care; those who required a more "structured" placement were placed in a group home.

SHORT-TERM FOSTER CARE

In 2011 I visited a transitional, short-term foster care program in Phoenix. In 2004, one year after ORR had assumed responsibility for unaccompanied alien children, Catholic Charities added these services to a well-established URM program so that "fragile" children and teens could be placed rapidly with a foster family pending release.[10] Dana Mercz, then the director, explained that the staff initially had misgivings about accepting the new ORR contract, fearing that the program might be perceived as an extension of border enforcement. She explained:

> It is not physical detention, but technically the children are still in custody. They are monitored 24/7 for escape risk or other behavioral issues and can't

attend public school. Under the terms of the FSA, we had to open and staff a classroom here. Children get the same medical and legal screenings as in the shelters. We gather the background information on the child's family and send it to ORR, and they make the determination for release and reunification. The reunification process can take a few days or last three to four months.[11]

The typical "short-terms" were younger children, age eight to thirteen, who had come to reunite with parents who were working in the United States. The parents' original plan to bring their children was frequently sabotaged by low wages, the high cost of living, and escalating smuggling fees. In many cases parents who had left behind toddlers were not able to send for them for years. Staff described the raw emotions of the children, who were angry with parents whom they hadn't seen for years, refusing to call them Mom and Dad. The hopeful anticipation of the reunion was marred by conflicting loyalties. Kids keenly missed their families in the home country, were apprehensive about joining parents who had new partners, and afraid to compete with younger U.S.-born siblings who spoke English perfectly and did well in school. These feelings emerged in written work displayed in the classroom. In one classroom assignment, the children had completed sentences that probed their hopes, dreams, and worries. They worried about absent relatives and elderly grandparents who were sick and poor. They dreamed of reuniting with long-absent parents and becoming part of new families but "felt sad" and "cried a lot." They hoped "to get an education" and vowed to try "to behave well" and "to do things the right way."

Short-terms were also "fragile youth" who had lived for years in undocumented or mixed-status families in the United States and were apprehended by ICE because of their unlawful status. They were removed from their families and transferred to the custody of ORR. Phoenix staff noted that they first saw such "internal apprehensions" in 2008. These were the most challenging cases because the children had spent years in the United States, had native fluency in English, were integrated in American society, and posed a greater "run risk."

Staff found it mystifying and counterproductive that children were placed in short-term foster care when immigration authorities were advised that they already had families in the United States who loved and supported them. They noted the increased scrutiny of immigrant parents as appropriate care providers, particularly when the children had been separated from parents for long periods and had disabilities, mental or medical health issues, or delinquency histories. To determine parental suitability in high-risk cases, ORR regulations required a home study. Until it was completed children remained in custody, either in closed facilities or in foster care. This policy is a radical departure from the domestic child welfare system that keeps children and parents together unless there is an accusation of abuse, abandonment, or neglect. Dana Mercz cited the case of a pregnant teenager who sought prenatal services at a California clinic. When the staff discovered that the teen was undocumented they alerted immigration authorities.[12] Despite the fact that she was attending high school, living with a two-parent family, and had no criminal background, the ICE agents who apprehended her refused to release her. Instead, they transferred her to ORR custody and deported her twenty-nine-year-old Mexican boyfriend. The ORR intake team cited her pregnancy at sixteen and relationship with "an older man" as significant risk factors and placed her with a foster care family in Phoenix pending the result of a home study. The director explained, "It was absolutely ludicrous. She came from a very supportive family. Her mother is Mexican and has no status, but her stepfather is a well-established businessman. He's an American citizen who runs a ranch and trains racehorses. They totally accepted her situation. So she spent forty-five days in a foster family home in Phoenix while caseworkers in California conducted a home study before releasing her right back to her family."[13]

One staff member described the troubling case of an eight-year-old then in short-term foster care: "They picked up the family, kept the child, and deported the parents to Nogales [a Mexican border town], where they have been waiting for two months. The parents are frantic, they call constantly hoping to get word on the child's release. The government denies other services after their release but keeps the kids when they already have families!"[14] Another case manager had similar concerns: "I feel the pain and desperation of the parents. What right does the government have to scrutinize these families and to prevent reunification with their kids? Yes, the families break the law, they are undocumented, but they are parents first. They want to be with their kids. I am from a poor country, and I have seen kids begging for food and heard their stories. How can I judge them?"[15]

A GROUP HOME

Unaccompanied minors who had behavioral issues in custody, were older and without family in the US could be released from custody to a group home. In early June 2011 KIND attorney, Megan McKenna, suggested that I try to speak with Manuel, "a really nice kid" who had received permanent legal resident status just two months earlier, in April. I made contact with Manuel's case manager and pro bono attorney.[16] Manuel had a traumatic family history in Honduras. He lost his mother to illness as a baby, was abandoned by his father, and was so neglected by his grandparents that he ended up on the streets, where, at the age of nine, he was coerced into serving as a lookout and running errands for a local gang. After escaping from the gang's long reach and crossing into the United States at sixteen, he was apprehended and detained in an El Paso shelter for a year where he received a diagnosis of major depressive disorder and PTSD and was prescribed psychiatric medications.

Manuel was granted a juvenile visa (SIJS) based on the abandonment by his family, his age, and the coercion by gang members. He was released from the shelter one day before his eighteenth birthday and initially placed in a group home because he "needed a more structured environment." He spent the first seven months there before being placed with a foster family. He exhibited "oppositional and defiant behaviors" at the group home, refusing to take psychiatric medication, to participate in counseling sessions, and to attend his high school classes. The program director felt his refusal to invest in school reflected negatively on her program. His case manager blamed his refusal to take his prescribed medication on his "Latino machismo" and fear of being seen as weak. "He was so damaged but couldn't open up and be in a psychological space. It was really sad," the case manager reported.[17] He was transferred to a foster family but stayed in the program only two months. As soon as he received his green card, he voluntarily emancipated and left Massachusetts to join family members living in South Carolina.

I visited the group home where Manuel was placed after his release from custody. The program had opened in 2009 and admitted teenage boys stepped down from secure, staff-secure, shelter, and residential treatment facilities throughout the country. Staff used a behavior modification program identical to the "strength-based model" implemented in ORR shelters. There was twenty-four-hour supervision of the clients and a ratio of four teenagers to one staff member. Clients earned daily and bonus points for their individual behaviors and group conduct both in the house and in the outside community. Points were given for speaking in English and displaying "independent living skills" such as cleaning bedrooms, doing laundry, and learning to cook. Privileges included earning a weekly allowance of $20 and spending time in the community. Staff also assigned points based on the "good" choices the boys made. If they spoke English, was it "an appropriate conversation"? If they received the maximum allowance, did they spend it right away or save it? If they got the maximum number of points for the week, what behaviors still needed to be improved? If they broke the rules by returning past curfew or damaged property, the staff assigned an essay in English or hours of labor.

Although I could not ask Manuel about his experience, Ernesto, who had spent six months in a similar group home, remembered his experience vividly. Unlike many other other kids, Ernesto had been transferred to a group home from a foster family. At eighteen he had aged out of the ORR system and could no longer remain in foster care. Because his legal case was still pending he was ineligible to enter the URM program. A Virginia NGO then under contract to ORR agreed to house him in a group home. Ernesto described the jarring transition and the searing betrayal he felt "at being kicked out of care at eighteen."

> That [foster] family was so different than the shelter. There were no rules and the foster mother was never there. She never spent time with us. We cooked, watched TV, and took care of ourselves. Then when I turned eighteen, the program kicked me out. I couldn't stay in that [foster] home anymore and I had to leave the school where I had friends and knew the teachers. Why do they help the kid and then drop him when he is eighteen? I don't understand how the system works. I had a case, but they didn't help me no more. They never explained that to me. I had no place to go. Then they said I could go to a group home.

Ernesto imagined that a group home would be different from a shelter but was crushed when he encountered many of the same restrictions.

> There were so many rules. You had to ask permission to go outside, to go to the kitchen, to do anything. I said, "Is this jail?" I was terrible, terrible. I said, "Too many rules!" They wrote me up and wanted to kick me out. I said bad words all the time, I was tough then. But I saw that I wasn't going to win acting like that. So I tried to get along. They put me on different levels in the group home. I was at the bottom, and it took me five months to get to the responsible level . . . I finished high school because I realized that the worse I behave the worse they treat me. So if I think before I say something I can control myself, and I did. After that the rules were nothing. They never wrote a report on me after that. I accept the house rules. I helped a lot of kids, I told them not to make mistakes, I tell the new kids to behave.

Given his lack of family support in the United States, his need to repay smuggling loans, and his commitment to support his mother and eight younger siblings, Ernesto had no choice but to accept "the house rules." He understood that "bad behavior" had no upside, and he was deeply grateful for the help he received from the group home. However, his abusive treatment and prolonged confinement in two shelters coupled with the abrupt termination of foster care services had given him a jaundiced view of human rights guarantees and American child welfare principles. It took him two and a half years to finish high school, become fluent in English, and get full-time employment. By that time, he saw his future prospects as a compromise between the American Dream he had imagined and what he could realistically expect given his limited education and impoverished background. Like most of the interviewees who were detained for long periods, Ernesto experienced the arbitrary rules and punitive restrictions in custody as a form of violence akin to incarceration. He chose to become a role model for the new kids not because he necessarily believed in the morality of the rules. Rather, he grasped the pragmatic benefits of compliance and wanted to impart those lessons to other kids.

EVALUATING A REFERRAL FOR LONG-TERM FOSTER CARE

Most of the young people I interviewed had been released from custody to foster care programs before their eighteenth birthday. LIRS staff and attorneys at KIND helped me identify young people who had received legal status, were over eighteen years old, and were building lives in the United States. I conducted focus groups and interviewed individual staff members in six nonprofit organizations that operated short- or long-term federal foster care programs for minors released from ORR custody.[18]

Staff saw the release, referral, and placement of older teenagers in foster care programs, particularly young men, as a complicated process. It involved finding a suitable foster family, easing the adjustment to life in a private home and in public school, and locating necessary social and medical service providers. The best referral was a teenager with no serious behavioral issues in custody, no criminal or delinquent history, successful or ongoing treatment for trauma, and a strong case for legal relief. Yet establishing that staff had a "good" referral was difficult.

"We Need More Information!"

Staff complained that they received only partial or inaccurate ORR reports on the child's family background, history in the home country, behavior in custody, and psychological profile. They needed to know if there were peer issues, if the child had regular contact with family members and performed well in the shelter classroom. Was the child being treated for a conduct disorder, and if so was he medically compliant? Was he committed to getting an education or just biding time until he could work? This information allowed the NGO agency staff to match the child with the right family. Foster care families were a scarce resource, particularly those with the experience and will to foster foreign teenagers. A clinician in Massachusetts explained:

> We don't get the necessary historical information in the referral report. There is no history of abuse or domestic violence, no information on [the youth's] current functioning. The documentation on the diagnosis is unclear. Who is writing the report? Sometimes a referral report from the shelter will list multiple mental conditions such as "reactive attachment disorder" and "bipolar" without a clear Axis I diagnosis. We have children who arrive from Texas with three different medications and a script [prescription] for thirty days written by an out-of-state psychiatrist. We can't get it filled in Massachusetts.[19]

A typical placement problem involved teenage boys with criminal charges or sketchy background information that raised serious questions. One program director noted, "The description in the ORR file doesn't match the kid at all. The behavioral problems are either minimized or exaggerated."[20] The most problematic referrals involved any purported gang involvement. One case manager was emphatic:

> Gangs? We don't even mention it because it is the kiss of death. We see kids who had past contact with gangs but didn't belong to the gang and typically had no involvement with criminal activities. The kids felt an emotional attachment to individuals in the gang because they had no family and lived on the street. Because of bad press and local attitudes about "illegals" we have to pretend they don't exist.[21]

A lead case manager who evaluated the new ORR referrals described a conference call she had with shelter staff. They wanted a foster care placement for a young man who had serious mental health issues and had spent ten months in custody.

> I needed to educate them about foster care. He really needed more treatment. Foster care is not a cure-all. There needs to be preparation for a placement. We need to know more about the child's ability to attach to others. Who were they closest to in custody? A teacher, a youth care worker, a case manager? We need to have a sense that they can tolerate the intimacy of family life. The shelter director couldn't understand why we would deny the child

the opportunity for the least restrictive setting and recommend a group home first. We have an excellent group home, and we recommend that some kids have that experience first so we can prepare them for foster care. Otherwise we set them up for failure.[22]

ORR FFS's were also wary of referring a minor with a background of drug abuse or gang activity for foster care and risking the loss of a limited number of tested and committed foster care families. Unlike the NGO staff, the FFS had access to the minor's full file and could strategically share or withhold confidential information that could affect acceptance of a referral.[23]

"Does he have a Legal Case?"

NGOs were instructed not to consider the minor's eligibility for legal status but rather to evaluate a referral solely on the child's needs and family background. Most staff found this requirement not only untenable but also unethical. The question of legal relief was inextricably linked to the psychological profile and social well-being of the child they needed to place. Teenagers in long-term foster care lived in a permanent state of anxiety if legal relief was uncertain. The "sword hanging over their heads" interfered with their ability to connect with foster families and to concentrate in school.[24] How could staff evaluate the referral of "a seventeen-and-a-half-year-old who would age out of the program at eighteen" if they had no information on the legal case? They needed to know if the youths were eligible for relief. Were they trafficked? Were they prostituted? Were they the victims of a crime? One case manager complained:

> Who benefits if we get a referral on a kid who turns eighteen in several months, has no attorney, no eligibility for status, and we can't find a foster home because there are criminal charges. It is cruel to keep them in care until they are deported. Does the good outweigh the bad?[25]

Helping kids find pro bono attorneys was a constant challenge given the limitations on federal funding of direct legal representation for undocumented minors, the heavy case loads, and the high turnover of underpaid immigration attorneys at legal service providers, as well as the cutbacks in pro bono services at private law firms since the 2008 recession. NGO staff worked hard to develop relations with legal service providers and pro bono departments and to educate juvenile and family court judges about the legal needs of immigrant youth. One director explained,

"We tap out the NGOs and pro bono attorneys. They get slammed with more cases than they could handle and can't accept any more."[26]

The most frustrating referrals were those with contradictory information on the child's eligibility for an SIJS visa. This visa provided a pathway to citizenship and admittance to URM support until the age of twenty-one, but the minor had to be declared a dependent of a U.S. family court before the age of eighteen because of abuse, abandonment, or neglect in the home. NGO staff complained about referrals that lacked specific symptoms but concluded with the statement, "This is a potentially good SIJ case." Even worse were reports stating, "The child qualifies for SIJS but lived with Mom and Dad and had a great home life."

"I am an Educated Person and I Find these Regs Confusing!"

All the staff expressed frustration at the constantly changing federal regulations. They were bombarded with confusing ORR memos announcing policy changes. One director explained, "I am an educated person and I find these reg[ulation]s confusing. For example, we receive memos every month with changes on reporting SIRs. Is it the FFS who gets notified or the project officer [in ORR headquarters]? If I make a mistake, there is big trouble."[27] Another director agreed: "We will get an email saying, 'This is the new regulation in effect at 5 p.m. EST today.'"

An additional challenge was identifying health care providers who would accept the government rate for services and comply with the onerous paperwork requirements. One staff member explained, "Our kids are eligible for health services through the Veteran's Administration. We need preapproval for standard medical procedures and we burn through service providers who get irate if they wait months for payments or don't get paid at all."[28] The biggest problems involved requests for mental health treatment. For example: "We have to push and push. We rarely get a formal no, but they wear you down with requests for more information and more justification. The [Division of Children's Services] director gets very involved and makes the final decision personally. There is no appeal process."

FINDING A FOSTER FAMILY

It was a constant struggle to find families willing and able to accept older male teenagers who spoke little or no English and had anger, trauma, and/or substance abuse issues. An ORR priority was to recruit "bi-lingual, bi-cultural staff and foster families." In many areas Spanish-speaking foster families were difficult to find. Failing that, staff looked for American families who would welcome the opportunity to host a child from a different cultural background. Some foster parents who regularly accepted domestic kids refused to have anything to do with the undocumented: if they were illegal, that meant they were bad.

Staff also encountered school authorities who were reluctant to enroll undocumented minors in public school. In politically conservative areas like Richmond, Virginia, and Phoenix, Arizona, anti-immigrant bias was a problem, and staff had to cite federal law to get their clients enrolled in school.[29] In upscale areas such as Arlington, Massachusetts, school authorities were reluctant to enroll "ORR kids" because they typically stayed for a year or less, had low graduation rates, and were ill-prepared linguistically and scholastically. One program director explained, "How do you convince a high school principal to accept a seventeen-year-old with a third grade education and no English? They say, 'Why should we invest in a kid who will leave school in a few months?'"[30]

Staff noted that the ORR kids were not like traditional foster care clients. Unlike domestic children or unaccompanied refugee minors who arrived in the United States with legal status and social service support, the UACs faced the pressure to send money to impoverished families back home as well as the threat of removal if they did not win legal status. One case manager insisted, "They came to work, not to go to school! They have managed their own lives, made their own decisions, and they have trouble accepting the constraints of foster care. Even though their stated goal is education, the pull from their family back home is too strong." Looking back over his cases, he noted that four of the nine ORR cases he had followed since 2008 ran away or chose voluntary emancipation at eighteen rather than enter the URM program and be required to stay in school.

Many staff members believed, as one person put it, that ORR kids had "attachment issues because they were so traumatized." One case manager described the serious emotional problems that trump the kids' own needs: "They are long past parenting. They see caregivers as mere providers, not as foster parents. They are seventeen going on thirty-five. They are not kids, that's the problem!" Two of her colleagues disagreed, explaining that the older teenagers had a limited time with the foster family and only got support services until eighteen. Why would the parents or the kids commit to one another if they stay only a few months? "Besides they need time to themselves," he said. "They were never alone in custody. After release they struggle to find themselves and to connect with people and organizations they choose."[31]

Foster care programs earned "black marks" and "bad press" with community leaders and school authorities if their kids acted out sexually, skipped class, took drugs, ran away, or refused to commit to schooling. Staff found it more difficult to recruit and keep foster families if the kids flouted their authority, had emotional issues, broke curfew, or refused to do chores. Foster care program staff had to file Significant Incident Reports, in particular, for kids who ran away, and to submit child welfare recommendations to ORR headquarters. However, they had no say in the final decisions involving allocation of medical and psychiatric services or transfers within the system, whether a step up from foster care to a residential treatment facility or a step down from a group home to placement in a family.

One director described her attempt to transfer a teenage girl engaging in self-destructive behavior to a local residential treatment facility where the teenager could stay connected to her foster family and continue her legal case. The ORR-contracted psychiatrist disagreed, ordering that she remain in the home. This provoked a crisis that resulted in her removal from the family, a ten-month stay in a residential treatment facility five hours away, and a request to return the teenager to a foster family. She concluded, "Had she improved? We really didn't know. There are too many cooks in the kitchen. It is so difficult to make sure that the focus stays on the kid, not on the potential liability for ORR."[32]

Staff reported that they had to minimize potential behavioral issues in foster care by declining referrals when there was a record of serious criminal behavior or severe psychological disorder and no legal case. A bad referral involved a combination of risk and safety factors. One staff member explained, "We got a referral for a kid who broke his placement with us by running away and ended up back in custody. He said he ran away because of gang pressure here. He needed help, so he turned himself in to the police, was put in a secure [ORR] facility, then stepped down, and referred to us again! We said, 'No way!'"

RELEASE

Maribel's Story

Maribel's view of her prospects for release was strongly influenced by the rights she thought she had as a Honduran minor. "They didn't kick out Hondurans, Salvadorans, or Guatemalans, only Mexicans," she said. "Everyone knew that those kids were immediately deported." Yet her relief at being able to stay in custody was undercut by her fear of turning eighteen there. Everyone knew that "aging out" signaled the end of ORR jurisdiction, a transfer to ICE custody, and disappearance into the black hole of adult detention. Federal staff, attorneys, and advocates all related accounts of ICE officers arriving without prior warning to handcuff and remove youths from ORR facilities on their eighteenth birthday—often right after midnight. Detained youths also heard these stories. Maribel was seventeen when she was detained in Texas in January 2007 and had a birthday in August. Her cousin was released in just four weeks because he had family in the United States. Months went by, and Maribel began to panic. She knew that "immigration for adults was hell" and was desperate to get out.

> Every Tuesday a lawyer came. When you see the lawyer you get so excited because you think something is happening on your case. It was the same with my caseworker. I was always wanting to see her to ask about my status [regarding release]. We would listen for her because anytime she pulled someone out of the house, she had news. Sometimes it was good news—that you would be released to your family or a foster family. Sometimes it was bad news. I got bad news. I have a million cousins and aunts in the U.S. and they make good money, but they have hard hearts. One aunt even has U.S. citizenship, but she didn't want to help. I begged her, but she said no. I felt so alone and I was scared.

Maribel's case was finally resolved in May 2007. Her lawyer petitioned the court for asylum based on her father's threat to kill her if she returned, and it was granted. She was released to a foster care program in Virginia just seven days before her eighteenth birthday. She remembered being met by her Catholic Charities social worker who took her out to dinner.

> I had never been to a restaurant in Honduras. I never ate what I wanted in the shelter. She said, "Eat what you want!" I was so excited. I couldn't believe it. She took me to the doctor, and the therapist. At first I went every week and then once a month. It was not therapeutic for me. What I needed was to find people from my culture, who speak my language. My foster family didn't speak Spanish. I had no English. I was about to go crazy. I spent time alone, crying in my room. Then one of the kids gave me the phone number of the pastor of a Hispanic church. I met her and so many kids. I got out and got involved . . . I upgrade my life in Richmond. While I was living with the foster family I was going to high school. My first year I got straight A's and my senior year I got into the National Honor Society with a 3.5 GPA. I applied for legal resident. It took forever. Some kids turn eighteen

and have no legal status. One day my social worker came to the foster family house where I was. I asked why she came and she said, "You got your green card!" I jumped up and screamed. I couldn't believe it. It took my cousin twenty years. I said, "Oh Lord, thank you." It was so hard at the beginning, but now I have my legal status [legal permanent residency]. I don't have to pay for a lawyer and nobody can kick me out! After that I left the foster home and went to independent living through Catholic Charities. I graduated from high school and started college courses. They gave me money for rent and bills and I worked part-time.

Corina's Story

Corina's release narrative was not as uplifting as Maribel's. She had left home at fifteen and had been apprehended in Arizona and detained in a Phoenix shelter for ten months before her release to a foster family in Michigan where she rapidly learned English and excelled in school. After a preliminary legal screening, her attorney had determined that she was potentially eligible for legal relief. He prepared the case for asylum and began the application process for the SIJS visa.[33] In 2004 she won her asylum case, a finding that the government attorney appealed. Her attorney applied for the SIJS four years before the passage of the TVPRA of 2008 instituted major protections for unaccompanied children like her. Before 2008 the U.S. attorney general, as the legal custodian of unaccompanied children in immigration custody, was required to give his consent before the guardianship of such children could be transferred from federal authorities to a local, state, or family court. At that time consent decisions were based on cursory investigations and subject to long delays. Some cases were decided only days before a child's eighteenth birthday, when it was too late to obtain the necessary findings from a juvenile court.[34] Corina's case fell through the cracks when her original attorney left his practice and gave the file to a colleague who did no further work on the case. Corina was released and sent to Michigan where she lived with several foster families. By the time the federal officer reviewed Corina's application for SIJS, she was over eighteen, and he denied consent. Corina aged out of the ORR system without legal status. A tenacious caseworker connected her with an attorney who ran the immigration clinic at the Mercer Law School in Detroit. He thought the case was salvageable, assigned it to his law students, and got it on the docket for a hearing at the Detroit immigration court in November 2011.

I first spoke with Corina in late October 2011, just days before her immigration hearing. She had been in the country for nine years and still had no resolution of her petition for legal status. With her case manager's help, she had graduated from high school and completed a training program to be a nurse's assistant. After leaving foster care at eighteen she moved several times but then was invited to stay in a "rent-free room" in the home of a local teacher. At nineteen she fell in love with a young man from her country and moved in with him. They had two daughters, ages four and one, who were U.S. citizens because they were born here. Corina worked for four years as a nurse's assistant on a temporary work permit, but it expired and was not renewed. She was frustrated and depressed.

> I am so afraid of getting deported to Guatemala because I have two daughters who were born here. Right now I can't work as a nurse's assistant and I am a stay-at-home mom. I have no work, no job, no college, and I can't get financial aid. I get cash assistance and food stamps, but I hate the government giving me all that. I want to work and take care of myself and my family. The U.S. doesn't always treat us good as immigrants. I know that they have their reasons. But I wish they would know my heart.

Ernesto's Story

Like Corina, Ernesto continued to confront obstacles with his legal case.

> When I got to Virginia, there were no papers. That white guy in Texas lied. The social worker asked me, "What is your record? I don't see anything about this in the file." Then my attorney said, "There is nothing in your record." I didn't know what to do. I had the card that the Latino guy in Texas gave me and I called him every day for two weeks. I was confused because he told me to call if I had a problem and then he never answered. Then the phone was cut. I did get a [U] visa, but it was much later. . . . When I came here to Richmond they put me in a foster home. It was so tough. The foster mom didn't speak Spanish and I didn't have any English. They sent me to a school with classes all in English. In Honduras it was so different, you walk, you ride a bike or a horse, and you get to school when you get there. Here you gotta wait for a bus. At school the teachers would talk to me and I didn't understand. I wanted to cry and disappear because it was so hard. I remember that one day I got lost in that school because all the halls looked the same. I didn't know where to go for lunch. They offer us a free lunch and put a number on a paper. I didn't have a clue how it worked. It was horrible, and I said, "Why did I come here?" I should have stayed home. But it got better.

A VOLUNTARY DEPARTURE

In spring 2012 a New York attorney shared a story sent to her by a young woman who had been apprehended and put into removal proceedings. The young woman had graduated from high school as an honors student and was arrested in 2011 after police stopped the car she was riding in.

As the new year approaches, with it comes new dreams and expectations. I remember 365 days ago when I was sitting home [in the U.S.] writing down my goals and objectives for that same year that had begun. Along with it was the hope of becoming a young adult living the American Dream. Originated in Brazil, I was brought to the U.S. over seven years ago after living through hard times being away from my dad who was then illegally in the country and was fighting to bring the rest of the family. In September of 2004, I finally got to see my father after over a year. . . . In that first year living as an "American" I struggled to learn English, to make new friends and adapt to the new life my parents had arranged for me to live. I am a high school graduate who loves to play soccer and loves to go to church to accomplish my voluntary occupations such as youth choir minister, choreographer, pianist, secretary, journalist, translator, babysitter, event planner, and organizer, as well as part of the church's media. As graduation approached this year, I began to face trouble trying to get enrolled in the College admission process because of my illegal status at the state of Massachusetts. My biggest dream has been for years the same, to go to college and build a career. As of today, I have chosen to become either a lawyer or a diplomat who will fight for the legal rights of courageous and strong kids and students who have lived as I have. Unfortunately, after arranging a trip to Florida last October, I was detained by immigration along with a friend and some family who were in the car . . . I was transferred to New York where I was detained for over two weeks until my dad worked to get me out of there the fastest possible. I had not only lost six pounds. I lost freedom and started to feel as if I was not welcomed at all in the U.S. as many ICE agents told me so. For two months I could say I was a hostage of depression. When I talked to my guidance counselor, she had told me that chances of me being admitted to a good college couldn't be better but because of my status, I would have hard time paying for everything since I couldn't apply for financial aid. I really couldn't pay for any of it and that all made me feel even worse. I started to think about what my life would've been if I stayed in that situation and it was then that I realized leaving the country was the only option to cure myself, leave the circumstances and fight for the future I have always dreamed of. It's been almost a month since an immigration judge granted me voluntary departure and I am back in Brazil. I have taken a placement test to start college and I am very happy because I was admitted to the best school in the state. . . . Unfortunately, I miss the US already because even to this day it is there where I grew up and became mature, formulated dreams and expectations. I love the USA! I have hope that one day I will still become a citizen of the place [where] I had the American Dream. For you kids still in the US facing this same situation, never give up! I didn't, I simply opted to live my dream somewhere else but I know I will be back soon. So I would like to encourage all young adults like I, don't let anything hold you back. Don't let anybody let you down. Keep your hopes up and your dreams high. Wherever you have the chance to succeed, if you believe, you will so. Best wishes!!

CONCLUSION

It has become common for NGO advocates, attorneys, and members of Congress to declare the immigration system is broken and to demand its reform. We have seen that the process of family reunification is riven with contradictions and confusing requirements. The child welfare perspective that is increasingly manifest in the policies organizing custody is driven by a moral imperative to protect the children, but paradoxically it can make them even more vulnerable and produce negative effects.[35] The enhanced protective mechanisms and intrusive background checks make it easier to identify risk factors and to deny or delay release or to place children in foster care, group homes, or treatment programs rather than allow them to join families already in the United States. At the same time, the pressure on staff to release children rapidly even as the number of new arrivals has exploded has meant less time for in-depth screening of family background, health needs, and potential legal relief. Although family reunification aims to serve the best interest of the child by prioritizing releases that are safe, in practice the best interest of the child must compete with other important considerations such as security, economics, available bed space, the need to ration services, and the threat of legal liability for ORR. As troubling as the stories of children who accept voluntary departure after long years of residence in the United States are the cases of minors who rotate in and out of the custodial system multiple times, acquiring criminal histories that set them on a path to permanent illegality.

Stakeholders have argued that the recent increases in admissions to ORR are not only unsustainable, but will exacerbate current problems with release. In the 2013 federal fiscal year, ORR admitted 25,041 unaccompanied minors into custody, a figure that had quintupled from the 2004 total of 5,238 and nearly doubled from the 2012 total of 14,721. ORR placed most minors in shelters (21,553) and sharply reduced the number of placements in medium-secure facilities (staff-secure and therapeutic staff-secure) from 886 in 2012 to 492 in 2013. The number of minors detained in high-security facilities fell by almost one-half, from 221 in 2012 to 107 in 2013. At the same time, the number of short-term foster care placements more than doubled, from 863 in 2012 to 1,938 in 2013 (reflecting higher admissions of children who were younger and/or had mental or physical disabilities) even as long-term foster care placements remained flat, group home placements inched up from 3 to 130, and those in residential treatment facilities fell precipitously from 70 in 2012 to 6 in 2013.[36] Despite the huge increases in admissions, less than 5 percent of 2012 and 2013 releases involved home studies. In both fiscal years, only 10 percent of the children who were released received recommendations for follow-up services.

In 2013, of the detained population from Central America (73 percent male, 27 percent female), 37 percent were from Guatemala, 30 percent were from Honduras, and 26 percent were from El Salvador, numbers that have remained relatively constant. Although most minors were between fourteen and seventeen years of age, ORR reported a worrisome trend. The percentage of minors under fourteen had increased from 17 percent in 2012 to 24 percent in 2013. In 2014 the number of border crossers under the age of twelve increased by 117 percent,[37] with girls representing 40 percent of the CBP apprehensions. The statistics on ORR admissions obscure the fact that the vast majority of those apprehended at the Southwest border are Mexican. Despite the additional protections legislated for unaccompanied Mexican minors in the 2008 TVPRA, most underaged Mexicans are immediately removed from the United States. As a result, the percentage of Mexican children in ORR custody plummeted from 17.6 percent in 2010 to only 3 percent in 2013.[38]

In response to mounting evidence of the corrosive effect of long periods of detention for minors, ORR has significantly reduced the average length of stay in custody. Between October 1, 2008, and September 30, 2010, 24 percent of youths were detained between 61 and 120 days and 9 percent from 121 days to a full year.[39] ORR announced that the average length of stay in 2013 had been further reduced to 50 days. In December 2013 ORR administrators outlined their 2014 goal of releasing minors more rapidly, a goal that could be met by "enhanced efficiency, a reduction of redundancy at the shelter level, and streamlined procedures for approving sponsors."[40] In the midst of the 2014 surge Mark Greenberg, acting assistant secretary of the Administration of Children and Family of the Department of Health and Human Services, testified before the Senate Committee on Homeland Security and Government Affairs that the average length of stay in ORR custody was 35 days.[41]

A number of stakeholders were concerned that the continued surge in admissions and the imperative to turn over beds more rapidly would have a negative impact on an already vulnerable population. One government official worried:

The whole system could collapse under its own weight. For those with a less generous view of immigration it is easy to cast blame. They could look at the way release works and say it is too easy for traffickers to get kids into the country and then get them released. Many [immigration authorities] will want to treat them like adults and subject them to expedited removal. It might start to work the same way for all kids as it does now for those from Mexico and Canada. It is only a matter of time with 40,000–50,000 kids coming in that a crime will be committed that will grab public attention. People would be shocked if ORR releases a kid to an approved sponsor one day and the next day a sweat shop is busted and the kid is found to be working there. Or let's say a young girl is released to a pimp who runs a brothel or to a criminal gang. In that case, there could be a push for more enforcement, not less.[42]

The day after we spoke, the same official sent me a Fox News article quoting Texas district court judge Andrew Hanen, who had issued a blistering court order in which he alleged a conspiracy on the part of the Obama administration to flout immigration laws. He claimed that immigration officers were permitting human smugglers to bring minors across the border and deliver them to their illegal parents already living in the United States.[43] In fall 2013, NGO personnel and immigration attorneys were already receiving reports of minors who had been released to sponsors who were trafficking them for labor or sex or were ill equipped to care for them.[44]

In a recent editorial Sonia Nazario, a journalist and the author of the national best seller *Enrique's Journey,* argued that huge investments in enforcement along the U.S.-Mexico border have not kept migrants out but sealed them in, separating them from their families on the other side. Border security policies beg important questions about the humane treatment of immigrant families in the United States. We should ask ourselves if it makes sense to deport 200,000 undocumented parents of American children and then to place 5,000 of those children in U.S. foster care because they are parentless.[45] Who does it benefit to detain undocumented children even for short periods when the vast majority— now 88 percent—will eventually be released to families or approved sponsors? Are they put at greater risk by release to undocumented family members rather than by placement in foster care? The well-known risks of the detention and deportation of undocumented parents explain why children who are apprehended by ICE agents often deny that they have families in the United States when the opposite is true. When parents without legal status refuse to act as sponsors it is not proof, as many enforcement officials claim, of their indifference to their own kids. Rather, parents must weigh the hazard of losing precarious sources of income, homes, and the custody of younger children if they are removed from the country.

Federal authorities insist on separating family reunification from immigration proceedings, citing the different goals and time lines involved in each process. Nonetheless, the two systems often work in tandem to amplify their control and containment effect. The decision to transfer a child to a facility or program out of state can compromise a legal case by disrupting the relationship with an attorney or even result in a deportation order if a youth in removal proceedings misses a scheduled hearing in immigration court. Conversely, the decision to seek a SIJS can catapult a child into adulthood by severing his family ties so that he can be declared a ward of the state. This pathway to citizenship precludes the youth's ability to petition for legal status for family members in the home country.

We have no answers to these questions. After a child's release there is only cursory follow-up and limited options for postrelease services. One case manager told me about a seventeen-year-old from California who was arrested after a neighborhood altercation. He stole a cell phone and threatened "to mess up" the victim. He was charged with a public order violation of "street terrorism," removed from his family, and placed in a secure facility in Oregon. The young man was released to his family after five weeks. I asked his case manager if he had any information about the young man. He exclaimed:

> Are you kidding? We never know what happens to the kid. We only get flyers from ORR with happy ending stories. We deal with kids who have lived here for years and are at risk from gangs in their own neighborhoods, right here in the U.S. They are poor, flunking out of school, and would really benefit from follow-up services. Local systems have services for drug and alcohol abuse and educational services. But these kids are not under their jurisdiction. There is no endgame to it. I would ask the FFS if he ever had any contacts with these kids after release, and he said, "Never."[46]

7

Immigration Court

Historically children have been neglected and often intentionally excluded in U.S. immigration policy and the law. When unaccompanied children are prosecuted for immigration violations, even the youngest respondents find themselves alone in removal proceedings before immigration judges and ICE trial attorneys without assistance from immigration attorneys or child advocates.[1] Although children can independently seek humanitarian forms of immigration relief, such as asylum and protection from removal under the Convention Against Torture, they are held to the same substantive criteria, evidentiary requirements, and burden of proof standards as adults. In the one-size-fits-all approach, children have to defend against removal by proving eligibility for forms of relief designed almost exclusively for adults.

The penalties and barriers that immigration laws impose on persons who enter the United States without authorization and remain without legal status apply to children as well as adults. This is true regardless of whether the child made the individual decision to immigrate or was carried across the border as a baby. Immigration law attaches punishing and permanent legal consequences for the decisions made by the child's parents or guardians as well as the bad choices children make prior to the age of majority.

The major pathways to lawful status provide no special recognition of the rights, interests, or perspective of the child.[2] Under immigration law the child is conceived as a "quasi-appendage" to an adult family member or caretaker.[3] The status of children as individual bearers of rights is discounted, their right to asylum is compromised, and their citizenship as a basis for family residency is denied.[4] In fact, the one form of immigration relief available specifically to children, Special Immigrant Juvenile Status, applies only to children who are declared dependent by a family or juvenile court.[5] It reflects a deeply held presumption that children lack an independent existence and the capacity to act rationally and effectively apart from adults.[6]

Immigration law diverges sharply from mainstream approaches in juvenile and family courts that mandate protective measures by considering mitigating circumstances, demanding less accountability, particularly for youths under the age of seventeen, and viewing juveniles as less deserving of the most severe punishments.[7] Beyond a set of voluntary guidelines that call for a child-friendly atmosphere in court proceedings,[8] immigration courts make no allowance for developmental immaturity, cultural incapacity, or special vulnerability. Immigration judges may not consider the child's best interests as a primary criterion for legal relief, an egregious departure from recognized international standards.

Immigration courts lack meaningful safeguards for children (or adults) with mental disorders and cognitive impairments who are in removal proceedings.[9] In a criminal or juvenile court, defendants cannot be tried or convicted if they lack the mental competence to understand and participate in the proceedings and to assist in their own defense. Immigration law lacks a similar standard for competency in proceedings. Immigration judges are not required to appoint lawyers or to alter procedures in order to accommodate a respondent with mental disabilities.[10] Given the adversarial nature of immigration court proceedings at the best of times, the obstacles to obtaining a fair trial and just ruling become virtually insurmountable for children whose mental disabilities make it impossible for them to comprehend legal procedures, to respond coherently to ICE trial attorneys, or to provide credible evidence without the benefit of legal representation.

In this chapter we follow unaccompanied children into immigration court proceedings, a system with arcane rules, staff shortages, hearing backlogs, powerful government attorneys, and disempowered judges. Children struggle to find pro bono attorneys familiar with immigration law and to weigh the best options given the limited remedies available to them. We begin with background on the immigration court system and then examine a first appearance in immigration court, followed by a complicated SIJS case, and end with a case that illustrates the potential pitfalls to winning asylum.

ASYMMETRICAL POWER RELATIONS

Every level of the immigration court system is marked by structural power imbalances that favor the government and undermine both judicial fairness and due process protections. The current structure of the immigration court is in constant tension with the legal mandate to exercise independent judgment, a mandate premised on the separation of the judiciary from the legislative and executive branches of government. The immigration court is part of the executive branch of government and is located in an agency, the Executive Office of Immigration Review, within the Department of Justice. Thus immigration judges work in an agency that prosecutes and judges violations of immigration law, a conflict of interest that commingles prosecutorial and review functions. Immigration judges not only adjudicate cases brought by the government attorneys, but they are beholden to the same boss, the U.S. attorney general, for their employment and tenure.[11]

ICE trial attorneys have virtually unfettered discretion to bring charges in court, to determine the conditions for release, and to control information central to the government's case.[12] Immigration judges lack contempt authority and, as a result, cannot control their own courtrooms by sanctioning ICE trial attorneys who arrive late, come unprepared, make misleading statements, or harass respondents. Compared to the meteoric rise in funding for enforcement activities and for the hiring of ICE trial attorneys, immigration judges must hear more cases at a faster pace with chronically inadequate resources.[13] Defense attorneys are similarly disempowered. Whereas their professional misconduct can result in disbarment, ICE trial attorneys face no such consequences. Judges' low professional status within the legal establishment is reflected in working conditions that compare unfavorably with their colleagues in district courts. Immigration judges carry heavier caseloads, spend more hours on the bench, hear cases without court reporters, and render decisions without adequate assistance from law clerks.

Although immigration judges are disempowered compared to ICE trial attorneys and district court judges, they wield enormous power over the adult and child respondents who seek legal relief. Only 40 percent of all respondents in immigration proceedings have legal representation, a figure that drops to 15 percent for those in detention. The majority of respondents must appear pro se, whereas ICE attorneys are always present to represent the government.

In contrast to criminal courts, where the facts of the case emerge from a strategic confrontation between the prosecution and defense, the facts of the immigration case are established by the enforcement branches of the government, not by the individual parties to the case. In contrast to the judge in criminal trials, who is intended to serve primarily as a neutral arbiter and to enforce adherence to legal procedure on both the prosecution and the defense, the immigration judge can take an active role, questioning the respondent and witnesses and building the record that results in a decision rendered at her individual discretion.

Between a Rock and a Hard Place

I interviewed both sitting and retired immigration judges who heard juvenile cases or presided over detained juvenile dockets.[14] They strongly supported the need for government-funded representation, "particularly for children with legal competency issues." According to one retired judge, "If we are not to perpetuate injustice we need appointed counsel for respondents. The pro bono system is hit or miss. Kids should all have attorneys and a child advocate. This is particularly important because of the penal mindset of ICE."[15] Another judge insisted that "no child's case should ever go forward without an attorney" and that those under fourteen should be excused completely from appearances in court.[16] Aside from the legal ethics, many insisted that funding legal representation would make court proceedings more humane, efficient, and cost-effective.[17]

Accepting that "immigration law was not designed for kids," judges criticized the structure of removal proceedings and the tenor of courtroom hearings. They advocated specialized juvenile dockets[18] staffed by volunteer judges whose training and experience would ensure that they see children first as developing human beings, not aliens.[19] One judge intoned, "We need judges who don't see them as delinquents or criminals. Many of these kids have been broken. They have been sold, beaten, or burned, or lived in a chicken coop. How do we interpret the hideousness of that experience? If we are sympathetic it lowers the level of stress. We need patience and time."[20] Some judges sought to create a child-friendly atmosphere by removing their black robes. As one explained, "I want the children to see that I am a person so they can gain trust and believe that they are getting a fair hearing."[21] Another judge stated, "There is no trust between judges and kids in detention. We can't just start asking questions in the first hearing and expect them to be honest! Maybe after the fifth or sixth hearing they'll start to tell the truth."[22]

Although over half of the judges I interviewed served as ICE trial attorneys or judge advocate generals (JAGs) before accepting positions on the bench, these same judges criticized the confrontational posture of ICE trial attorneys whose primary goal was deportation. One recently retired judge described how the mind-set of ICE trial attorneys changed after the creation of the Department of Homeland Security in 2002: "Before they saw themselves as civil prosecutors, as having a prosecutorial role, not a punishing role. Now there is a very different mentality. They have no acceptance of their role as anything other than a road-block—whether it means providing copies of documents or the careful preparation of the case."[23] A senior immigration judge with three decades of experience, first in the private bar and then as a trial attorney, decried the "Clarence Darrow" types "who treat removal proceedings like a football game" in which aggressive tactics score a win: "Hostility is a stupid tactic because the whole process goes downhill and justice is not served."[24] Another opined, "We have to keep reining them [ICE attorneys] in, but there is only so much you can do if you can't control what cases you hear and you have no contempt authority."[25] Another lamented, "They want to deport them all and let God sort out the details."[26] Many judges condemned the aggressive conduct of ICE trial attorneys, badgering children with hostile questions and accusing them of lying, concealing important facts, or faking psychological trauma.

The interviewees who presided over juvenile dockets agreed on the need for "extrajudicial information." They wanted to know who the child is and where he or she comes from. What is the family like in the home country? How much schooling does the child have? One senior judge insisted, "We need to know what is going on in their lives. You can't sit in this court and pretend you are disconnected from dependency issues, crime, prostitution, drug abuse, or gang violence."[27] Many expressed frustration that time and structural constraints prevented them from getting a more complete picture of the child's background. One judge, who worked on the Flores Settlement Agreement and later served as a trial attorney, described his discomfort when a child appeared with an unidentified adult: "I always put those adults under oath and I question them. I need to confirm the facts before they are released.[28] Another judge, who spent eleven years at the Arlington immigration court, explained, "I always wondered if the kids' legal screening was adequate. Did I get all the facts? I worried about the Chinese girls because of the huge increases in the smuggling fees. Were they prostituted or exploited in dangerous sweatshops?"[29]

Burnout and Stress

The limited avenues of legal relief combined with exploding caseload burdens, intrusive administrative oversight, diminishing resources, and relentless exposure to horrific persecution stories created symptoms of stress and burnout among judges. One study concludes that immigration judges work under stress levels that compare to those of emergency physicians and prison wardens. They report that female judges are more symptomatic than their male counterparts.[30] It is no accident that the female interviewees mention the lack of attention by the EOIR to the psychological costs of judging "the equivalent of capital cases with the resources of a traffic court," especially when the respondents are "children alone."

This issue exploded into public view in 2010. An *L.A. Daily Journal* article described the unprofessional conduct of Lorraine Muñoz, the immigration judge handling the detained juvenile docket at the Los Angeles immigration court.[31] Julianne Donnelly, program director of Esperanza Immigrant Rights Project, alerted the judge's superior to "the climate of overwhelming hostility, sarcasm and intimidation" in the courtroom. Donnelly warned that such treatment risked further damaging children "already suffering from severe abuse and psychological trauma." The judge, an eleven-year veteran of the bench, had served for only eight months when complaints emerged. Donnelly described judicial conduct "that was completely antithetical" to the child-sensitive questioning and age-appropriate language and tone set forth in EOIR Operating Policies and Procedures: cynical asides "that parents should be prosecuted for not sponsoring their kids," angry outbursts, abrupt adjournments, harsh retaliation against children who refused to divulge sensitive family information, and sarcastic remarks about the honesty of child trafficking victims. Even more troubling were examples of action that potentially compromised a petition for legal relief.[32]

What went unsaid in media reports were the unusual pressures associated with the Los Angeles detained docket, which saw 8,000 to 10,000 children a year in removal proceedings. The judge handled a crushing load of 1,500 cases with woefully inadequate resources. One Los Angeles immigration attorney familiar with the juvenile docket insisted that structural constraints and systemic failures were to blame, "not the individual judge."[33] One of the judge's colleagues remarked that "the pressures were overwhelming and she underwent a complete transformation."[34] Like the traumatized children who appeared before her, the judge appeared to exhibit symptoms of extreme stress and psychological trauma: emotional exhaustion, erratic outbursts, deep cynicism, and depersonalization.[35]

A major cause of burnout is the lack of judicial independence and the imposition of "performance goals that are more suited to assembly-line work than to the complex nature of the law and the life and death consequences" in removal proceedings.[36] Interviewees complained that their colleagues in the legal establishment did not view them "as real judges."[37] One judge spoke for many of her colleagues when she said, "I have no First Amendment rights because I work for the executive branch of government."[38] It is no small irony that the liminal status and weak structural position of immigration judges mirror the disempowerment of the very children whose cases they hear.

A MASTER CALENDAR HEARING

In October 2010 four youths held at an ORR staff-secure facility appeared for their first hearing—a master calendar hearing—scheduled on the detained juvenile docket. Three of the four were first-time arrivals, but the fourth, a sixteen-year-old Mexican boy I will call Jorge, had been apprehended once before. During his previous sojourn, he lived in the Phoenix area and worked at a fast-food restaurant. Jorge was arrested during a traffic stop and immediately deported to Mexico without a hearing in immigration court. This time ICE agents alleged that Jorge was caught with a group of Mexican men while selling drugs. They designated him an "Unaccompanied Alien Child" and transferred him to ORR custody.

Most master calendar hearings are perfunctory proceedings that last only minutes and offer little opportunity for judges to observe or question the individuals before them. Master calendar hearings in juvenile dockets usually involve a request for a continuance of removal proceedings without pleading to immigration violation charges. Continuing the proceedings is intended to give detained youths time to find pro bono representation, wait for release to an approved sponsor, or consider the option of returning home. Some hearings, like this one, had much higher stakes for youths like Jorge who had no possibility of release or eligibility for legal relief.

Jorge's case was called, and he came forward, standing alone at the table for respondents, opposite the elevated dais of the immigration judge and across from the ICE trial attorney. The Vera Institute of Justice contracts with ORR to recruit local legal service providers to screen detained youths for possible legal relief and to inform them of their rights in detention and in court. Since only a small percentage of detained youths get legal representation[39] and few if any find pro bono attorneys to advise them in the first court hearing, they must appear pro se or obtain assistance from an attorney who serves as a "friend of the court." This arrangement has been described as a benign procedure that typically involves an attorney from an ORR/Vera-contracted legal service provider speaking on behalf of the youth in court but not acting as the attorney of record.[40]

The friend of the court (FOC) model arose as a response to scarce free legal services and the challenges judges face adjudicating the cases of pro se respondents who need extra assistance. Although individual judges have the discretion to determine the scope of the FOC role in their courtrooms, there is considerable uncertainty about the nature and extent of this role. Many judges want more explicit guidance from EOIR; they are wary of the potential for attorneys to exceed their prescribed role by acting like legal representatives.[41] This immigration judge instructed the attorney from the legal service provider to stop acting as an FOC. He believed that detained youths were adversely affected by appearing with a lawyer who did not enter a formal appearance with the court.[42] The local attorney admitted that she had been functioning "almost like the attorney" during master calendar appearances.[43]

In 2010 administrators of the ORR/Vera Institute's Unaccompanied Children Program were clamping down on attorneys who appeared to be breaking or bending the federal rules prohibiting direct legal representation. One Los Angeles immigration attorney explained, "We were never supposed to enter an appearance in court. We only have [federal] funding to screen for legal relief and to inform the kids of their rights." Addressing the challenges posed by master calendar hearings, she added, "Judges shouldn't question pro se kids on the record, not ever."[44]

Because of the dilemmas posed for detained youths with criminal charges, an attorney from the Vera Institute had asked the immigration judge to permit the local attorney to attend the master calendar hearing. My visit coincided with the first hearing where the attorney served in a modified friend of the court role.

The attorney had advised Jorge to ask for voluntary departure because he was implicated in a drug offense and had no prospects for family reunification. Voluntary departure, unlike a deportation order, has been described as the most common form of relief, albeit the most limited in terms of the status it affords.[45] It is considered a legal benefit because it returns unaccompanied minors to the home country at government expense but imposes no long-term restrictions on legal reentry to the United States.[46] It is a discretionary ruling that depends on the background—or good moral character—of the petitioner as well as the circumstances of the apprehension. EOIR rules stipulate that voluntary departure is reserved for "aliens" with no record of aggravated felonies or terrorist activity.[47] Before rendering a decision judges typically want answers to key questions. Is this the first entry without authorization? Where and with whom was the child apprehended? How long has he been in the country before his apprehension?

Attorneys familiar with this judge's courtroom had registered serious concerns about the routine shackling of minors from secure facilities, which was done at the insistence of the ICE trial attorney. They also objected to the judge's practice of questioning pro se minors on the record about criminal activities and family reunification issues. A major problem was the judge's unfamiliarity with the enhanced legal protections afforded unaccompanied minors under the TVPRA of 2008.[48] Nikki Dryden, then an attorney with the Vera Institute, related the story of a sixteen-year-old minor who had appeared at a master calendar hearing in 2009 without legal counsel or an FOC and asked to return home. Unaware of the youth's eligibility for government-funded voluntary departure, the judge informed him that unless he had the money to pay for his trip he would have to take a deportation order.[49] The ICE trial attorney strenuously objected to voluntary departure, citing the minor's theft of a blind person. Because there was no attorney to contest that assertion or to ask for evidence, the teenager received a deportation order.[50] That was not an isolated occurrence according to the case manager at the secure facility where Jorge was detained.

A Detained Juvenile Docket

Among the challenges of presiding over a detained juvenile docket, the judge cited the need to create a child-friendly atmosphere but added, "The best interests of the child cannot override the law. As an immigration judge I owe service to young people but I cannot be their benefactor or advocate. . . . My role is to deemphasize the adversarial nature of the proceedings, to reduce nervousness, and to establish the trust that leads to effective communication."[51] His priority in the first hearing was to get information rather than to take pleadings.

> That way I can determine the next steps. The [detention] system is good. The kids are removed from a [potentially harmful] adult environment and given the chance to decompress. . . . Should the youth be released and reunified with the family? What if the mother is undocumented herself, poor, and doing menial work? What choices will her son have? Would a return to the home country be a better outcome? There are very limited resources for the kids who get out of custody.[52]

Addressing the issue of children who express a fear of persecution if they are returned to their home country, the judge insisted, "If I denote the slightest unease or fear [on the part of the minor], if they are victims of abuse or have issues that would qualify them for asylum or trigger the need for other services, I will have those discussions in court."[53]

Jorge's Hearing

The judge began the hearing by noting that a representative of the legal service provider was present "to provide information on the youth's behalf." Through questions to the attorney, the judge ascertained that Jorge had been notified of his rights, was informed of the immigration charges, had no possibility for family reunification, and was asking to return home. Turning to Jorge, he verified that Jorge did not fear returning to Mexico. Then the judge turned to the ICE report.

Judge: Last year you had contact with ICE in Phoenix. Could you explain how you were arrested?

Jorge: There were several of us in a car. They stopped us and put us in a patrol car.

Judge: I see [that this time] there are some pretty serious charges. The government report says that you were arrested after transporting drugs across the border, is that correct?

Jorge: Yes.

Judge: Have you been talked to your mom in Mexico?

Jorge: Yes.

Judge: What did she tell you to do?

Jorge: She told me to come back and to study.

Judge: Last year you were sent right back. This time you are in front of an immigration judge. We will go over the facts so there are no mistakes and so we can see whether the information the government has is correct, OK? You don't have to agree. If anything is wrong will you tell me?

Jorge: Yes.

The judge verified Jorge's birthdate and nationality as well as those of his parents. He then had Jorge admit to the factual allegations of "coming across without documents, entering the U.S. illegally, without being inspected." Next he questioned Jorge on the record, and Jorge explained that he had "crossed the border on foot" with four other men. Together they carried four backpacks with "20 kilos of drugs" and were each paid "$1,800." He planned to use the money "to help his family." The judge asked for the government's position on the case. This time the ICE attorney indicated that she would not oppose a grant of voluntary departure. The judge granted it but delivered a stern warning.

> I will grant voluntary departure because you will be in custody [and no flight risk exists]. You came into this country illegally and were smuggling drugs. This is very serious. It is more than being caught with a lot of money, regardless of whether you intended to use it for yourself or your family. I will give you this opportunity because I hope you will leave this kind of life. It is more than deportation or jail. You surely put your own life at risk. I see that you are a boy. You will be no good to your family if you begin that life. They can't replace you if you lose your life.[54]

Later I met with the attorney and the director of the ORR/Vera Institute legal service provider. They had seen cases involving impoverished street kids who had been trafficked and forced to serve as drug mules or smuggled across the border with the understanding that they would repay their debt by selling drugs. What were Jorge's prospects given his testimony about transporting twenty kilos of drugs? Would that be a permanent bar to obtaining legal relief? The attorney responded, "Unfortunately, yes, in cases like this there are no positive outcomes. The master calendar is an evidentiary hearing. The judge inquires about the individual background and the kid has no attorney. If I were the attorney, I would never allow him to say those things on the record. But we know what this judge expects. This judge insists that the kids answer all his questions. If they refuse, he issues a deportation order."[55]

This case illustrates the hazard of requiring children who face deportation to appear in court proceedings without appointed counsel or an independent child advocate. It also reveals the limitations of a model that relies on legal screenings in detention and on limited access to immigration attorneys. Children and adults face ICE trial attorneys whose agenda is often to avoid delays in the disposition of cases. They may have an interest in emphasizing offenses that are aggravated felonies or crimes of moral turpitude because these would result in deportation orders and long-term or permanent bars to legal reentry.

Despite the creation of juvenile dockets, significant problems remain. The judge adopted the well-intentioned, paternalistic admonitions more suited to a juvenile or family court judge but in a context that provided no due process protections. Despite the judge's apparent concern, he relied on an ICE report alleging criminal activity. At that point relatively little was known about Jorge's family circumstances or his motivation for crossing the border a second time. In the press of preparing youths for court, ORR case managers in the facility conduct rapid, preliminary interviews that provide only basic biographical information. They rely on the ICE reports that influence ORR placement decisions. Many youths reveal detailed and sensitive information only if or when they develop a rapport with a caseworker or clinician.

Even the scant background information in this case begs important questions. Why did Jorge risk crossing the border with a large quantity of drugs? Was he a victim of trafficking? Had he been smuggled into the United States and forced to sell drugs to repay his debt to a coyote or a gang? Did his family need money for medical care or to pay kidnappers a ransom? Only an in-depth investigation would have provided the answer, and that did not happen.

Several years later I interviewed a young Honduran, Martin, whose story could have been Jorge's. Martin had been abandoned by his mother and lived on the street before leaving for El Norte with his only friend, José. Near the U.S. border they met a smuggler who took them across. As a result they incurred a debt of $2,500 and were forced to pay it off by working for a drug cartel operating in the United States. The cartel boss warned Martin that if he got arrested he should "keep his mouth shut." Martin was arrested in 2008, transferred to a secure detention facility in California, and deported to Honduras. He was there for less than a week before the cartel contacted him and demanded that he return to repay his debt or be killed. Because he feared for his life, Martin returned to California. Over a sixteen-month period he was apprehended, placed in secure ORR detention, and deported twice more. On one stay in Honduras Mara Salvatrucha gang members murdered Martin's friend, José, and Martin narrowly escaped the same fate while attending José's funeral. Despite meeting weekly with ORR case managers in custody, Martin had never revealed any details about the drug cartel or their death threats. Given their long reach, he was sure that if he informed on them they would find out and kill him. During three periods in ORR custody, no one had ever fully explained the possibility of applying for a trafficking visa until Martin arrived at a facility in Portland. Martin knew that this was his last chance to tell his story before he turned eighteen, and with an attorney's help, he applied for the visa. A decision is pending on his case.

"This is Why We Need a Child Advocate!"

Many adjudicators and attorneys agree on the need to have a court-appointed child advocate to speak for the best interest of the child. I saw this firsthand in a hearing in the detained juvenile docket of the New York immigration court.[56] After her arrest for soliciting sex and transfer to ORR custody, an undocumented fifteen-year-old I will call Marcy appeared in immigration court. She was born in Sierra Leone and had a tumultuous childhood, fleeing first to Gambia to escape violence and then to London, where she spent three years with her mother, stepfather, and siblings. At fourteen she joined her biological father who was living in the United States. When conflicts developed between them, Marcy attempted to fly back to London on her own but was turned away because she lacked the proper documents. Two narratives emerged to explain her situation.

First, according to Marcy's ORR case manager and the Catholic Charities attorney who screened her in custody, she had been stranded at the airport, broke and alone. A young man who helped her turned out to be a pimp. He held her against her will and pressured her to turn tricks for money. In ORR custody Marcy had been identified as a severely traumatized trafficking victim who required intensive therapy and medication for anxiety and depression. The attorney requested that the judge terminate the removal proceedings and grant voluntary departure so she could return to London where her mother was "desperate" to be reunited with her.

The ICE trial attorney offered a different narrative. She opposed terminating the proceedings, citing an ongoing investigation into "glaring inconsistencies" in Marcy's story that "would likely lead to her arrest for prostitution." She introduced serious questions about Marcy's past, adding that she "was the mother of a two-year-old child." Who was caring for that child? Why had Marcy left to come to the United States? What was the nature of her relationship with her mother and stepfather? If they were so concerned why hadn't they come to the United States to get her? Tempers flared when the attorney demanded that the government produce evidence. Throughout the proceedings Marcy remained motionless in her seat. She was so heavily medicated that she sat with her head lolled back, eyelids drooping, her mouth open and drool pearling on her chin, oblivious to the heated exchanges swirling around her. The judge refused to grant voluntary departure, citing TVPRA requirements.

After the hearing, he explained, "I could not make an independent decision given the conflicting versions. She could not be released because there is no guardian or sponsor. This case is a perfect example of why we need a child advocate to determine the child's best interest. My concern is that she apparently conceived a child at thirteen, gave birth at fourteen, and came to the U.S. alone. She may have been neglected or abused. These issues are not related to her immigration status but belong in the realm of a family court." Two months later Marcy's mental health issues had worsened, and she was transferred to a therapeutic staff-secure facility in Texas.

A SPECIAL IMMIGRANT JUVENILE STATUS CASE

Background

The SIJS is unlike all other forms of immigration relief because it combines state child welfare and federal immigration procedures[57] to provide a pathway to citizenship specifically for undocumented children who suffer abuse and whose best interest would preclude a return to the country of origin. SIJS requires action and coordination by two statutory systems, a dependency finding in a domestic juvenile or family court, approval for legal permanent residency from U.S. Citizenship and Immigration Services, and the termination of removal proceedings in the immigration court.

Created in 1990, SIJS was originally intended by Congress to be available to all undocumented, abused children regardless of their detention status[58] and to prevent a return to their abusers in the home country.[59] In the 1997 context of widespread anti-immigration sentiment, Congress tightened qualification criteria and limited benefits by barring a child who obtained legal status through the SIJS provision from sponsoring a parent or sibling for legal status.[60]

In their landmark 2006 report Jacqueline Bhabha and Susan Schmidt identified serious procedural flaws in the SIJS statute that disqualified otherwise worthy applicants.[61] Reforms were implemented in 2008 with a U.S. district court decision[62] and the passage of the TVPRA, resulting in expedited processing times, waivers of costly filing fees, expanded eligibility provisions, and limited exclusions to family reunification."[63]

Despite these reforms, detained youths continue to face obstacles. State judges and social service departments[64] have denied their access to domestic courts for protective purposes, saying that they lack jurisdiction over immigrant children.[65] Detained children have been eligible for SIJS since 2008, but such denials are commonplace. Unfortunately, many state court personnel believe that child protective proceedings are unnecessary when children are in federal custody. A case in point involved an abused minor in Westchester County, New York, who was denied access to the family court because he was in ORR custody. His attorneys trenchantly noted "the cold logic that implies that youth are safe from abuse while being housed and fed by the agency [ORR] that will eventually return them to ICE [at the age of eighteen] for removal to their abusers."[66]

Although the abused child's best interest is supposed to be the paramount consideration in declaring him a dependent of the state court, in reality unlawful immigration status frequently trumps the need for protection. State courts cite jurisdictional and funding issues as the rationale for denying dependency orders, claiming that the federal government is the legal guardian and is, therefore, responsible for undocumented children. For this reason, SIJS continues to be underutilized or even out of reach in certain states.[67] The risks are increased for children who have histories of severe abuse as well as mental disabilities.

The Case of Javier

Javier was born in Mexico and suffered sustained physical abuse from a father who was ashamed of having a son who was slow. When Javier was seven his parents left their four children with their grandparents and headed to find work in El Norte. They settled in New York City and the following year sent for Javier's older brother. Two years later, with their parents' help, his two sisters also went to New York. Javier's parents never sent for him or provided support for him. With his siblings gone Javier grew desperate, and when he was ten years old, he set out alone to find his family. He crossed the border at Tijuana and eventually made his way to New York—a possibility his parents had never expected. The abuse continued until his parents returned to Mexico one year later, leaving Javier behind. By that time Javier's older brother was married, had a young family, and reluctantly allowed Javier to live with him.

Javier alternated between sleeping in his brother's living room, staying with friends, and living on the street. He had a chaotic adolescence. He avoided school, worked at menial jobs, hung out in a rough neighborhood, and engaged in petty theft in order to eat. At seventeen he was arrested for robbery and sent to the Riker's Island detention center.[68] He spent two months there without ever seeing an attorney or appearing before a judge. When the Riker's facility processed his release, ICE agents moved in, issuing a detainer and a notice to appear in immigration court. They designated him as unaccompanied and transferred him to ORR, where the intake team placed him in a secure facility in Richmond, Virginia, based on "his criminal charges." The ORR placement order was signed on December 31, 2008, just five months before his eighteenth birthday.[69]

In custody Javier was screened for legal relief and evaluated by a psychiatrist, who described his cognitive function in the mental retardation range. Javier eventually revealed an "extensive history of abuse by family members." He was reassessed by an attorney from a legal service provider who deemed him eligible for a SIJS visa and agreed to represent him pro bono. Meanwhile, the ORR case managers requested background information from Riker's but received only an FBI report listing an arrest and a charge for robbery. There was no record of a hearing in juvenile or immigration court.

Javier's condition deteriorated rapidly in secure detention. He was stressed and severely depressed and became increasingly withdrawn. In therapy sessions at the facility Javier had great difficulty remembering dates and details about his past. Nonetheless, he was consistent in describing the family abuse, displaying facial scars from frequent whippings. His parents repeatedly kicked him out. He was sure that they abandoned him because of his "problems."

Due to his special needs, potential legal relief, and looming eighteenth birthday, the facility staff sought different placement options.[70] They explored the possibility of family reunification, first with his older brother, who "was unresponsive and refused to help," and then with the family of a friend, which also declined to sponsor him. By the end of

February, with no family reunification options, Javier's case manager requested a step down to a therapeutic staff-secure facility in Chicago. She hoped that the transfer could lead to placement in a transitional living program where Javier could pursue his SIJS case and receive services after he turned eighteen. The step down was denied because the transitional living programs were at capacity and had long waiting lists. Increasingly desperate, the case manager sent an urgent appeal to the county Division of Social Services, explaining that she needed a therapeutic placement for a Mexican minor with special needs. She explained that there was no appropriate facility within their network, so the minor would age out of the federal custody and likely would be transferred to adult immigration detention. Such a transfer would compromise his legal case and do "real damage," given "his mental and cognitive deficits." In April 2009, just one month before Javier's eighteenth birthday, the county agency refused, explaining that Javier's custodial needs were a federal matter.

In the first step of the SIJS application process, a state court must declare the child a dependent and issue an order finding that reunification with one or both parents is not viable due to abuse, abandonment, or neglect. The refusal of state, family, or juvenile courts to file cases for abused immigrant children is an insurmountable barrier to obtaining SIJS protection. Children like Javier are in a catch-22 situation. A state court may refuse to take jurisdiction over minors as long as they are in federal custody.[71] Yet ORR only releases minors to approved sponsors, citing the need to protect them. If there is no possibility of family reunification they remain in custody. Javier had no sponsor, despite his eligibility for SIJS relief. He faced the real prospect of languishing in ORR custody until his eighteenth birthday, after which ICE agents would transport him in handcuffs to the nearest adult detention facility.

Two weeks before his eighteenth birthday his case manager heard about a Catholic family who ran a homeless shelter and contacted them to see if they would provide a temporary placement for Javier. They agreed, and just two days before he turned eighteen Javier was released from detention and went to live in their home. The arrangement worked well, and Javier stayed with them for eighteen months.

Javier's foster mother remembered the call she received about a traumatized young man in immigration custody who needed a home until his legal issues could be resolved. As it happened she and her husband had regularly visited a Nigerian man who was detained at the adult immigration center where Javier would end up.

They told me that he had a mental handicap. He had grown up in New York and had an arrest. When they told me his age I thought of a vulnerable eighteen-year-old in that hell hole. I told them that I would do anything to prevent that. There is really no Latino community in this area, but my husband and I agreed because we could not let him go to that horrible place. I'll never forget the first time we saw him. He had longish hair, a mustache, tattoos, scars on his face, and a gang boy uniform with the white tee and baggy pants. He looked really tough, and we had some trepidation because he had been exposed to some bad stuff, but then we also saw the extreme vulnerability. He raised himself, he came alone to the U.S., and then found no family help.[72]

During the frantic search for a sponsor, Javier's attorney proceeded with his petition for a dependency order from the local juvenile and domestic relations court. The SIJS petition was heard by one of two judges who had fluctuated in their approach to detained minors. Midway through 2009 the judges stopped signing dependency orders, citing both a procedural concern and a jurisdictional issue. Alarmed that increasing numbers of SIJS petitions were arriving in their court, they reversed course and asserted that they lacked jurisdiction and could not make findings for a noncitizen minor. Javier's was one of the last orders they signed in May 2009. The order declared him a dependent of the court and stipulated that it was not in his best interest to return to Mexico.[73]

Having surmounted this legal hurdle and with the dependency order in hand, Javier's attorney began the second step for the SIJS visa. She petitioned for adjustment of status and legal permanent residency with the United States Citizenship and Immigration Service (USCIS) while requesting continuances in immigration court. In mid-December 2009 Javier's SIJS petition was approved by USCIS. By that time he had been in custody for almost one year, first at Riker's, then in the secure ORR facility, and later in the care of the foster family.

His foster mother described his anxiety each time they returned to the immigration court to request continuances. On one occasion she said, "The people at Riker's had threatened him with deportation. It was so cruel. Then he went to a secure facility. After that the kid didn't trust anything that was official. He got so frustrated waiting and waiting and he wanted to quit and we had to convince him to hang on." The case was slated to return to the immigration court where the judge would rule on the approved petition and grant legal permanent residency, placing Javier on a five-year pathway to citizenship. It would be another eight months before he had that hearing in immigration court.

While prepping for the immigration court hearing Javier's attorney found a potentially damaging psychological report in which he had described living on the street and being used as a drug courier by older guys. These new details were worrisome given his criminal charges. Immigration law provides that many criminal convictions and some conduct bar applicants from demonstrating the good moral character that is required for most forms of relief.[74] This was a serious concern given Javier's impaired ability to defend himself. Unlike criminal or juvenile courts, there is no clear standard for mental incompetency and judges are not required to accommodate a respondent who is mentally disabled.[75]

Javier suffered from two disabilities that are often confused,[76] mental health problems resulting from his childhood trauma and cognitive impairment that limited his ability to function normally. His attorney explained that these conditions raised serious mental competency concerns.

> Could a sixteen-year-old mentally retarded boy be a drug trafficker? Given his cognitive issues and memory gaps, could he even remember exactly what he did? Was it coercion? Were they really drugs? Did he have the mental capacity to understand and meaningfully participate in the court proceedings? We knew that he didn't. Even though a juvenile delinquency disposition does not constitute a crime in immigration law, we still had a freak-out moment. He could not be prepped for the immigration hearing because he would say anything and admit to anything. If the ICE trial attorney introduced the drug issue in court it would have opened a can of worms.

Javier's lawyer contacted the ICE trial attorney before the hearing to request that Javier be excused from testifying in court because of his mental disability. She agreed. Just two weeks before the hearing a new ICE attorney took her place and accepted the deal negotiated by her predecessor on the condition that she receive written proof of Javier's low IQ. The only proof his attorney had was the damaging psychiatric evaluation, and there was no time to have him retested. Her one option was to request that Javier's IQ not be presented in open court. During the hearing, to her surprise, the ICE attorney explained in a sidebar to the judge the need for sensitivity. The judge agreed but raised the issue of Javier's arrest and detention in New York. That introduced "a scary moment of doubt" until the ICE attorney indicated that the charge had been dismissed.

Before ruling the judge insisted on questioning Javier's foster parents. Worrying that they had not been prepped, his attorney objected that Javier was not giving testimony. The judge insisted, and they testified, saying that they would have adopted Javier if he had been younger. The hearing ended with a grant of legal permanent resident status and a celebration at a local IHOP. Javier could now get a social security number and work legally.

SIJS is viewed as a generous form of relief that waives punishing grounds of inadmissibility, does not consider juvenile delinquency dispositions as a bar to legal status, and makes permanent residency status immediately available because it is not a family-based visa subject to yearly caps and long waits.[77] At the same time, it engages two statutory systems that continue to present procedural obstacles and jurisdictional conflicts. Youths like Javier with mental disabilities and criminal issues remain at risk of losing their legal status if they reoffend. Such cases would have no chance of success without representation by experienced immigration attorneys.

Despite the advantages of pursuing an SIJS, there are also drawbacks, namely, the permanent bar on sponsoring family members who seek legal entry into the United States. In an immigration system based on family sponsorship, SIJS introduces rules that effectively undercut kinship bonds. Although SIJS does not formally terminate parental rights, it substitutes the state as the legal guardian of the child, perpetuates the dependency of the youth, and threatens future attempts to repair damaged relations and restore family ties. For the government, the child who is rescued from abuse is also severed from his entire family in the home country. He no longer has biological siblings or family members who could benefit from his legal status. Despite the abuse he suffered from his parents and siblings, Javier's first decision as a legal adult was to reestablish contact with his brother and sister in New York.

Javier faced a rocky road on his own. Despite eighteen months of English classes, he was barely literate. His foster mother worried about his ability to keep even menial jobs and to avoid bad influences without a structured family life. How would someone with Javier's handicaps get schooling and health care? Reflecting on her experience, she said, "Life shouldn't be so scary and uncertain for a young person like Javier with cognitive limitations. The whole system is broken. Detention and deportation are not the answer."[78]

WINNING ASYLUM

I interviewed a retired immigration judge shortly after the *New Yorker* published an article that we both had read on the embellished persecution stories told by some asylum seekers.[79] The article came up when I asked the judge about credibility determinations. Such determinations are central to an asylum proceeding since the grant or denial is frequently based only on the applicant's testimony. Although a self-described conservative in granting asylum, the judge recognized the challenges faced by undocumented youth from poor, minority backgrounds. She described granting asylum to a severely mentally disabled minor who was convicted of writing bad checks as a minor. In another case that "broke her heart," she had no choice but to deny an asylum claim of a petitioner convicted in criminal court of selling drugs with his brother—an aggravated felony. She believed that he had been wrongly convicted and described how he had fled violence in Haiti and overcome abandonment by his parents and abuse in a group home to become a scholar-athlete in college.[80]

The asylum cases of children are particularly challenging under U.S. immigration law. Asylum petitions must establish a well-founded fear of persecution for a child on the basis of one of the protected grounds, race, religion, nationality, political opinion, or membership in a social group. Because children are not a protected class under this structure most claims are made on a "social group" ground. Asylum adjudicators have been wary of a claim based on membership in a social group because they view it as ill defined and ambiguous.[81]

A social group is defined as persons who share a characteristic that is immutable and so fundamental to their individual identities or consciences that they cannot or should not be required to change it in order to avoid persecution.[82] The primary definition of immutability can be an innate characteristic or a shared experience. An additional criterion relates to the social recognition of the group. Over time, the interpretation of social perception has shifted from determining the social attributes shared by members of a group to requiring that the group be socially visible and particular.[83] Recently the social visibility standard was renamed "socially distinctive" to clarify that the group must be set apart, or distinct, from others in a significant way;[84] the group need not be visible literally but must be recognizable by society.[85] There are unique challenges in adjudicating asylum claims based on membership in a protected social group.

In 2009 I observed an asylum hearing in the San Francisco immigration court that involved a Mexican transgender person. The attorneys explained that the youth, born Abraham Gonzalez (not his real name), had always identified as a female. In the area of Mexico where he grew up it was common knowledge that acting gay could invite ridicule, harassment, and even violent retribution. His family earned a living from drug trafficking, and *maricones,* "faggots," were particularly reviled. As an adolescent Abraham did not know that sexual minorities existed or that he could change his physical appearance, become a woman, and legitimately claim a transgender identity. He did not understand that the abuse he had suffered as a child counted as persecution or that he had the right to protection under U.S. immigration law based on sexual orientation.[86]

After crossing the border alone as a sixteen-year-old and struggling for months, Abraham made his way to San Francisco. A staff worker in a homeless shelter connected him with legal and social services for transgender youth. This was the beginning of a new life; Abraham learned the language of transnational rights-based movements and the entitlements of sexual citizenship articulated by the activist LGBT support organizations in the Bay Area. He acquired a new vocabulary, including terms such as "homophobia" and "heteronormative behaviors." Three years later Abraham became Cecilia. With help from the Transgender Law Center, she found excellent pro bono legal representation.

LGBT Status and Immigration Law

Many adjudicators fail to recognize that discrimination based on "homosexual conduct" is really directed at transgender status. Whereas sexual orientation is recognized as a basis for asylum, childhood is not a protected class. The reported cases regarding LGBT youths suggest that applicants rarely receive special consideration due to their status as minors.[87] Pervasive stereotypes based on white, heterosexual norms may also condition the way adjudicators assess the claims of nonwhite LGBT asylum seekers.[88] As a result, LGBT youths are subject to overlapping forms of discrimination: racism, homophobia, and antiyouth bias. The testimony that they provide is frequently not accepted as adequate proof of their sexual identity, and the very notion of an LBGT child is treated as a paradox.[89]

LGBT Status and Membership in a Social Group

Winning asylum has been called a game of refugee roulette,[90] because there are significant disparities in grant rates across and within immigration courts. Significantly, an asylum grant is not determined on the merits of the case alone. Rather, the background and gender of the judge, the composition of cases, the nationality of the asylum seeker, and the availability and quality of the legal representation all affect asylum decisions. Between 2004 and 2009 the immigration judge hearing Cecilia's case granted 35.7 percent of the asylum claims she heard. Her denial rate of 64.3 percent was higher than that of her colleagues in the San Francisco immigration court (55 percent) and of immigration judges nationwide, who denied asylum claims 57.3 percent of the time.[91]

To establish that LGBT youths and persecuted minors in general have a "well-founded fear of persecution," it must be shown that they belong to a "particular social group." While a claim of homosexuality is now an accepted means of establishing membership in a social group for asylum purposes,[92] the courts have yet to recognize a claim of transgender identity. The Ninth Circuit Court in San Francisco has come the closest to affording protection to transgender applicants but has not explicitly stated that those who possess such an orientation constitute a distinct social group for asylum purposes.[93] Moreover, many adjudicators use North American sexual and gendered terms that conflate "transgender" with "gay." They fail to appreciate that transgender individuals can identify as any sexual orientation and that many are heterosexual.[94] The persistent misconceptions of transgender issues unfairly narrow the notion of social group and ignore the unique threats facing transgender individuals. Cecilia's attorneys had to establish a nexus or show the connection between the persecution she suffered and her membership in the social group recognized in the Ninth Circuit Court: "gay boys with female characteristics in Mexico." This legal requirement has an impact on LGBT petitioners who share an immutable characteristic but must often conceal their sexual orientation and remain socially invisible in order to avoid discrimination or persecution.

Assessing the fear of persecution is complicated, and many asylum cases are decided on the basis of incomplete or limited evidence. Immigration attorneys warn that establishing truth for asylum purposes is different from recording what really happened. The goal is to present evidence that supports a coherent and credible account of the persecution. Frequently the nuances of a case must be set aside in order to produce an unassailable persecution narrative.[95] In fact, an ambiguous narrative is inherently problematic. Christopher Nugent, an immigration attorney whose specialty is arguing complicated asylum cases for children, emphasizes, "We can't use postmodern notions of culture. We need holistic descriptions of culture and absolute statements—in the present tense—of what people think and how they act."[96]

To meet the burden of proof, corroborating evidence is desirable but not required. Recognizing that such corroboration may be impossible to obtain, particularly when the persecutors are criminals, police, soldiers, or politicians, immigration law stipulates that credible testimony is sufficient. In this case, Cecilia's attorneys had no written corroboration of her story from her Mexican classmates, extended family, school authorities, or municipal officials. Moreover, her undocumented relatives in the United States declined to testify on her behalf. The case relied on her credible testimony alone.

Constructing the LGBT Asylum Narrative

Cecilia's attorneys provided a narrative that revealed the deep wounds of a childhood spent within warring branches of a violent drug family. As a three-week-old infant Cecilia was sent by her parents to be raised in a distant town. Cecilia was only nine years old when her father and uncle were murdered by a rival family faction. Given the rigid demands of machismo, she testified that if either branch of the family discovered her sexual orientation they would kill her.

Cecilia's attorneys had to show that her sexual orientation was an immutable characteristic central to her gender identity and to establish a pattern of abuse based on the social visibility of her "effeminate characteristics." Using the rights-based language and the sexual terms recognizable to the court, Cecilia described the discriminatory treatment she had received in the Catholic school she attended, particularly when she began to dress as a girl. She was harassed and beaten by classmates and discriminated against by the principal and teachers, "who couldn't stand gays." At sixteen Cecilia was expelled from the school and fled across the border on her own. After a brief sojourn with her mother's family in Southern California, she was thrown out because of her "transgender life." Cecilia was on her own, "destitute, homeless, with no friends, no family."

Cecilia testified to "a certain inclination that she had, since an early age, for all things having to do with women." This inclination led to a horrific incident soon after her seventh birthday. After a day spent swimming at a river with her siblings and cousins, she attracted the attention of soldiers who were patrolling nearby. In halting testimony, broken by sobs, Cecilia described what happened next.

Cecilia: I realized their intentions were not good and tried to run. The four of them came after me and raped me. They said things to me that I had never heard. They didn't care that they were hurting me. To them I was like a toy. At the time they were raping me I fell and struck my chin on a rock. I have a scar here.

Immigration judge: Was anything said?

Cecilia: Yes, they called me *cochon, puto* [whore], *maricon*. They said they were fucking me because I was gay.

Immigration judge: They used that language?

Cecilia: Yes, and they said, "Do you want more? We have more to give you." [Long pause and visible effort to speak] After they were done, they said that if I told anyone they would cut me up. So they left this [pointing to her lower back], they cut me here to remind me.

Immigration judge: Did you tell anyone what had happened?

Cecilia: No, out of fear and shame I never told.

In their brief her attorneys included news articles and U.S. State Department country condition reports noting the elevated risk of harassment and violence that transgender individuals face across Mexico and Central America. Drawing on anthropological research, the attorneys described how a culture of machismo shapes views of homosexuality.[97] They explained that men who have sex with other men but who are perceived as sexually dominant (*activo*) are generally not considered homosexual and suffer little social stigma. They presented a cultural worldview to show that even seven-year-old boys are at risk of violent retribution when their effeminate behaviors violate hypermasculine norms and expose them as gays, or worse, as transgender individuals.

In her testimony Cecilia explicitly identified herself as a transgender female. She emphasized the process of transformation through medical treatment and education that led from her status as a gay boy to that of a transgender woman. Her attorneys stressed the enduring threat from her Mexican relatives and the lack of safe areas anywhere in the country for a transgender person.

WAIVING THE ASYLUM FILING DEADLINE

Cecilia's asylum claim was initially heard in an affirmative hearing before an asylum officer in the U.S. Citizenship and Immigration Services. It was denied because she had not filed her application as required within one year of her 2005 entry into the United States.[98] As a result, she was placed in defensive removal proceedings in the San Francisco immigration court. The court would have to waive the one-year bar before deciding on the merits of the asylum case. Even a deserving claim must be denied if the court declines to grant an exception based on changed or exceptional circumstances. Making a credible case for a waiver is critical, but the asylum decision remains at the discretion of the judge.

Cecilia's attorneys relied on expert witness testimony and the government's own regulations to argue that Cecilia qualified for a waiver.[99] She was an unaccompanied minor, was confused about her gender identity, and suffered from PTSD because of the abuse and abandonment she endured. One of the most commonly accepted reasons for a late filing is an exceptional circumstance involving a serious medical or mental health issue such as PTSD. Cecilia's attorneys contacted a child psychiatrist whose specialty is the diagnosis of trauma among refugees. He determined that Cecilia had PTSD and if forced to return to Mexico, "She would suffer further depression and quite possibly become suicidal."

DISQUALIFYING THE CLAIM

The ICE trial attorney vociferously opposed waiving the one-year filing rule. He rejected the testimony that Cecilia suffered from PTSD and the evidence of persecution based on her gender identity. Some legal scholars argue that the rationale for requiring extrinsic evidence to confirm oral testimony lies in the belief that a sexual orientation claim is uniquely vulnerable to fraud and lies. Questions posed to determine the respondent's "real" sexual orientation utilize language that reveals unconscious adherence to racialized sexual stereotypes of Latino masculinity and white gay norms in the United States. They note that evidentiary requirements focus more on external conduct than on actual experience and culturally relevant markers.[100] Here the ICE trial attorney's questions about homosexual conduct and cross-dressing revealed his confusion about transgender identity. He erroneously conflated sexual orientation with gender identity, and as a result, he viewed Cecilia as an effeminate gay man rather than a transgender woman. At one point the immigration judge had to correct this misperception, saying that "transgender and homosexual are not the same thing."

In rejecting the claim, the ICE trial attorney made no allowance for Cecilia's status as an unaccompanied minor who crossed the border at sixteen and became homeless. On the one hand, he held her to an adult standard without allowing for her diminished capacity or limited experience as a teenager suffering from trauma. He rejected the claim of past persecution, implying that the Cecilia was largely responsible for her own misfortunes. Tellingly, although she considered herself a female, the ICE trial attorney continued to refer to Cecilia as "he."[101] On the other hand, he showed antiyouth bias by discrediting the very notion of a transgender child. This approach is consistent with a dated developmental paradigm that views children as incomplete persons who are incapable of bearing witness, of formulating independent opinions, or of adopting non-normative gender identities.

The ICE trial attorney began his cross-examination of the psychiatrist by asking him to explain the term "malingerer." He intended to show that Cecilia had faked her distress by parroting PTSD symptoms in her psychiatric interview in order to get the right diagnosis for her asylum claim. He suggested that the psychiatrist had been fooled by a clever trauma performance. Couldn't that happen, he asked?

> *Psychiatrist:* Certainly I could be fooled. A malingerer may, in fact, look up the symptoms, but there is little likelihood that an asylum applicant will read and understand the full psychiatric diagnosis. Such a person is not familiar with the diagnostic nosology. Her behavior was consistent with the presentation of trauma found in a survivor of abuse. I witnessed her reluctance to remember. I observed the shaking of the hands and the tearing of the eyes.
>
> *ICE attorney:* In your expert opinion is the respondent a malingerer?
>
> *Psychiatrist:* No.

The ICE attorney also dismissed Cecilia's claim on the basis of membership in a social group. His questions were hostile and repetitive. He circled back again and again to demand elaboration of the facts relating to the rape. He not only pressed Cecilia on painful details but also discounted the distress that such violence would inflict on a child. Refusing to call the attack a rape, he questioned Cecilia about the "incident," wondering why the soldiers believed that he was "gay or different from another boy." He taunted Cecilia about wearing girls' clothing, peppering her with sarcastic questions.

> *ICE trial attorney:* So you didn't wear a girl's clothes that day? Oh, come on, which is it? Looking feminine or wearing a girl's clothes? What was it that made the soldiers think that at the river?
>
> *Cecilia (clearly angry, more upset and raising her voice):* I DON'T KNOW.

THE DECISION

After an adjournment for lunch, the judge heard closing statements and rendered the final decision. The attorneys argued that Cecilia had a well-founded fear of persecution based on the past abuse she suffered and on the expectation of future persecution as a transgender person in Mexico. They also argued that she qualified for a waiver of the one-year deadline due to exceptional circumstances related to her case.

In his closing statement the ICE trial attorney emphatically argued for a denial.

> Nothing changes the law or the facts of the case. We have only his testimony. Can we say that there was persecution on the basis of the protected ground of membership in a social group? What is it? Being a member of a drug family? The only incident that rises to the level of persecution is the rape. But it occurred when he was seven years old! What is the particular social group for a seven-year-old? Is it a seven-year-old with effeminate characteristics? He was not a transgender male. How is the rape relevant? There is no nexus to the protected ground of membership in a social group.

The immigration judge ruled that Cecilia met the definition of a refugee and had suffered past persecution. Importantly, she accepted the argument that "Cecilia is a member of a particular social group: transgender females in Mexico." She addressed both the immutability requirement that defines membership in a social group and the exceptional and changed circumstances rule that waives the bar on asylum applications submitted after one year. She wove both strands into her decision, arguing that Cecilia "has always identified as sexually different than a male." Yet the judge also asserted that Cecilia has "matured and changed . . . she is growing into what she always was."

Citing a landmark case in asylum law, *Cardosa-Fonseca,*[102] the judge argued that the evidence met the burden of proof. She held that Cecilia's status as an unaccompanied minor, age, rejection by her family, and mental health issues had the cumulative effect of creating a legal disability under immigration law, a fact that the government attorney incorrectly dismissed.

The judge affirmed the defense counsels' arguments distinguishing between sexual orientation and gender identity in order to argue that Cecilia belonged to the particular social group of transgender individuals. The judge rejected the government's contention that "a rape by four soldiers, who gave verbal reasons for the attack, has no relation to the claim of persecution." She found it entirely "reasonable that Cecilia was targeted because of her effeminate characteristics, her sexual characteristics." She granted asylum to Cecilia.[103]

I interviewed the judge after her retirement. She described the ICE attorney's flagrant dismissal of accepted law and discriminatory treatment of the young respondent. In her mind the case easily met the standard. Both the judge and Cecilia's attorneys were alert to the ways homophobia differs across social, cultural, and political terrains.

In contrast, the ICE attorney tried to disqualify Cecilia's claim by conflating transgender identity and homosexual orientation—a notion that is prevalent in American popular culture. He also dismissed Mexican concepts of sexuality where similar conflations are likely at work and where machismo shapes how gender is performed, particularly in the area where Cecilia grew up. Gay and lesbian identities cannot be understood as universals but are embedded in local and culturally specific gender relations.

The ICE attorney evaluated the case through an American lens where homosexual conduct substitutes for identity. He appeared to apply a number of competing tests based on conduct and status, relying, like some adjudicators, on controversial Euro-American psychological theory that conceives of status and conduct as easily distinguishable and readily understandable. This theory approaches the question of LGBT identities with the preconception that being gay is mutable conduct and an intentional choice. Thus LGBT status and conduct reflect the same choice.[104] The ICE attorney argued that "Abraham" chose a gay identity by acting like a homosexual. Being gay was, therefore, not an immutable characteristic signifying membership in a social group.

While rejecting the immutable characteristic standard for "Abraham" as a gay, the ICE attorney still applied the social visibility test. He assumed that Cecilia's outward demeanor and gay mannerisms would have been visible and easy to decode by others in Mexican society. Paradoxically, he also implied that Cecilia was not gay enough because others—in particular, members of her family—did not recognize the sexual orientation based on her behavior. Thus, he argued, there was no connection between the incidents reported and Cecilia's membership in the social group of effeminate gays and no persecution.

What is equally striking here is the predatory view of young teenagers as socially disruptive and threatening. From this perspective, they generate no sympathy because they make fraudulent claims and drain public resources. On the one hand, some adjudicators "adultify" children by ascribing malicious intention to them and making them accountable for their actions.[105] On the other hand, they resort to specifically Euro-American terminologies that view children as innocent, unformed, and without the ability to interpret their own social worlds. They deem children incapable of expressing their own sexual orientations or of being targeted for rape on that basis. They do not credit young people's testimony regarding their gender identity even when it is sincere and consistent. In this view, children are expected to refrain from sexual activities. Those who express a non-normative sexual orientation or who commit certain acts are no longer considered children deserving of special treatment or of asserting their right to protection through an asylum claim.

This and other cases suggest that some groups like sexual minorities experience multidimensional subordination, not just sexism and racism, but heterosexism and antiyouth bias as well.[106] To produce a convincing persecution narrative Cecilia had to become conversant with new categorical markers and knowledge of specialized sociolegal terminology based on Euro-American sexual and gendered models. Given the legal ambiguity surrounding membership in a social group and the claim of transgender identity, as well as the judge's low asylum grant rate, her petition could easily have failed. Asylum claims can be successful when discretion is exercised by adjudicators who are attentive to culturally specific and evolving understandings of discourses of gender, sexuality, and youth and notions of pathology within the United States and abroad.

CONCLUSION

A recent NGO report has uncovered the systemic impediments to justice in U.S. immigration courts.[107] Countless immigrants are swept up in a byzantine legal process and face a courtroom experience in which they are subjected to "degrading treatment" and held in detention awaiting trial so long that many choose to leave even when they are entitled to stay. In 2014 the delay for case hearings in court was as long as 587 days.[108] The risks are even higher for children. Immigration judges are keenly aware of the legal obstacles children face in immigration law but are largely powerless to prevent "assembly line injustice" in defensive court proceedings. Many judges rightly question if removing the black robe and avoiding legalese makes any difference given the absence of government-funded legal representation and the limited options for legal relief. Can a relaxed courtroom atmosphere and a child-friendly manner mask the power imbalances of proceedings sufficiently to build the trust needed to elicit the truth? How far does empathy go in a legal structure that does not incorporate the best interest of the child as a basis for legal relief? Accepting that "lots of kids are going to end up having to go back because they lost the case or couldn't make it in U.S. law"[109] offers little solace when arbitrary rules disqualify the most vulnerable petitioners from obtaining legal status. One judge asked, "What do we do with children who have been abused or persecuted but are not eligible for asylum or any other relief? Do we terminate the case? Can we offer some kind of withholding of removal?"[110] Although the numbers of unaccompanied children in removal proceedings applying for asylum have remained roughly the same,[111] new child arrivals have skyrocketed. At the same time immigration prosecutions—the majority for simple illegal entry—and deportations have reached record highs, a policy that has yielded "nothing but more broken families and interrupted lives."[112]

From the moment of apprehension until release from custody, children's cases are mired in administrative complexity and bureaucratic delays. Despite a rhetorical commitment to operational efficiency and standardized regulations that promise protection, the federal custodial system lacks transparency, enhances redundancy, restricts information flows, and concentrates power hierarchically in the hands of a few senior administrators whose decisions are difficult to review or appeal. The previous director of the Division of Children's Services at ORR prided herself on her hands-on approach to resolving complicated cases. Unfortunately, her agency never implemented a formal appeal process for the decisions she personally made on transfers or release, and Congress has failed to establish an independent oversight body charged with monitoring the entire system. Practitioners and advocates complain that the current administration of ORR is even less inclined to share information on operations.

Detention regimes, like the custodial system for unaccompanied children, rely on a thicket of national and local laws, policy directives, and tracking systems that are implemented by a bewildering array of personnel in immigration enforcement, citizenship services, federal and state courts, police forces, and NGOs. These systems frequently work at cross-purposes and in haphazard ways to amplify or mitigate their punitive effects on children. In Jorge's case there was a complete failure to accord due process, during a first apprehension when he was inadequately screened and subjected to expedited removal and a second time when he was forced to appear in court and answer self-incriminating questions without an attorney. In contrast, the cases of Javier and

Cecilia illustrate both the importance of having competent legal representation and the serendipitous nature of obtaining a successful outcome in immigration proceedings. The luck of the draw determines the courtroom where the case is heard, yet the single best predictor of winning legal relief is the identity and background of the judge.[113]

A 2009 Appleseed report noted that undocumented immigrants come to the United States because they "are all inspired by the American promise of opportunity and our traditions of fair play and equal justice under the law."[114] Yet the report's authors concluded that the court's failure to uphold America's legal ideals means that individuals and communities on the margins—the working poor, minorities, and undocumented children—are unfairly denied their opportunity to "pursue the American Dream."[115] In the final chapter we turn back to the young people who shared their stories and, at a remove of some years and with the security of legal status, revisit what the American Dream means for them.

8

The New American Story

This book began with a quote from the undocumented Dreamer activist Benita Veliz at the 2012 Democratic National Convention. She had seized every opportunity and succeeded against all odds. Yet compared to other young Americans from humble beginnings who surmounted daunting obstacles, Benita could expect no reward, only the prospect of permanent temporariness. Her situation reflects the porous boundary between legality and illegality in immigration law, illustrating how shifting legal categories work to transform otherwise worthy insiders into criminal outsiders. Her very presence on a national stage pointed to the contested use of the law to criminalize the undocumented and to deny them basic human rights.

Dreamers and the young people who land in detention share similar migration histories but are rarely considered part of the same population. The risks they share should give us pause. Both groups are subject to the arbitrary and often haphazard enforcement of immigration laws that sweep up, detain, and deport undocumented youth and U.S. citizens alike. Despite their moral worthiness, serendipity has an outsized role in the stories of young Dreamers. Citlalli, one of the Georgetown University Dreamers, explained, "I am lucky that I grew up in an accepting immigrant community. My family could, in a sense, blend. We could 'stay out of trouble' if we tried hard enough, though it was always on my mind that I could not ever have a close encounter with the law." Dreamers are just one wrong move or accident away from detention and removal proceedings. One example illustrates the fragility of their position. Since 2012 the attorneys who screen young people in immigration detention and determine their eligibility for DACA have had to battle ICE agents and DHS detention officers who blocked their efforts to apply for this temporary relief from deportation. One attorney with a client who was eligible for DACA reported that his undocumented client was detained in ICE custody. Despite being eligible for DACA, ICE officials pressured his client to sign his own deportation order on the strength of a form from a probation officer alleging "gang membership."[1]

Despite facing similar risks, the two groups are viewed differently. Young people like Maribel, Carlos, and Javier come to the attention of immigration authorities when they run afoul of immigration or criminal law, are placed in federal custody, and are prosecuted by the government. Even after winning legal status, they avoid public activism and remain largely invisible. Their claims to citizenship rights, critique of immigration law, and reform advocacy do not command the same respect. As children crossing the border alone or young people apprehended internally, they are viewed first as lawbreakers and treated like security threats. There is no ready narrative to counter the stigma of detention and to argue against deportation.

It has been five years since I began to collect the stories of young people who experienced the federal custodial system firsthand. With the benefit of legal status and at a remove of some years from federal custody and immigration courts, I asked them to comment on that experience and on their futures. It is no accident that I could only locate some of those who had legal relief. I regret not being able to include the voices of young people like Antonio or Orlando who spent long years in this country but were ineligible for legal relief and slipped under the radar. Whether they remained in the shadows or were deported, I hope that if they read what follows it will resonate with them.

As we saw, the majority of young migrants had to leave home to survive socially and economically. They witnessed or experienced violence during the journey north from ruthless smugglers, corrupt border guards, criminal gangs, or racist cops. Most suffered extreme deprivation and wrenching isolation. A few narrowly escaped death on Mexican trains, at the hands of criminal gangs, or during desert treks only to be mistreated in U.S. federal custody. Others spent long months in detention and waged an anxious uphill battle for legal status. Their lives after release—placement in foster families or group homes and attendance at public schools—were often marred by stress, anti-immigrant discrimination, and dashed hopes. The relief of being free from custody led to other struggles—mastering the language, navigating American schools, finding a welcoming community, fighting their removal proceedings, and gaining a foothold in a tough job market. Most had smuggling fees to repay and remittances to send home so their families would not lose title to land and houses. Their high expectations for employment and decent wages were frequently compromised by poor English proficiency, inadequate job skills, and insufficient training opportunities. The desire to get on with their lives and the need to find work took priority over clearing the many hurdles of staying in school. Many had to let go of the dream of a middle-class lifestyle in a climate of limited access to stable jobs, affordable housing, and health care benefits.

When asked what they would do if they could start over again, half said they would never have left home because they had suffered too much. They had survived a grueling rite of passage, a period of isolation and sacrifice, when they left behind family and journeyed alone to El Norte only to end up in detention. Yet in the same breath these same young people expressed optimism about the future.[2] Like other extended and arduous rites of passage, "winning their case" moved them to a new status, out of the shadows of illegality and into the light of legal personhood. They saw themselves as highly resourceful and adaptable, not as victims.[3] As one young man explained, "We were men in our country, working and making money. They treated us like children in the shelters. Maybe we had to have a childhood first before we could become adults again, American adults."

TRANSFORMATIONS

The young people understood the journey from homeland to resettlement in the United States not only as a real experience spanning space and time but also as a metaphor for the transformations that occurred along the way. They described where it had taken them and at what cost, sharing important lessons for themselves and for all of us.

In 2011 I met Jairo, a very thoughtful twenty-two-year-old who spoke excellent English. He had begun a "second life" in the United States, rising like a phoenix from the ashes of his life in Guatemala. He insisted that "the principles of the U.S. like freedom and rights were implanted on us," even as he described experiences that belied those ideals. Like so many others he fled violent gangs and abject poverty "doing what was necessary to survive" before crossing the border and losing his way in the Arizona desert. His group had run out of water when they saw a sign in Spanish and English warning that "illegals" would be shot for trespassing. Just beyond lay a cattle trough. Mad with thirst, they scrambled over the fence and drank from the stinking yellow water. When Jairo looked up he was staring down the barrel of a gun. "It was a white lady, the ranch owner," he said. "We begged her to let us go. She spoke Spanish and said, 'You don't understand, wetbacks, I have a 9 millimeter and I will put a bullet in your head if you run.' She locked us in a garage like dogs until Immigration came and arrested us."

Once in custody Jairo became angry, "behaved bad," and got stepped up to a staff-secure facility. "While I was there one of the staff, a former military guy, beat me real bad in a bathroom. His wife worked there too, and he thought I was cheating with her. I wasn't." That was a low point. His second life began years later with legal relief, a green card, and a steady job. "Put this in your book," he said. "I spent eight days in the desert and I still have the pants I wore. I will keep them always to show my kids and grandkids in case they think about doing something stupid. They are dirty, with holes from cactus needles and barbed wire, but I don't touch them. They remind me of everything I went through to get here." When I asked him what he would change if he could, he insisted, "I would change nothing, not the fear, the trains, the desert, not even the beating. I am who I am because of what I went through. All the things I suffered made me stronger and they are part of me." When I asked him to suggest a title for this book he hesitated, "I don't know, but it should have something to do with aiming for the stars."

I met Ángel, the young Mexican who was apprehended after working for months to repay his smuggling debt, and his Honduran friend Ernesto in 2011. Their former caseworker and surrogate parent, Mr. Bob,[4] had counseled them, harangued them to study, helped them find pro bono attorneys, made sure they had health care, assisted them with legal forms, and arranged for them to stay temporarily in a rent-free house on campus so they could finish school and find work. Ángel had a green card and was attending a nearby public school, studying science, math, and English and participating in a vocational track for auto mechanics. A year later, in 2012, Ángel graduated from the high school vocational program as a certified auto technician and was named the Outstanding ESL Student of his class. By 2013 he had a steady girlfriend and was hopeful about his prospects.

Like Jairo, Ángel described a life divided into two phases, before and after his journey to the United States and placement in an ORR group home. He could cite the exact date and time when he arrived there and remembered being warned, "'You gotta go to school in here.'" "I say, 'Man, are you kidding? I want to go to school.' When I was working in the fields [in Florida] I saw a school bus go by. I wish one day I am on that bus with a backpack going to school, learning the language. I say to myself, 'I gotta do it. I am young and smart. But how?'" He mistrusted his first case manager, believing that she wanted to close the case and send him back. He also resisted seeing a therapist because he wasn't "crazy." He had been granted voluntary departure and was scheduled to leave when he finally revealed the abuse he had endured in Mexico. His clinician helped him find a pro bono attorney. After two years and five continuances in an immigration court, he had SIJS status and became a legal permanent resident. Looking back, he explained:

> I am not the same person I was when I came. This place helped to change me, my personality. When I first came I didn't know who I was. Now I have more opportunities to have a better future. I learned two languages, Spanish and English. I am a new person with my legal papers and education. I respect people, I am not talking the same way. This experience was hard, but it gave me what I didn't have in my country. I have something now. I am not just working in landscaping or at McDonalds. I want to work for the government. I have a dream to maybe join the American air force or the navy.

Language and Race

These young people recognized that learning English and becoming educated were the tools they needed to navigate the white mainstream world and to deflect racialized perceptions of them as foreigners. They had lived in the United States for a period of between four and fourteen years when I met them and had been influenced by American racial thinking. They interpreted their social position in relation to an American racial classificatory system that marks difference along a continuum from blackness to whiteness.[5] Because they came alone, were from impoverished families, had no legal status, and were unable to speak the dominant language they were viewed and viewed themselves as racially different by the "whites" they encountered in the CBP, ICE, and FBI, in the immigration and criminal courts, and in the federal shelters.

Maribel expressed this most powerfully when she realized that her lack of economic and cultural capital put her in a structural position similar to disadvantaged American minorities. She had excelled in her Honduran school and helped run her mother's grocery business, but in custody she felt humiliated and "dumb, like a nobody around all those gringos who spoke English and Spanish. I could only speak Spanish." After winning legal status and release, then graduating with honors from an American high school, she combined college study with a part-time job in retail sales. She worked in an upscale children's shop where she was the only "Hispanic." That experience taught her how minority groups are differentiated from the mainstream middle class on the basis of their language, class, and racial background. She got angry when she described how the other part-time help, "white gringa salesgirls," picked on her, mocking her accent and her ambition to excel in a dead-end job. They used their paychecks for frills; she used hers to buy necessities.

At a remove of five years she viewed her past through different eyes: "Life in that shelter was so hard and so lonely, but I turned it into my blessing. It was the beginning of a new life. It forced me to learn English and without it I would not be where I am today. Life in the shelter was like a puzzle. I had to find all the pieces and put them together before I was ready to live in this country. Now I speak English and I feel like I even think like a gringa!" She explained, "At first I was afraid to correct people or let them know when they were crossing a line. No more! Now I make them treat me right!" Learning colloquial English, earning college credits, building up savings, and being a responsible person "with no credit card debt" were efforts to change her class position and claim the status, if not the respect, of middle-class whites. Yet she never forgot where she came from and why she left.

Both Modesto and Corina came from indigenous communities in Guatemala and spoke dialects at home. Once in custody they had to learn two languages, first Spanish and then English. Indigenous peoples have been stigmatized and racially marked as different from "mestizo" populations at home as well as in Hispanic immigrant communities in the United States.[6] Corina experienced this discrimination firsthand when she was placed in a Cuban foster family who cheated her out of the spending money allocated for her by the ORR-contracted service provider. She never complained but also never forgot what had happened to her. Modesto hit the jackpot with his foster family, an upper-middle-class couple who had lost their only son in a car accident. They opened their home and their hearts to him, and he considers them his parents. Both Corina and Modesto went on to independent living programs, continued their education, and gained valuable job skills.

Religion and the Power of Belief

Language and education were central elements in these youths' adjustment to a new American life. Equally important was the power of religion as a redemptive force and as a belief system linked to Hispanic communities of faith. Hispanic evangelical churches have played a prominent social role in the lives of many immigrants. A number of the young women I interviewed were active members of Pentecostal churches, but Ernesto had a unique experience. He had become a born-again Christian, committing his life to evangelical preaching. When I first met him in 2011 he seemed to be in a good place. He had learned English, passed the GED equivalency exam, and, with legal assistance from a Texas attorney, had obtained a U visa. He also worked full-time at a car repair shop as a licensed inspector. Despite persistent worries about making enough money and a serious injury on the job, he insisted, "I am healthy, I have food, I work, I have a life here."

When we met the following year, he described the protracted existential crisis that had led to his religious conversion. Despite his accomplishments in the United States, Ernesto continued to suffer from deep wounds inflicted during his formative years: the biological father who refused to recognize him, the stepfather who mistreated him, the Zetas who tortured him, the shelter worker who abused him sexually, and the federal officials who lied about his legal status.

> I was so angry and frustrated. I was afraid of the future and of death. My childhood was so hard because I grew up on the street. It was easy to buy alcohol, and at seven years old I was drinking and smoking. I was terrible, saying bad words all the time. I was filled with hate for my father and my stepfather and after I got kidnapped by the Zetas I was thinking that I would go back and kill them. Then, when I was in the group home and had to follow so many rules, I thought when I get out I'm gonna get drunk. But I realized that I had to change my life. I needed to let all that go and find peace.

This emotional crisis was the prelude to what fundamentalists call "coming under conviction," or converting.[7] It begins with an acute awareness of one's sinfulness and of the imperative to address it. As an inner rite of passage it transforms the sinner into a new person who is freed from the bondage of sin and reconciled with God. That afternoon Ernesto witnessed his faith to me, narrating his life in Christian terms— "a life washed in the blood of Christ." As a born-again Christian he accepted the meaning of the gospel: "The Bible tells us to forgive others, and if I don't forgive my stepfather or the lady who abused kids in the Texas shelter God won't forgive me." He spoke the language of faith: "I accept the power of the Father, Son, and Holy Ghost, and I am at peace. Things happen for a reason. God has a purpose for me and I try to do his will and sin less." For Ernesto, as for other converts, conversion provoked a shock that altered the very terms of his life and set him on a new path.[8]

Maribel too believed that she had been redeemed by her faith and participation in a Pentecostal Hispanic church where she headed the youth ministry. She remembered being filled with hate and blaming her father for the terrible suffering he had inflicted on his family. By 2013 she had married her boyfriend, become a U.S. citizen, and given birth to a beautiful little boy. She insisted, "I am so thankful to heal inside. It took a long time, but the bitterness is gone. Before my heart was hard, but now I can't hate anymore. God did it."

PUTTING DOWN ROOTS

When I first spoke to Corina in 2011, she was frustrated and depressed. She had made a substantial down payment on the American Dream by starting a family and building a new life with her Guatemalan boyfriend of five years. She had two healthy, beautiful daughters, her fiancé had steady work, and after being evicted from a mobile home park because they were undocumented, they found and rented a comfortable apartment. Her case manager described Corina as a model immigrant—mature, responsible, and kind—whose case had fallen through the cracks. She had been plunged into a nine-year legal purgatory when the government appealed her grant of asylum and denied her petition for SIJS status. The long legal battle and the interminable wait for a resolution of the case had forced her to postpone higher education, a professional career, and marriage to the father of her children.

When we met in person in Grand Rapids, Michigan, in early November 2011, Corina was exuberant. Just a few hours earlier her attorney had called her to say that the Detroit immigration court had finally approved her petition for permanent residency. We spoke again in 2013, and she had more news to report. She had married the father of her girls, was studying to become a dental hygienist, and was planning to apply for citizenship. Her daughters were learning to read and speak in Spanish and English, and her long-term plan was to continue with college courses. "After my release," she explained, "I was mad and tough because I had no family. Now I wanna do it for my kids and for me. I get so mad when I see young people who don't wanna work and study, who don't think about the future and waste their time. I tell them, 'Learn, Go to work. There are so many opportunities here!'"

I met Modesto and Veronica in early June 2011 in Worcester, Massachusetts. They had found one another after their placement in foster families in the same Lutheran Social Services program. Modesto was excited about starting his freshman year that fall at Leslie University. He borrowed a phrase from a TV ad—"a body in motion tends to stay in motion"—to describe the exceptional journey he had made from an indigenous Quiché-speaking community in Guatemala to matriculation as an education major in an American university. He finished one year of college, but when Veronica got pregnant he "prioritized his family life" and went to work full-time to provide for his baby daughter and Veronica.

Modesto was working at FedEx for $8.50 an hour when he met an immigrant making good money as an interpreter for a private translation company. As one of only a few Quiché speakers with excellent English skills in the United States, he became certified as an interpreter and was soon making an excellent living as a freelancer with private clients and immigration courts. He liked the work because it allowed him to travel all over the country and to interpret for all kinds of cases, including for kids in detention. "I am on the other side now. I have to translate what they say, I can't comment. I can't tell them what to do. I just interpret. But I can clarify things for minors to help them out, say, to reunify with a family or to go with a foster family."

Modesto planned to become a citizen as soon as he was eligible in 2015 and to teach his daughter English as her first language. He had returned to Guatemala to meet his wife's parents for the first time and to visit his elderly father. He supported his father and sent money to his siblings but also considered his foster parents in Massachusetts family. "I am their son, and my daughter is their granddaughter," he told me. He planned to go back to college and was considering an interpreter program offered by Boston University. Near the end of our conversation he insisted:

> This interpreter job is not the end. It is just the beginning. I plan to go forward. My real dream is to become an attorney. I really like immigration law. I can relate it to my own experience. I want to give something back, to represent young people at a low cost or for free. I have learned a lot about the law by watching attorneys in court. I can see how it works and I really want to help.

When I spoke with Ernesto in late 2013, his church had grown to fifty people and he was working every day "to be a better person and to get closer to God." He spoke only about his faith and desire to live a blameless life. He had no girlfriend or future plans, explaining that he had a very bad year. His U visa and work permit had expired, and he was thrown out of work for three months waiting for a twelve-month extension pending approval of his green card application. This added enormous pressure because "the bills don't care if you have a job or not." He was unable to send money to his mother, who was fighting to retain title to her house because lenders were demanding repayment of the loans she had taken out for his smuggling fees. Although his lawyer had assured him that his application was in order he wouldn't believe it until he held the green card in his hands. Until then he had to defer his dream of joining the air force and returning home to see his family.

MOVING FORWARD

When I asked the young people how they would change the immigration system if they could, they offered astute analyses of detention and the law. Modesto had a good experience at the border and in the shelter, but he felt that it was essential for young people to get appointed counsel and to shorten the time spent in detention. Commenting on immigration policy, he noted, "The only thing I know is that immigration is big business. Illegals are a big business. The people who run the private prisons make a lot of money. The longer they keep you in jail, the more money they make. . . . There are lots more deportations now. There were 38,000 Guatemalans deported last year [2012], and this year they are expecting to deport 50,000. There are also many minors coming to the U.S. from my country." He added, "It is a bit ironic since if there was no immigration system, no illegals, I wouldn't have a job!"[9]

Ángel remembered his first caseworker lecturing him about "crossing the border without papers and breaking the law." He said, "But if I had asked for their permission they would have said no. I had no choice because to survive I had to leave." Maribel too reflected critically on anti-immigrant bias.

> I understand the American point of view that it is unfair for immigrants to come here and to take advantage. They don't think immigrants have the right to get benefits when they weren't raised here and didn't pay taxes. But I would tell them that I came here to change my crazy life and to provide for my children. I wanted to come to a place with laws. People don't understand

what we suffer to get here. I had to leave my country and my mother because she couldn't help herself. But I can and I am strong.

Reflecting on what he had experienced, Ernesto said, "Once you realize that the rules are there to educate you it makes you a better person. When we are young we don't understand and we think things are against us. I know that there are people in the shelters who did bad things, but most of them are there to help. Here in the U.S. nobody can touch you. There are laws and rights. The attorneys are good and the judges are respectful." By 2013 Ernesto was less sanguine about his future. He had just returned to work and had not followed the debates on immigration reform. When I asked how he would improve government custody for minors, he advised "the government to give each kid a Bible." Six years after entering the country he was still waiting for his legal status to be resolved and teetering on the edge of despondency.

When I asked Maribel what advice she would give to new migrants she didn't hesitate.

Don't be too scared to change. You may cry and want to go back to your country, but stay, be independent, and work hard. You have opportunities here. Don't throw them away. Don't live like you are back in your home country. Your children will be born here and they will make their life here. I can see my whole life in my past and in my present and I am accomplishing my dream.

On October 29, 2013, Georgetown University alumna Sen. Dick Durbin returned to campus to speak about immigration reform. He was introduced by Kim, the Georgetown undergraduate and DACA recipient discussed in chapter 1. She thanked him for fighting for immigration reform "for me, my family, and my community." Durbin related the sad case of Juan Gomez, an undocumented Georgetown undergraduate. In the 1990s Gomez's parents had traveled from Colombia to the United States on tourist visas with their two young children, Juan and his older brother, and fought unsuccessfully for asylum. The appeal process dragged on for years as they grew up and excelled in school. In 2007 ICE agents conducted a surprise raid on their Miami home and detained the entire family, ultimately deporting the parents. Thanks to the advocacy on the brothers' behalf, Democratic senator Christopher Dodd introduced a private bill requesting a review of the case. ICE officials temporarily deferred their removal orders, and Juan received a full scholarship to Georgetown University, graduating Magna Cum Laude from the business school in 2011. With a six-figure position at J.P.

Morgan and a temporary work permit, Juan "was living the American Dream in New York." But the dream collapsed in May 2013. With a DACA application still pending, the firm could not renew his work permit. Juan accepted a lucrative offer from a Brazilian investment firm and left the United States without ever being able to return. This cautionary tale, Durbin explained, illustrates the need for comprehensive immigration reform.

Immigration reform stalled in 2013 and the Congress recessed for five weeks in August 2014 without taking action on the administration's request for funds to address the humanitarian crisis involving thousands of young migrants. Several legislative proposals were introduced that would modify current immigration law by applying the same legal standards to all unaccompanied children. These proposals would shorten the time frame for deportation proceedings, expedite removal from the United States, limit judicial review of cases, end the possibility of reunification with family in the United States, and, the most extreme proposal by Rep. Jason Chaffetz, expressly bars the government from paying for counsel for aliens, keeps children in detention pending consideration of an asylum claim, and ends the special provisions under current asylum law for unaccompanied children.[10]

We should all ask ourselves if it makes sense to continue to prosecute and detain unsustainable numbers of unaccompanied minors, 61,340 in 2014, almost 90 percent of whom will be released to families already living in the United States. Who does it benefit if we spend hundreds of millions of dollars to inform them of their rights, to improve their mental and physical health, and to teach them English only to put them in removal proceedings and cut them loose with minimal or no services after their release? Why build insurmountable hurdles to legal status and deny them the opportunity for legal work? Wouldn't it be in our best interest to welcome young people like Juan Gomez, Citlalli Alvarez, Kim Maima, and Francisco Gutierrez who grew up in the United States and were educated in our finest universities? Why shouldn't we protect all young people who escape violence and work hard to realize the tantalizing promise of the American Dream?

Appendix

RESEARCH METHODS

I combined five years of on-site ethnographic fieldwork with in-depth archival research on the identification, treatment, and representation of Unaccompanied Alien Children in the United States. The ethnographic portion of the research involved on-site visits to twenty federal facilities at all security levels in eight states and to six federal foster care programs in five states; observation of 120 hours of master calendar and merit proceedings in fifteen federal immigration courts; and attendance at a variety of public and private events related to unaccompanied, undocumented minors. I conducted 140 in-depth interviews with immigration authorities, a designation that refers to the people who currently work or have worked in the federal custodial system. This includes thirty-one sitting and retired immigration judges as well as 109 federal staff working under contract to ORR, including facility/program directors, case managers, clinicians, floor staff, immigration attorneys, accredited representatives, and law school students; advocates affiliated with nongovernmental social and legal service providers and community organizations; and outside experts on refugee populations. I conducted on-site focus groups and/or individual interviews—in person and by telephone—with (1) social workers in the SAFE Haven program, which was administered by Lutheran Immigrant and Refugee Services and under contract to ORR until September 30, 2010, in Arizona, California, Florida, Illinois, and Texas; (2) professional staff in six nonprofit organizations that operated short- or long-term federal foster care programs for minors released from ORR custody in Phoenix, Arizona; Grand Rapids and Lansing, Michigan; Richmond Virginia; Tacoma, Washington; and Worcester, Massachusetts; and (3) foster parents in Phoenix, Arizona; Worcester, Massachusetts; Tacoma, Washington; and Virginia. I also interviewed forty formerly detained young adults, thirty-eight of whom had obtained legal status and were building lives in this country.

In the shelters and in the foster care programs, I observed case review meetings, intake interviews, legal orientation presentations, and shelter classrooms. I conducted semidirected interviews and spoke informally with a range of staff members, including directors, clinicians, case managers, teachers, youth care workers, and kitchen staff. At the immigration court I observed intake screenings of detained minors as well as master calendar and merit hearings and interviewed court staff, detention officers, and judges. The president and vice president of the immigration judges' union, Dana Leigh Marks and Denise Noonan Slavin respectively, granted in-depth interviews and shared their publications on evolving immigration law and policy as well as the challenges facing judges. Chief Immigration Judge Brian O'Leary met with me in 2009 and approved my request to observe immigration court proceedings in 2009. Judge O'Leary made it clear that immigration judges could not speak to outsiders and that any requests for information on courtroom proceedings, policy, or adjudicators should be addressed to the Office of Public Affairs at the Executive Office for Immigration Review. Nonetheless, a number of senior sitting judges agreed to interviews on the condition that their names remain confidential.

I attended numerous events focusing on unaccompanied, undocumented minors, including public briefings, eight stakeholder conferences between 2008 and 2012, and student-organized events on behalf of would-be Dreamers. I attended a training session for LIRS social workers in April 2009, and in June 2009 I led a workshop on unaccompanied children with funding from the Radcliffe Institute for Advanced Study at Harvard University. The workshop was intended to bring together two populations—academics and practitioners—with similar interests but little professional contact. Over a three-day period social scientists, immigration attorneys, legal scholars, immigration judges, and service providers shared research findings, practitioner expertise, best practices, and recommendations on improving custodial care, facilitating access to legal representation, and protecting minors' rights in detention and in immigration court. The journal *International Migration* published workshop findings in an article written by immigration attorney Aryah Somers with critical commentaries by anthropologist Elizabeth Krause, child psychiatrist Stuart Lustig, sociologist Cecilia Menjívar, and former director of Children's Services at LIRS, Olivia Faries. Finally, I audited an Immigration Law and Policy course at Georgetown Law School taught by my colleague, Andy Schoenholtz, in order to better understand how attorneys are trained in immigration law and policy.

The archival component of my research included examining material on the history and evolution of immigration law, policy, and courts in the Executive Office for Immigration Review; the system of detention for unaccompanied, undocumented children in the United States; the migration of Mexican and Central American immigrants in the postwar period; and the representation of unauthorized immigration in scholarly publications, popular culture, mainstream media and blogs, think tanks, NGO reports and websites, political speeches at public events, and the advocacy efforts on behalf of this population by public and private stakeholders.

ACCESS AND CONFIDENTIALITY

In order to gain access to closed federal facilities and the staff who worked in them I submitted a detailed research plan in 2009 to the director of the Division of Children's Services at ORR, who approved the number, timing, and duration of the visits I made to federal facilities between September 2009 and the May 2011. The director, project officers at the Washington, DC, headquarters, and managerial staff introduced me to local staff and provided statistics on admissions, bed space, type of facility, and release. Access was premised on the condition that I not identify the name or specific location of any of the closed federal facilities where children were detained. In the book I have identified only the city and state of the facility. The one exception was NORCOR in The Dalles, Oregon. I contacted the director of the facility and received his authorization to visit and interview staff in October 2010 after ORR had terminated the contract with NORCOR. I visited six foster care programs from January 2011 to March 2012 with the assistance of staff from USCCB and LIRS.

My requests for permission to interview federal field specialists and the director of the Division of Children's Services and the director of ORR were denied or ignored. One ORR administrator explained off the record that in the context of intense scrutiny of the federal custodial system by public agencies such as the Office of the Inspector General, the Congressional Research Service, NGOs, professional associations, and academics, as well as ongoing lawsuits alleging abuse of children in federal custody, FFS personnel were not permitted to speak to the press or to academics. However, one FFS whom I met agreed to a short telephone interview and five FFS's spoke informally with me during on-site visits. All of the staff members I interviewed requested anonymity in order to be able to speak frankly about the methods for evaluating behavior and assessing risk and the practices that identify qualified sponsors and govern release.

I refer to federal staff only by their job titles but include the security level of the facility and in some cases relevant biographical information to provide the context needed to interpret their statements. Most immigration attorneys also requested that their names not be used because of their contractual relationship with the government through the Unaccompanied Children's Program at the Vera Institute of Justice. Oren Root, director of the Unaccompanied Children's Program at the Vera Institute of Justice, would not allow me to attend national stakeholder meetings. I note that even attorneys who no longer worked in the Vera Institute program insisted on anonymity, fearing unspecified repercussions. Only one attorney who had worked in the Vera Institute's Unaccompanied Children's Program in 2009–10, Nikki Dreyden, agreed to be quoted by name.

It was difficult to locate young adults after their release from detention because there is no comprehensive process to track minors after release. The directors of Unaccompanied Refugee Minor programs, who placed minors in foster care or independent living arrangements, and KIND attorneys were particularly helpful in connecting me with potential interviewees. I worked only through front-line service providers and immigration attorneys to identify young people who were willing to share their stories with me. To protect their privacy I have changed their names and identifying characteristics. Only one young man, Modesto Antonio Boton-Rodriguez, indicated that I could quote him by name.

Notes

CHAPTER 1

1. www.durbin.senate.gov/DREAMERS, accessed January 30, 2012.
2. www.cbp.gov/newsroom/stats/southwest-border-unaccompanied-children.
3. www.cnn.com/2014/07/02/us/california-immigrant-transfers.
4. www.chron.com/news/houston-texas/houston/article/League-City-seeks-to-ban-undocumented-children-5607794.php.
5. Frydman, Dallam, and Bookey 2014; UNHCR 2014: 4.
6. Brané, cited in Gordon 2014; McKenna 2014; see also Young 2014.
7. Robles 2014.
8. Frankel 2011; Somers et al. 2010a.
9. Terrio 2009.
10. Adams [1931] 1947: 374.
11. Ibid.
12. Mitt Romney, nomination speech, PBS, August 30, 2012.
13. Barack Obama, nomination speech, PBS, September 6, 2012.
14. Saulny 2012.
15. Mitt Romney, nomination speech, PBS, August 30, 2012.
16. Matt Barreto, interview, *Race 2012*, PBS, October 16, 2012.
17. Ngai 2004: 3.
18. Ibid., 7–8.
19. Ibid., 4.
20. Arendt [1951] 1966.
21. Schrag 2011: 118.
22. Ibid., 124–25.
23. Ngai 2004: 259.
24. De Genova 2002.
25. Sen 2012.

26. Chavez 2008.

27. Rich Benjamin, interview, *Race 2012*, PBS, October 16, 2012.

28. Huntington 2004: 45.

29. Steve King, interview, *Newsmax,* July 23, 2013.

30. U.S. Customs and Border Protection 2014.

31. See Agamben 2005.

32. Flores v. Meese 934 F. 2d 991, 994 (9th Cir. 1990).

33. Flores v. Meese, No. CV 85–4544-RJK (Px) (C.D. Cal. July 11, 1985).

34. Reno v. Flores 507 U.S. 292 (1993).

35. Flores v. Meese No. CV 85–4544-RJK (Px), at 6, 7 (C.D. Cal. Filed Jan. 17, 1997) (stipulated settlement agreement).

36. Office of Refugee Resettlement briefing on detention and removal, Institute for the Study of International Migration Roundtable, October 6, 2014.

37. Staff figures indicate only administrators and managers, not local staff in shelters, treatment facilities, detention centers, or group homes under contract to the government. Administrators of the Division of Children's Services within the Office of Refugee Resettlement gave these statistics in a Power Point presentation at the 2010 annual meeting for ORR staff and service providers (Author's files).

38. U.S. Department of Health and Human Services, Administration for Children and Families, Office of Refugee Resettlement, Division of Children's Services, *Statistics on Operation,* 2012, 2013.

39. UAC Program Facility Contact Information, External List, *Houston Chronicle* FOIA request to ORR, October 2, 2013.

40. McKenna 2014; UAC Briefing to Appropriators, HHS, DHS, DOJ, DOS, OMB, April 22, 2014.

41. USCCB, email communication, December 2, 2014.

42. Krogstad, Gonzalez-Barrera, and Lopez 2014.

43. U.S. Customs and Border Protection 2014.

44. Only 8 percent of minors in federal detention in 2012 were Mexican. In 2013 that number dropped to 3 percent. U.S. Department of Health and Human Services, Administration for Children and Families, Office of Refugee Resettlement, Division of Children's Services 2012, 2013.

45. Contracted facilities are located in Arizona, California, Florida, Illinois, Massachusetts, Michigan, New Jersey, New York, Oregon, Pennsylvania, Texas, Virginia, and Washington. In 2014 the government has been scrambling to open additional shelters, numbering 114 as of September 30, 2014, and housing young migrants in temporary facilities on military bases in California, Oklahoma, and Texas.

46. This is the reason ORR administrators cited for withholding basic statistics on the type and location of facilities and the average length of custody. This rule is applied inconsistently as some academics and advocates are provided information that journalists can only obtain by submitting Freedom of Information Access requests.

47. Office of Refugee Resettlement Provisional Policy and Procedures Manual 2008.

48. Agamben 2005; see also Fassin 2005: 382.
49. See Heidbrink 2014: 15–20 for a critical discussion of children's agency.
50. Thronson 2006.
51. Semple 2014, A11; 79 Fed. Reg. 62159 (October 16, 2014).
52. Thronson 2006.
53. Fassin 2005; Redfield 2005.
54. Agamben 2005.
55. Ibid.
56. Bhabha 2014: 11.
57. Lancaster 2010: 63.
58. Welch 2012: 19–21.
59. De Genova 2002.
60. Peutz and DeGenova 2010: 23.
61. NYU School of Law and New York Civil Liberties Union 2011.
62. Carbado and Crenshaw 2013.
63. Kanstroom 2007: x. The subhead, "Deportation Nation," is taken from the title of Kanstroom's book. See also De Genova and Peutz 2010.
64. Wessler 2012.
65. Meissner et al. 2013.
66. Gupta 2013: A21.
67. Meissner et al. 2013: 8.
68. Ibid., 9.
69. Rosenblum and Meissner 2014: 1.
70. *TRAC Immigration Reports,* ICE, Prosecutorial Discretion Program, June 28, 2012. http://trac.syr.edu/immigration/reports/287/.
71. White House Press Secretary, November 19, 2014. www.whitehouse.gov /the-press-office/2014/11/20/fact-sheet-immigration-accountability-executive-action.
72. www.wilsoncenter.org/event/dreamers.

CHAPTER 2

1. Thanks to the efforts of Ms. Cammisa, Kevin found an attorney and won asylum in January 2011.
2. www.acf.hhs.gov/programs/orr/programs/ucs, accessed June 12, 2014.
3. The interview sample comprises 40 young adults over the age of eighteen, 13 girls and 27 boys. Fourteen came from Guatemala, eighteen from Honduras, three from Ecuador, three from El Salvador, one from Brazil, and one from Mexico. All had been in the United States for at least two years; one remained without legal status, and the other has been returned to Brazil. One of the young women I interviewed was born in the United States to Honduran parents and was a U.S. citizen. All but one of the names have been changed.
4. Ward 2004.
5. Adams 2012: 12.
6. World Bank 2011: 7.
7. Adams 2012: 22.
8. Vigh 2006.

9. Coutin 2005.

10. USCCB 2014.

11. Stoll 2013.

12. *Cachuco,* which translates as "dirty pig," is a derogatory term used for Central Americans in Mexico.

13. Vogt 2013: 765.

14. Ibid.

15. Given the increase in CBP arrests along the Southwest border in 2011, then-secretary of DHS, Janet Napolitano, pressed Mexico's president, Enrique Peña Nieto, to secure its southern border (Archibald 2013).

16. Urrea 2004: 60.

17. Heymann 2011: 7.

18. The 2000 election of Vicente Fox inaugurated a new era of "unprecedented bilateral action by Mexico and the US to fortify the border with personnel and surveillance technology" (Priest 2013: A12).

19. Urrea 2004: 62–63.

20. Ibid.

21. Andreas 1998.

22. Cave 2013: 33; Priest 2013.

23. Vogt 2013: 776.

24. Adams 2012: 22.

25. Ibid., 29.

26. Anderson 2013: 1–2; see also "Bodies Pile up in Texas as Immigrants Adopt New Routes over Border," *New York Times,* September 23, 2013, A12.

27. The number of Mexican children who were apprehended after crossing the border without papers went from 13,000 in fiscal year 2011 to 15,709 in 2012 and reached 18,754 in 2013 (UNHCR 2014: 5).

28. UNHCR 2014: 6–7.

29. Cavendish and Cortazar 2011.

30. The coyote may accept part of the smuggling fee up front, with the balance to be paid upon a successful crossing. If, as was the case with Ángel, the migrant cannot pay, the debt must be paid off on the U.S. side of the border (Cavendish and Cortazar 2011:14).

31. Byrne and Miller 2012: 11. All but five of the interviewees were caught within one week of crossing the border, and most were apprehended within hours.

32. Ibid., 4.

33. No More Deaths/No Mas Muertes 2011: 4.

34. American Immigration Council, National Immigration Project, Northwest Immigrant Rights Project, and ACLU of San Diego and Imperial Counties 2013.

35. The OIG report specified that the Office of Border Patrol (OBP) policy required medical assistance to be provided to the individuals *they* identified as in need of attention (OIG 2010: 12). The report identified "the biggest gap" as the training of CBP agents, saying "We were unable to determine whether all CBP employees who are responsible for handling UACs have the sufficient training to do so" (21).

36. Michelle Brané, telephone interview with author, April 30, 2013.

37. Woman's Refugee Commission 2012: 22–23.

38. An Arizona attorney describes the Border Patrol as an "occupying army" because of illegal stops and searches, bullying treatment and excessive use of force (Lyall 2014).

39. National Immigrant Justice Center et al. 2014.

40. Carroll 2014.

41. The OIG made unannounced visits to CBP facilities housing unaccompanied children on July 1–16, 2014, and published a report on July 30, 2014, indicating that in terms of infrastructure the facilities were largely in compliance with the Flores Settlement Agreement requirements (Roth 2014).

42. Woman's Refugee Commission 2012: 14.

43. In 2011 and 2012 the CBP allowed the WRC access only to selected stations and consistently denied interviews with detained children for monitoring purposes. In contrast, ORR and ICE provided relatively open access to WRC attorneys until 2012 (Woman's Refugee Commission 2012: 21).

44. Ibid., 23. Beginning in 2013 ORR no longer permitted NGO monitors access to closed detention facilities.

45. See Stephen 2007: 224–25.

46. Chavez 2008.

47. Stephens 1995: 11–13.

48. Chavez 2008: 2–3.

49. The Illegal Immigration Reform and Immigrant Responsibility Act and the Antiterrorism and Effective Death Penalty Act.

50. Meissner et al. 2013; Rosenblum and Meissner 2014.

51. Fassin 2005; Ticktin 2011; Terrio 2008. See also Uehling 2008.

52. Napolitano 2013.

53. Shear 2013: A1, A9.

54. See the account of Mark Lyttle, a diabetic who has spent much of his adult life in mental institutions, jails, and group homes (Finnegan 2013); and District Court for Eastern District of New York, *American Immigration Council*, March 8, 2013. In 2011 CBP agents at Dulles airport outside Washington, DC, detained a four-year-old girl with a U.S. passport who was returning from vacation in Guatemala with her grandfather. CBP agents held her for more than twenty hours without adequate food or drink and chose to deport her to Guatemala rather than release her to "illegal" parents.

CHAPTER 3

1. Flores v. Reno, No. CV 85-4544-RJK (Px), at 7 (C.D. Cal. Filed Jan. 17, 1997) (stipulated settlement agreement). The agreement was reached in 1996 and implemented in 1997.

2. Ibid., 6, 7.

3. Bhabha and Schmidt 2006: 46 n. 17.

4. At that time, the Community Relations Service (CRS), an agency within the Department of Justice and distinct from the INS, was responsible for the care and placement of unaccompanied children who entered the United States

without authorization. In 1996 the CRS was absorbed into the INS, which became the custodian and prosecutor of unaccompanied children detained while crossing the border or within the interior of the country (Bhabha and Schmidt 2006: 38).

5. Flores v. Meese 934 F. 2d 991, 994 (9th Cir. 1990).

6. The private corporations that operated detention facilities under contract to the INS and were named in the lawsuit were Behavioral Systems Southwest in Pasadena, California, and the Corrections Corporation of America in Laredo, Texas. Flores v. Meese, No. CV 85–4544-RJK (Px), at 1 (C.D. Cal. July 11, 1985).

7. Ibid., 3.

8. Zatz and Smith 2012; Zilberg 2011: 30–35.

9. Flores v. Meese, No. CV 85–4544-RJK (Px), at 16 (C.D. Cal. July 11, 1985). There were a number of squalid detention facilities in Texas and California where detainees were "fenced into shacks, tents, and make-shift shelters deemed more dangerous and less habitable than those used for Japanese Americans during World War II (Olivas 1990: 3)."

10. Carlos Holguin, telephone interview by author, May 22, 2013.

11. Flores v. Meese, 681 F.Supp. 665 (C.D. Cal. 1988). The lawsuit argued that routine strip searches violated the Fourth Amendment prohibition against unreasonable searches and seizures. In two earlier cases the district courts found that the INS had deprived unaccompanied minors of their right to full hearings and other due process rights. In *Perez-Funez* the court had enjoined the INS from employing threats, misrepresentations, subterfuge, or other forms of coercion. Perez-Funez v. INS, 619 F.Supp. 656, 670 (C.D. Cal. 1985). The judge in *Orantes-Hernandez v. Meese* also found "a persistent pattern of misconduct, use of intimidation, threats and misrepresentation," and evidence of widespread abuse of detainees. Orantes-Hernandez v. Meese, 685 F.Supp. 1488, 1504–5 (C.D. Cal. 1988).

12. Flores v. Meese, No. CV 85–4544-RJK (Px) (C.D. Cal. July 11, 1985).

13. Ibid., 4.

14. Ibid.

15. Flores v. Meese, No. CV 85–4544-RJK (Px), at 24–28 (C.D. Cal. July 11, 1985).

16. Flores v. Meese, 942 F.2d 1352, 1355 (9th Cir. 1991). Beginning in the mid-1980s there was a rapid influx into California of youths from El Salvador, Nicaragua, Guatemala, and Honduras who were seeking family members already in the United States. In 1990 alone the INS apprehended 8,500 undocumented children, 70 percent of whom were unaccompanied and in their mid-teens (National Immigration Center 502 U.S. 183, 1991 at 9, n. 12).

17. Holguin, interview.

18. Flores v. Meese, 942 F.2d 1352, 1355 (9th Cir. 1991).

19. Ibid., 1356.

20. Flores v. Meese, 942 F.2d 1352 (9th Cir. 1991) *rev'd sub nom.* Reno v. Flores, 507 U.S. 292, 113 S. Ct. 1439, 123 L. Ed. 2d 1 (1993).

21. The class consisted of all "aliens under the age of 18 who are detained by the INS Western District because a parent or legal guardian fails to personally appear to take custody of them."

22. See the Memorandum of Understanding Re Compromise of Class Action: Conditions of Detention, Flores v. Meese, No. 85–4544-RJK (Px), (C.D. Cal. Nov. 30, 1987) (referred to as the "Juvenile Care Agreement").

23. 53 Fed. Reg. 17449 (May 17, 1988).

24. Flores v. Meese, 934 F.2d 991, 1014 (9th Cir. 1990).

25. Flores v. Meese, 942 F.2d 1352, 1365 (9th Cir. 1991). Initially a divided panel of the court of appeals reversed the district court in Flores v. Meese, 934 F.2d 991 (9th Cir. 1990). The Ninth Circuit voted to rehear the case and selected an eleven-judge en banc court. That court vacated the panel opinion and affirmed the district court order. Flores v. Meese 942 F. 2d 1352, 1365 9th Cir. 1991).

26. While affirming the legality of detention, the Court remanded the case to the district court for resolution of the plaintiff's complaint. The parties reached the FSA in 1996 before the court could issue a final ruling.

27. Flores v. Meese, 942 F.2d 1352, 1362 (9th Cir. 1991).

28. Bersani 1992: 873.

29. Flores v. Meese, 942 F.2d 1359 (9th Cir. 1991).

30. Yick Wo v. Hopkins, 118 U.S. 356, 374, 6 S.Ct, 30 L.Ed. 220 (1886).

31. Flores v. Meese, 942 F.2d 1352, 1359 (9th Cir. 1991) *rev'd sub nom.* Reno v. Flores, 507 U.S. 292, 113 S. Ct. 1439, 123 L.Ed. 2d 1 (1993) (citing Wong Wing v. United States, 163 U.S. 228, 229, 16 S. Ct. 977, 978, 41 L. Ed. 140 (1896)).

32. Flores v. Meese, 942 F.2d 1352, 1360 (9th Cir. 1991).

33. Ibid., 1362.

34. Ibid., 1378; original emphasis.

35. Ibid., 1380.

36. Ibid., 1381.

37. Ibid., 1365; original emphasis.

38. "The Fourteenth Amendment of the Constitution is not confined to the protection of citizens. . . . These provisions are universal in their application, to all persons within the territorial jurisdiction, without regard to any differences of race, of color, or of nationality; and the equal protection of the laws is a pledge of the protection of equal laws. . . . [I]n our system, while sovereign powers are delegated to the agencies of government, sovereignty itself remains with the people, by whom and for whom all government exists and acts."

39. Flores v. Meese, 942 F.2d 1352, 1366 (9th Cir. 1991).

40. Ibid., 1370.

41. Reno v. Flores, 507 U.S. 292 (1993).

42. Ibid., 305–6.

43. Reno v. Flores, 507 U.S. 292, 302 (1993).

44. Ibid., 309.

45. Ibid., 322.

46. Justice Stevens referred to Section 242(a) of the Immigration and National Act providing that any "alien taken into custody may, at the discretion of the Attorney General and pending (a) final determination of deportability, (A) be continued in custody; or (B) be released under bond . . . .containing such conditions as the Attorney General may prescribe; or (C) be released on conditional parole. 8 U.S.C. § 1252 (a)(1)."

47. Reno v. Flores, 507 U.S. 292, 333 (1993).

48. Ibid., 337.

49. Ibid., 341.

50. Flores v. Meese, 942 F.2d 1352, 1355 (9th Cir. 1991) (en banc), rev'd 113, S.Ct. (1993).

51. Ibid., 1361.

52. It also accorded with the Federal Juvenile Delinquency Act, which specifies that detention, if necessary, should be in a "foster home or community-based facility" instead of an institution. Flores v. Meese, 942 F.2d 1352, 1361 (9th Cir. 1991).

53. Ibid., 1383.

54. Flores v. Meese, 934 F.2d 991, 1023 (9th Cir. 1991) (Fletcher, J., dissenting).

55. Flores v. Meese, 942 F.2d 1352, 1370 (9th Cir. 1991).

56. Ibid., 1375.

57. Reno v. Flores, 507 U.S. 292, 294 (1993).

58. Ibid., 295.

59. Ibid., 301.

60. Ibid.

61. Ibid..

62. Ibid., 298.

63. Flores v. Meese, 942 F.2d 1352, 1362 (9th Cir. 1991).

64. Ibid., 1362.

65. Ibid., 1364.

66. Ibid., 1363.

67. Reno v. Flores, 507 U.S. 292, 304 (1993).

68. Ibid., 305.

69. Ibid., 329.

70. Ibid., 327–28.

71. Holguin, telephone interview by author.

72. Flores v. Reno, No. CV 85–4544-RJK (Px), at 7, 9 (C.D. Cal. Filed Jan. 17, 1997).

73. Ibid., 7.

74. Ibid., 13, 21.

75. Women's Refugee Commission 2012.

76. Flores v. Reno, No. CV 85–4544-RJK (Px), at 16–17 (C.D. Cal. Filed Jan. 17, 1997).

77. Ibid.

78. OIG 2001.

79. It would have created the Office of Children's Services independent from the INS and provided government-appointed counsel to unaccompanied minors, in addition to incorporating the best interest of the child standard. Unaccompanied Alien Child Protection Act of 2000, S. 3117, 106th Cong. (2000).

80. Senate Subcommittee on Immigration, Senate Committee on the Judiciary, Hearing 107–867: 1–3 (2002) (statement of Sen. Edward Kennedy).

81. Although the original bill never became law, a substitute amendment passed by the Senate in November 2003 downgraded the provision for govern-

ment-funded counsel in the original bill to pro bono representation only. This was a political calculation intended to head off the opposition sponsors expected from their fellow senators (Young 2005, quoted in Bhabha and Schmidt 2005: 49).

82. Senate Subcommittee on Immigration, Senate Committee on the Judiciary, Hearing 107–867: 34–49 (2002) (statement of Wendy Young).

83. Senate Subcommittee on Immigration, Senate Committee on the Judiciary, Hearing 107–867: 28 (2002) (statement of Edwin Larios Munoz).

84. Ibid.

85. Compare the 2001 report by the Office of the Inspector General.

86. Senate Subcommittee on Immigration, Senate Committee on the Judiciary, Hearing 107–867: 31 (2002) (statement of Wendy Young).

87. The NGO changed its name to the Women's Refugee Commission.

88. Women's Commission for Refugee Women and Children 2002.

89. Senate Subcommittee on Immigration, Senate Committee on the Judiciary, Hearing 107–867: 16 (2002) (statement of Stuart Anderson).

90. Senate Subcommittee on Immigration, Senate Committee on the Judiciary, Hearing 107–867: 20 (2002) (testimony of Judge Michael Creppy).

91. The INS guidelines that preceded the TVPRA of 2008 are still in effect. They state that while the best interests of the child principle is a "useful measure for determining appropriate interview procedures for child asylum seekers," it can play no role in "determining substantive eligibility under the U.S. refugee definition" (Weiss 1998).

92. Center for Human Rights and Constitutional Law, Latham and Watkins, and National Center for Youth Law 2003.

93. These include immigrants' and children's rights organizations, practitioners, legal scholars, and the U.S. Office of the Inspector General.

94. Somers is wary of the enormous power of a bureaucratic behemoth like the Department of Homeland Security to influence an evolving custodial system without legislative oversight or procedural safeguards (Somers et al. 2010a: 353).

95. In late 2011 the name was changed to the Division of Children's Services.

96. The TVPRA introduced several major advancements in the processing of children's asylum cases. First, it permitted unaccompanied alien children to initiate their asylum claims in a nonadversarial proceeding before the Asylum Office of the United States Citizenship and Immigration Services. Second, it exempted unaccompanied alien children from safe third country agreements, assuring that children could not be required to return to the last safe country through which they traveled and to submit their asylum petition there. Third, it improved the age determination process by ending the sole reliance on X-rays and requiring that multiple forms of evidence be considered as part of a comprehensive assessment (Bhabha and Schmidt 2011).

97. Currently only one child advocate program exists, the Immigrant Child Advocacy Project, directed by Maria Woltjen and housed at the Young Center at the University of Chicago. The project recruits, trains, and supervises advocates assigned to children who are detained in Chicago-area ORR centers and also operates a small pilot program in Harlingen, Texas.

98. William Wilberforce Trafficking Victims Protection Reauthorization Act of 2008, Pub. L. 110–457, 122 Stat., at 377 (2008).

99. Center for Human Rights and Constitutional Law, Latham and Watkins, and National Center for Youth Law 2003: 5.

100. Bhabha and Schmidt 2006: 39.

101. Byrne and Miller 2012: 6.

102. Young and McKenna 2010: 251.

103. Office of Refugee Resettlement, 2010 Annual Conference, Powerpoint Presentation.

104. Office of Refugee Resettlement, Statistics on Operation, 2012 and 2013.

105. ORR Briefing on detention and removal to the Institute for the Study of International Migration Roundtable, October 6, 2014, Washington, DC

106. Bhabha and Schmidt 2006: 3; Byrne and Miller 2012: 5.

107. ORR Briefing on detention and removal to the Institute for the Study of International Migration Roundtable, October 6, 2014, Washington, DC.

108. USCCB, an ORR service provider, reported this figure for 2014 (email communication, December 2, 2014). In response to a request for 2014 data on total admissions, ORR administrator Elaine Kelley reported that "57,496 children were in care in 2014 in approximately 110 sites, at all levels" (email communication, December 5, 2014).

109. Somers 2010a: 353.

110. Bhabha and Schmidt 2006: 40.

111. Ibid., 33.

112. Haddal 2007.

113. Women's Commission for Refugee Women and Children 2009.

114. Young and McKenna 2010: 253; see also Frankel 2011.

115. Weiss 1998.

116. Young and McKenna 2010: 252.

117. Byrne and Miller 2012: 24. The Vera Institute estimates that a much higher proportion of children—70 percent—whose cases conclude while they are in ORR custody received legal representation. However, the majority of those cases resulted in removal orders or voluntary departure.

118. The government inspectors outlined the criteria for holding minors in a secure facility: they were charged or are chargeable with criminal or delinquent actions; they committed or threatened to commit violence; their conduct in (low-security) shelter care becomes unacceptably disruptive; they present an escape risk; or they pose a danger to themselves. The least restrictive care provision of the FSA required the transfer of youths who did not meet the secure detention requirements to a licensed shelter within a period of 3 to 5 days (OIG 2001).

119. Interviews at NORCOR, October 22, 2010, with the director, Jeff Justesen, and staff.

120. Ibid.

121. Three Lutheran Immigration and Refugee Services social workers (district field coordinators [DFCs]) under contract to ORR and attorneys from the Vera-contracted legal service provider in Portland, OR.

122. According to Jeff Justesen, ORR regional personnel provided limited monitoring and little regulatory guidance. Justesen insisted that NORCOR procedures had been misrepresented in the complaints regarding detention conditions by Vera Institute attorneys, DFCs, and NGO advocates. In his view the problems resulted from conflicting federal and state regulations. Oregon permitted shackling and strip searches of detained domestic juveniles, whereas the federal requirements under the FSA precluded manual restraints. Jeff Justesen, interview by author, October 22, 2010.

123. Unaccompanied Children's Program, Vera Institute, attorney, Nikki Dryden, telephone interview by author, November 6, 2010, and in-person interview by author, New Orleans, LA, November 20, 2010; DFC, telephone interview by author, September 3, 2010.

124. Nikki Dryden, telephone interview, November 6, 2010.

125. The immigration lawyer and legal scholar David Cole cites Moynihan in his editorial in the *Washington Post,* February 10, 2013, B2.

126. Bhabha and Schmidt 2006: 34.

127. Wendy Young, telephone interview by author, June 6, 2013.

128. Theodoredis 1994–95: 433.

129. Carroll 2014.

130. Lopez 2012.

131. Baum, Kamhi, and Russell 2012: 622.

132. Somers 2010a.

133. Frankel 2011: 82.

134. Kanstroom 2007: 46–63.

135. Ibid., 5–6.

CHAPTER 4

1. Haddal 2007.

2. Homeland Security Act of 2002, 462(g)(2).

3. The original study by Greulich and Pyle dates to the 1930s and was based on a sample of upper-middle-class white youth. It did not account for ethnic or class variation or for diet and child rearing practices that result in differences in skeletal development.

4. Heidbrink 2014: 125–26.

5. Women's Commission for Refugee Women and Children 2009: 7.

6. A small percentage of children are placed in transitional foster care. Children under thirteen, pregnant and parenting teens, and those with special needs are given priority for short-term placement with foster families (Byrne and Miller 2012: 14). In 2012 transitional foster care beds comprised only 5.8 percent of total ORR beds.

7. This new placement tool was introduced in the 2009 federal fiscal year and was announced at a national stakeholder meeting on November 3, 2009, in Washington, DC. The tool was used in the ORR facilities I visited in 2010, and an amended version was incorporated into the ORR operations manual in 2012. I had access to two ORR provisional policy manuals, both written in 2008 and neither made public. I quote from the version that was distributed for

comment to the NGO subcontractors at the annual ORR conference held in San Diego, CA, in 2008. Both are identical in substance, but the ORR conference manual includes longer narrative sections. I also quote from September 1, 2010, amendments to the provisional policy manuals that were provided to federal staff and sent to me by a confidential source.

8. The initial placements of children in high-security facilities as well as placements in medium-security facilities based on a borderline score of 6–7 were subject to mandatory review within thirty days. This review, the Further Assessment Swift Track, or FAST, was intended to address the problem of lengthy stays in restricted facilities by evaluating the possibility for a transfer to a less secure setting.

9. Young and McKenna 2010: 251.

10. Lisa Raffonelli, ORR communications liaison, provided data on 2013 total admissions by type of facility but declined to update the 2012 data she had provided on the number and distribution of funded beds by state.

11. Byrne and Miller 2012: 13–15.

12. All federal facilities were operated by private contractors and licensed by the state, Lisa Raffonelli, personal communication, May 21, 2013.

13. Women's Refugee Commission 2012: 18.

14. Site visit, Los Fresnos, TX, March 8, 2010.

15. Office of Refugee Resettlement Provisional Policy and Procedures Manual 2008: 37.

16. Ibid.

17. Somers 2010a: 339–40, 349–50.

18. Ariès 1962; Bluebond-Langner and Korbin 2007; Le Vine 2007; Stephens 1995; Terrio 2008.

19. Office of Refugee Resettlement Provisional Policy and Procedures Manual 2008: 48.

20. Ibid., 24–25.

21. Bluebond-Langner and Korbin 2007; Scheper-Hughes and Sargent 1998; Somers 2010a: 349–50.

22. Office of Refugee Resettlement Provisional Policy and Procedures Manual 2008: 75.

23. The Division of Children's Services (DCS) was formerly known by the acronym, DUCS, or Division of Unaccompanied Children's Services. It was changed in 2011.

24. Greta Uehling, a national program coordinator for a Washington-based nonprofit organization under contract to ORR, reported this case (2008: 848–49). She interviewed thirty children.

25. Site visit, Harlingen, TX, March 9, 2010.

26. In 2008 ORR awarded a $1.8 million grant to the Latino Health Institute to implement the Trauma Initiative, a thirty-month project to augment the delivery of trauma services to youths in custody (Women's Commission for Refugee Women and Children 2009: 17).

27. Interview by author, Harlingen, TX, March 9, 2010.

28. Interview by author, on-site visit, Phoenix, AZ, January 13, 2010.

29. Office of Refugee Resettlement, Division of Children's Services, 2010; Power Point presentation, ORR conference (April), author's files.

30. Byrne and Miller 2012; Frankel 2011: 81.

31. Carroll 2014.

32. Texas Standards Violations in ORR facilities, data obtained through a Freedom of Information Request and shared by Susan Carroll, journalist at the *Houston Chronicle*, June 15, 2014.

33. The forty-one-year-old shelter worker, Belinda Leal, was convicted of child abuse and sentenced on state charges to a seven-year prison term. FBI agents went to the Nixon facility to investigate the allegations. But federal prosecutors ultimately determined that they lacked jurisdiction to charge Leal with sexual abuse under federal law because it applies only to inmates in federal facilities, not to underage children in federal care (Susan Watson, telephone interview by author, April 1, 2011).

34. Susan Watson, an attorney at Texas Rio Grande Legal Aid, represented Ernesto. ORR first contracted with the Nixon facility in 2003. The staff were locally recruited, were minimally educated, and had no experience or training in child welfare approaches. Initially, the shelter had no full-time therapist and no state-licensed director. ORR did not assign a FFS to monitor shelter operations until after 2006, one year before a whistleblower reported the abuse. Serious problems arose in part because over a very short period the shelter capacity increased from 16 to 136 beds (Susan Watson, interview by author, April 1, 2011).

35. Illegal Immigration Reform and Immigrant Responsibility Act of 1996.

36. Frankel 2011: 68–69.

37. Resistance to federal and state enforcement programs has increased over the past few years. Fearing lawsuits, sheriffs around the country have started to refuse to honor ICE detainers on undocumented immigrants (Medina 2014). The Obama administration's November 19, 2014, executive order eliminates the secure communities program encouraging enforcement partnerships (www.whitehouse.gov/the-press-office/2014/11/20/fact-sheet-immigration-accountability-executive-action).

38. ICE, *Civil Immigration Enforcement: Priorities for the Apprehension, Detention, and Removal of Aliens* 2011.

39. ORR Placement Tool, rev. February 28, 2012.

40. Frankel 2011: 71.

41. Interview by author, RAICES, San Antonio, TX, March 11, 2010.

42. Interview by author, Portland, OR, October 20, 2010.

43. Interviews by author, on-site visit, Brownsville, TX, March 8, 2010.

44. Interview by author, on-site visit, Portland, OR, October 20, 2010.

45. Interview by author, on-site visit, Chicago, IL, June 2, 2010.

46. C. J. Toole, telephone interview by author, October 29, 2010.

47. Case managers, interview by author, on-site visit, Staunton, VA, May 18, 2011.

48. C. J. Toole, telephone interview by author, October 29, 2010.

49. This facility had just opened a therapeutic staff-secure unit.

50. Interview by author, on-site visit, Brownsville, TX, March 8, 2010

51. Judith Reifsteck, interview by author, on-site, Staunton, VA, May 18, 2011.

52. Jason Skeens, interview by author, on-site, Staunton, VA, May 18, 2011.

53. Judith Reifsteck, interview, May 18, 2011.

54. Case managers, interview, May 18, 2011.

55. Ibid.

56. Judith Reifsteck, interview, May 18, 2011.

57. Attorney, interview by author, October 20, 2010.

58. See Frankel 2011; Somers 2010a.

CHAPTER 5

1. In 2010 the long-standing tension over the role of SAFE Haven social workers as critical monitors of transfer and release decisions within the ORR system came to a head. On May 27, 2010, the president and CEO of LIRS, the Baltimore-based NGO that operated the SAFE Haven field coordination program, announced the decision to end their subcontractor relationship with ORR. In a letter to stakeholders, she cited the "inadequate weight" given by ORR to LIRS staff recommendations and the "failure to ensure that decisions regarding care and release are consistently grounded in children's best interests" (Author's files).

2. Foucault 1982, 1997.

3. Interview by author, on-site visit, San Antonio, TX, March 11, 2010.

4. Office of Refugee Resettlement Provisional Policy and Procedures Manual 2008: 37.

5. Ibid.

6. Interview by author, on-site visit, Miami, FL, September 25, 2009.

7. Ibid.

8. Interview by author, Houston, TX, March 5, 2010.

9. Interview by author, on-site visit, Harlingen, TX, March 9, 2010.

10. Interview by author, on-site visit, Phoenix, AZ, January 14, 2010.

11. Interview by author, Miami, FL, September 25, 2009.

12. Interview by author, Harlingen, TX, March 9, 2010.

13. Office of Refugee Resettlement Provisional Policy and Procedures Manual 2008: 79–80.

14. Interview by author, on-site visit, Phoenix, AZ, January 13, 2010.

15. Interview by author, San Antonio, TX, March 11, 2010.

16. Interview by author, Phoenix, AZ, January 13, 2010.

17. Interview by author, San Antonio, TX, March 11, 2010.

18. Interview by author, Phoenix, AZ, January 14, 2010.

19. Interviews by author, Phoenix, AZ, March 8, 9, 2011.

20. Interview by author, on-site visit, Chicago, IL, June 2, 2010.

21. Quotations are from facility staff members and DFCs in the seven staffing meetings I attended in 2010: two facilities in Phoenix, one in Chicago, one in San Antonio, three in Southern California, and one in Harlingen.

22. Castenada and Buck 2012.

23. Interview by author, on-site visit, Worcester, MA, June 13, 2011; and see the account of attachment therapies in Stryker 2010.

24. Interview by author, San Antonio, TX, March 11, 2010.

25. Interviews by author, SAFE Haven office, Houston, TX, March 5, 2010.

26. Interview by author, San Antonio, TX, March 11, 2010.

27. See also Heidbrink 2014: 121–22.

28. Interview by author, Phoenix, AZ, January 13, 2010.

29. Interview by author, Georgetown University, March 2, 2011.

30. Office of Refugee Resettlement Provisional Policy and Procedures Manual 2008: 24.

31. Heidbrink 2014: 125.

32. Women's Commission for Refugee Women and Children 2009: 21.

33. OIG 2008: 13.

34. Office of Refugee Resettlement Provisional Policy and Procedures Manual 2008: 56.

35. Interview by author, San Antonio, TX, March 11, 2010.

36. Interviews by author, on-site visit, Portland, OR, October 20, 2010.

37. Interviews by author, Phoenix, AZ, January 14, 2010.

38. Women's Commission for Refugee Women and Children 2009: 16.

39. The Women's Commission for Refugee Women and Children reported that "the level of monitoring conducted by federal field specialists is "inconsistent, unclear, and does not appear to allow for substantive review" (2009: 34).

40. Interview by author, Catholic Charities, Richmond, VA, March 21, 2011.

41. Email communication with Carlita's case manager, Estelle Junod, October 17, 2013; and interview, Anita Prasad, Commonwealth Catholic Charities program director, Richmond, VA, March 21, 2011.

42. Office of Refugee Resettlement Provisional Policy and Procedures Manual 2008: 11–12.

43. A *Houston Chronicle* investigation of SIRs between 2011 and 2013 revealed disturbing reports of sexual contact between children and staff in ORR facilities in Texas, Florida, New York, and Illinois and corroborated cases of children in Texas who were molested, sexually harassed, and assaulted. The *Chronicle* also discovered that cases routinely fell apart after law enforcement was involved (Carroll 2014).

44. This additional detail was provided in a version of the ORR Policy and Procedures Manual provided to the Women's Refugee Commission in 2008 in section 1.03 on p. 19.

45. Interviews by author, SAFE Haven offices, Harlingen, TX, March 8, 2010.

46. Interviews by author, SAFE Haven offices, Houston, TX, March 5, 2010.

47. Ibid.

48. Ibid.

49. Placement: Transfers Memo, ORR/DUCS Transition Procedures Review, September 1, 2010.

50. A step up from a shelter involves an increased emphasis on security for undocumented minors who are evaluated as likely threats and/or potential

offenders. Supervision is upgraded from line-of-sight checks at 15- or 30-minute intervals in low-security shelters to "constant line-of-sight and sound" monitoring by staff. Additional precautions include outdoor recreation within a secure perimeter, "no-climb fences," increased client to staff ratios, and restraints during transportation to and from court proceedings (Office of Refugee Resettlement Provisional Policy and Procedures Manual 2008: 41).

51. Interview by author, SAFE Haven offices, Houston, TX, March 5, 2010.

52. Interview by author, SAFE Haven offices, Miami, FL, September 25, 2009.

53. Interviews by author, Chicago, IL, June 2, 2010.

54. Interview by author, Georgetown University, March 2011.

55. Interview by author, Seattle, WA, March 7, 2012.

56. Interviews by author, SAFE Haven offices, Harlingen, TX, March 8, 2010.

57. Interview by author, on-site visit, San Diego, CA, July 13, 2010.

58. Interview by author, SAFE Haven offices, Miami, FL, September 25, 2009.

59. Ibid.

60. Interview by author, Seattle, WA, March 7, 2012.

61. Ibid.

62. Office of Refugee Resettlement, Statistics on Operation, 2012.

63. Interview by author, San Diego, CA, July 14, 2010.

64. Telephone interviews by author, September 9 and 19, 2010.

65. Interview by author, Phoenix, AZ, March 7, 2011.

66. Gozdziak 2010: 171.

67. Perry 2013.

CHAPTER 6

1. Uehling 2008: 848.

2. Byrne and Miller 2012: 18.

3. LIRS 2010: 7–12.

4. Byrne and Miller 2012: 19.

5. On-site visit, Phoenix, AZ, January 13, 2010.

6. Interviews by author, SAFE Haven office, Phoenix, AZ, January 13, 2010.

7. The TVPRA requires an assessment of the suitability of a proposed sponsor in four situations: when the child is a victim of a severe form of trafficking; when the child has a disability; when the child has been the victim of physical or sexual abuse; or when the proposed sponsor is deemed to present a risk of the abuse, maltreatment, exploitation, or trafficking of the child (TVPRA, sec. 235(c)(3)(B)).

8. LIRS 2010: 7–12.

9. Ibid., 11.

10. The program operated only ten beds in part because of the higher per diem costs per child and unique requirements imposed on short-term foster families. One family member had to be a full-time, stay-at-home parent, speak the child's language, complete extensive training, coordinate closely with case

management, receive a new arrival day or night, and provide 24/7 monitoring of the child.

11. Dana Mercz, interview by author, Phoenix, AZ, March 7, 2011.

12. Immigration attorney Angie Junck reported that probation officers routinely referred juveniles to ICE. In fact, San Mateo County, where this teenager lived, was second only to Orange County in California in the high number of referrals of juveniles to ICE officials according to statistics obtained by Immigrant Legal Resource Center from the Office of Refugee Resettlement (Junck, email, April 11, 2012).

13. Dana Mercz, interview, March 7, 2011.

14. Clinician, interview by author, Phoenix, AZ, March 8, 2011. Postrelease follow-up services continue for only six months or until the child's eighteenth birthday (LIRS 2010: 10).

15. Case manager, interview by author, Phoenix, AZ, March 8, 2011.

16. Email communication from attorney Joshua Lipshutz, June 7, 2013.

17. Case manager, telephone interview by author, June 10, 2011.

18. I conducted focus groups and/or interviewed staff members in six nonprofit organizations that operated short- or long-term federal foster care programs for minors released from ORR custody in Grand Rapids and Lansing, MI; Phoenix, AZ; Richmond, VA; Tacoma, WA; and Worcester, MA.

19. Clinician, interview by author, Worcester, MA, June 13, 2011.

20. Anita Prasad, interview by author, Richmond, VA, February 3, 2011.

21. Case manager, interview by author, Richmond, VA, February 3, 2011.

22. Lead case manager, interview by author, Worcester, MA, June 13, 2011.

23. Heidbrink (2014: 100–101) notes that in one case an FFS based his decision to exclude a recommendation for foster care on information that a detained youth had disclosed in confidence to a facility clinician about sniffing inhalants and negotiating with gangs while living on the street.

24. Interviews by author, Phoenix, AZ, March 7, 2011.

25. Case manager, interview by author, Richmond, VA, February 3, 2011.

26. Anita Prasad, interview by author, Richmond, VA, February 3, 2011.

27. Program director, interview by author, Grand Rapids, MI, November 3, 2011.

28. Anita Prasad, interview by author, Richmond, VA, February 3, 2011.

29. *Plyer v. Doe;* see Olivas 2012: 19–22.

30. Program director, interview by author, Worcester, MA, June 13, 2011.

31. Interviews by author, Richmond, VA, February 3, 2011.

32. Program director, interview by author, Lansing, MI, November 2, 2011.

33. SIJS is a visa available to children in care due to abuse, neglect, or abandonment who could not, as a best interest determination, return to their home country. See chapter 7.

34. Bhabha and Schmidt 2006: 52–53.

35. Uehling 2008: 845.

36. U.S. Department of Health and Human Services, Administration for Children and Families, Office of Refugee Resettlement, Division of Children's Services 2013.

37. Krogstad, Gonzalez-Barrera, and Lopez 2014.

38. U.S. Department of Health and Human Services, Administration for Children and Families, Office of Refugee Resettlement, Division of Children's Services 2013.

39. Byrne and Miller 2012: 16.

40. Stakeholder Meeting, Washington, DC, December 12, 2013.

41. ORR Senate-Testimony-HHS Acting Secy Greenberg-2014–07–09.pdf.

42. Telephone interview by author, December 19, 2013.

43. Berger, Fox News, December 19, 2013, www.foxnews.com/politics/2013/12/19/judge-claims-dhs-parents-smuggle.

44. Anna Ciesielski, telephone interview by author, January 9, 2014.

45. Nazario 2013; Wessler 2011.

46. C. J. Toole, telephone interview by author, October 29, 2010.

CHAPTER 7

1. The Young Center at the University of Chicago, directed by attorney Maria Woltjen, is the sole child advocacy program in the United States making child advocate assignments to children in Chicago and Harlingen, Texas.

2. Thronson 2006.

3. Nugent 2005–6: 219.

4. Bhabha 2006: 210.

5. Thronson 2010–11: 400–401.

6. In 2014 attorneys interviewing Central American families detained in Artesia, New Mexico, reported that children were being "piggybacked" onto a parent's asylum claim. Children who could have petitioned for asylum if they were unaccompanied were denied that opportunity if the parent was deemed not to have a credible fear of persecution. Child Immigration Listserve posting, July 16, 2014.

7. Scott and Steinberg 2003.

8. Memo, from Neal 2007.

9. See Human Rights Watch and ACLU 2010.

10. Ibid., 5–6.

11. Keener and Slavin 2002.

12. Ibid.

13. Marks 2012: 27.

14. Between 2009 and 2012 I interviewed thirty-one immigration judges. I quote by name only judges who were retired or who spoke as representatives of their union, the National Association of Immigration Judges. I respected the wishes of retired judges who did not want to be identified.

15. Judge Harry Gastley, telephone interview by author, August 3, 2011.

16. Judge Chris Grant, telephone interview by author, April 3, 2009.

17. Judge 6, interview by author, March 19, 2010; and Judge 20, telephone interview by author, October 27, 2009.

18. Of the 59 immigration courts nationwide, only 25 had specialized juvenile dockets in 2013. Of that number, 8 courts held hearings for nondetained minors, 8 for detained minors, and 9 for detained as well as nondetained minors (Executive Office of Immigration Review, Juvenile Docket Data, 2013).

19. Judge 4, telephone interview by author, June 11, 2009; Judge 9, telephone interview by author, March 26, 2009; and Judge 22, telephone interview by author, November 28, 2009.

20. Judge 23, interview by author, January 15, 2010.

21. Judge 9, telephone interview by author.

22. Judge 4, telephone interview by author.

23. Judge 25, telephone interview by author, August 5, 2011.

24. Judge 20, telephone interview by author, October 27, 2009.

25. Judge 4, telephone interview by author.

26. Judge 23, interview by author.

27. Judge 9, telephone interview by author.

28. Judge 27, interview by author, July 16, 2010.

29. Judge Grant, telephone interview by author.

30. Lustig et al. 2008: 29.

31. Hernandez 2010.

32. Confidential letter, December 8, 2009, to Immigration Judge Lorraine Muñoz, Julianne Donnelly, Esperanza Immigrant Rights Project, Catholic Charities of Los Angeles, Inc.

33. Attorney, interview by author, July 16, 2010.

34. Judge 9, telephone interview by author.

35. Lustig et al. 2008.

36. Ibid., 30–31.

37. Judges Gastley and Grant and Judge 4, telephone interviews; Judge Dana Marks, March 16, 2009; and Judge Denise Slavin, telephone interviews by author, March 24, 2009.

38. Judge 4, telephone interview by author.

39. In 2010 only 28 percent of detained children served by the ORR/Vera Institute Legal Access Project received direct or pro bono representation (Byrne and Miller 2012: 24).

40. Ibid., 23.

41. EOIR is developing guidelines for Friend of Court best practices. A draft document reminds parties appearing in this role that they have no authority to admit factual allegations, enter pleadings, seek relief (including voluntary departure), or seek appeal on behalf of the respondent. Confidential draft document, "Using the Friend of the Court Model for Unaccompanied Minors and Respondents with Indicia of Mental Incompetence" (EOIR 2013: 2).

42. Judge 2, interview by author, October 20, 2010.

43. Attorney, interview by author, October 21, 2010.

44. Attorney, interview by author, July 16, 2010.

45. Marks and Slavin 2012: 111.

46. Voluntary departure allows the child to reenter the United States lawfully after one year if he or she can obtain a visa.

47. EOIR 2012: Q1.

48. Nikki Dryden, telephone interview by author, November 6, 2010.

49. Before the 2008 passage of the TVPRA, a child granted voluntary departure was statutorily required to have the funds necessary to pay for his repatriation and

could be required to post bond. These requirements disqualified many children (INA 240B9a), 8 USC 1229c(a), 8 CFR 240.25).

50. Nikki Dryden, telephone interview by author, November 6, 2010.

51. "The concept of the best interest of the child does not negate the statute or the regulatory delegation of the Attorney General's authority and cannot provide a basis for providing relief not sanctioned by the law" (Memorandum from David L. Neal, May 22, 2007).

52. Judge 2, interview by author, October 20, 2010.

53. Ibid.

54. Master calendar hearing, October 21, 2010.

55. Attorney, interview by author, October 21, 2010.

56. Master calendar hearing, April 29, 2009.

57. Lloyd 2006: 238.

58. Ibid.

59. Baum, Kamhi, and Russell 2012.

60. Lloyd 2006: 258.

61. Bhabha and Schmidt 2006.

62. Perez-Olano v. Chertoff, 248 F.R.D. (C.D. Cal, 2008).

63. Immigrant Legal Resource Center 2010.

64. This occurred in cases pursued in social service departments, in Baltimore County, Maryland; Cook County, Illinois; or Westchester County, New York (Baum, Kahmi, and Russell 2012).

65. Baum, Kahmi, and Russell 2012: 624–25.

66. Ibid.

67. Bhabha and Schmidt 2011.

68. A *New York Times* investigation documented the brutal treatment of mentally ill inmates at the Riker's Island jail where attacks by officers have been commonplace and perpetrators are rarely prosecuted (Winerip and Schwartz 2014).

69. Confidential legal file; interviews by author, May 10, 2011; October 28, 2013.

70. Case manager, telephone interview, June 3, 2011.

71. See the SIJS case rejected by a Chicago state court (Heidbrink 2014: 102–8).

72. Foster mother, interview by author, June 10, 2011.

73. Confidential dependency order, Juvenile and Domestic Relations Court, May 18, 2009.

74. Marks and Slavin 2012.

75. Human Rights Watch and ACLU 2010: 6–7.

76. Ibid., 13.

77. Jackson 2012.

78. Foster mother, interview by author, June 10, 2011.

79. Mehta 2011.

80. Judge 25, telephone interview by author, August 5, 2011.

81. Young and McKenna 2010: 253–54.

82. Matter of Acosta, 19 I & N Dec. 211 (BIA 1985).

83. In re C-A, 23 I & N Dec. 951 (BIA 2006).

84. Matter of M-E-V-G, 26 I & N Dec. 227 (BIA 2014).

85. Matter of W-G-R, 26 I & N Dec. 208 (BIA 2014).

86. Jenkins (2009: 68) notes that, in contrast to the successful litigation of the rights of transgender and transsexual individuals in U.S. state courts, there is a dearth of case law recognizing transgender asylum applicants in immigration courts.

87. Hazeldean 2011–12: 382.

88. Morgan 2006: 150.

89. Hazeldean 2011–12: 377–78.

90. Ranji-Nogales, Schoenholtz, and Schrag 2007.

91. http://trac.syr.edy/immigration/reports/judgesreports/.

92. Tobaso-Alfonso, 20 I. & N. Dec. 819 (B.I.A. 1990).

93. Jenkins 2009: 75.

94. Benson 2008–9.

95. Good 2007.

96. Christopher Nugent, personal communication, June 18, 2009.

97. Carrier 1995; Lancaster 1998; Paz 1961.

98. The 1996 passage of the Illegal Immigration Reform and Immigrant Responsibility Act changed asylum law by requiring, for the first time, that asylum applications be submitted within one year of arrival in the United States. The asylum regulations finalized in 2000 include two categories of exceptions to the one-year ruling, "changed circumstances" or "exceptional circumstances." They also specifically mention the arrival of an unaccompanied minor as an example of the "extraordinary circumstances" exception to the one-year deadline (Neilson and Morris 2005: 255–56). Harsh restrictions on eligibility criteria essentially foreclosed relief for "untold numbers of otherwise eligible and deserving asylum seekers" (234).

99. "Asylum Officer Basic Training Manual" 2009.

100. Morgan 2006: 154–55.

101. The pervasive "pronoun problem" refers to adjudicators who refuse to use the pronoun that corresponds to the individual's gender identity (Benson 2008–9: 62).

102. Cardosa-Fonseca, 480 U.S. 421 (1987), establishes that if there is a 1 in 10 chance that the respondent faces persecution this is the standard to grant.

103. The judge also held that Cecilia qualified for the additional benefit of withholding of removal. Whereas the grant of asylum is discretionary, the finding of withholding of removal is mandatory and involves a higher legal standard, holding that there must be a clear probability of persecution.

104. Southam 2011: 1379.

105. Ferguson 2001; Terrio 2009.

106. Hazeldean 2011–12: 401–10.

107. Graythorn, Glad and Goldstein 2009. Available at http://appleseednetwork.org/wp-content/uploads/2012/05/Assembly-Line-Injustice-Blueprint-to-Reform-Americas-Immigration-Courts1.pdf.

108. *TRAC Immigration Reports,* July 10, 2014, trac.syr.edu/whatsnew/email.140710.html.

109. Judge 4, telephone interview by author.

110. Ibid.

111. Bhabha and Schmidt 2011: 20.

112. Morgenthau 2013.

113. Ranji-Nogales, Schoenholtz, and Schrag 2007.

114. Graythorn, Glad, and Goldstein 2009: 1. Available at http://appleseed-network.org/wp-content/uploads/2012/05/Assembly-Line-Injustice-Blueprint-to-Reform-Americas-Immigration-Courts1.pdf.

115. Ibid., Acknowledgments.

CHAPTER 8

1. Personal communication, September 4, 2012.

2. This optimism was reflected in a Washington Post–Miller Center poll conducted with Hispanics in September 2013. The results showed that Hispanic Americans are more likely to embrace the American Dream than other minorities (Constable and Clement 2014: A1, A8).

3. See Gozdziak 2010 on migrant girls who were trafficked.

4. Bob Larkin, interview by author, Virginia Home for Boys and Girls, March 21, 2011; and telephone interview by author, June 27, 2012.

5. Hartigan 2010: 150–52.

6. Stephen 2007.

7. Harding 2000: 34–39.

8. Ibid., 38.

9. Modesto Boton-Rodriguez, telephone interview by author, November 4, 2013.

10. See H.R. 5137, Asylum Reform and Border Protection Act of 2014, www.congress.gov/bill/113th-congress/house-bill/5137.

Acronyms and Abbreviations

BP	Customs and Border Protection's Border Patrol: charged with patrolling the U.S. border between ports of entry and enforcing U.S. immigration and customs laws.
CBP	Customs and Border Protection
DCS	Division of Children's Services, formerly Division of Unaccompanied Children's Services
DFC	District field coordinator: social worker in the SAFE Haven program administered by Lutheran Immigration and Refugee Services and under contract to ORR to provide screening and prepare the release of detained children until September 30, 2010.
DHS	Department of Homeland Security
EOIR	Executive Office for Immigration Review
FFS	Federal field specialist: regional ORR supervisor
FOC	Friend of the Court: an attorney who speaks on behalf of the minor in court but does not act as the attorney of record
FSA	Flores Settlement Agreement
HHS	Department of Health and Human Services
HSA	Homeland Security Act of 2002
INS	Immigration and Naturalization Service, prior to HSA of 2002
ICE	Immigration and Customs Enforcement (Division of Homeland Security)
INA	Immigration and Nationality Act

KYR   Know Your Rights

LIRS   Lutheran Immigration and Refugee Services

NTA   Notice to Appear: notice initiating removal proceedings in immigration court

ORR   Office of Refugee Resettlement

SIJS   Special Immigrant Juvenile Status: a visa designed for children under eighteen who have been abused, abandoned, or neglected by one or both parents in the home country.

TVPRA   William Wilberforce Trafficking Victims Protection and Reauthorization Act of 2008

UAC   Unaccompanied Alien Child

UNHCR   United Nations High Commissioner for Refugees

URM   Unaccompanied Refugee Minor

USCCB   United States Conference of Catholic Bishops

USCIS   U.S. Citizenship and Immigration Services

Bibliography

Adams, James Truslow. [1931] 1947. *The Epic of America.* New York: Blue Ribbon Books.

Adams, Tani Marilena. 2012. "Chronic Violence and Its Reproduction: Perverse Trends in Social Relations, Citizenship, and Democracy in Latin America." Latin American Program, Woodrow Wilson International Center for Scholars.

Agamben, Giorgio. 2005. *The State of Exception.* Trans. Kevin Attell. Chicago: University of Chicago Press.

Amnesty International. 2001. "Crimes of Hate, Conspiracy of Silence: Torture and Ill-Treatment Based on Sexual Identity." Available at www.amnesty.org/en/library/info/ACT40/016/2001. Accessed January 10, 2013.

———. 2003. "Unaccompanied Children in Immigration Detention" 1–2. Available at www.detentionwatchnetwork.org/node/286. Accessed December 1, 2012.

———. 2009. "Jailed without Justice: Immigration Detention in the USA." Available at www.amnestyuse.org/pdfs/JailedWithoutJustice/pdf. Accessed January 5, 2013.

Anderson, Stuart. 2013. "How Many More Deaths? The Moral Case for a Temporary Worker Program." NFAP Policy Brief, National Foundation for American Policy. 1–2 (March).

Andreas, Peter. 1998. "The Political Economy of Narco-Corruption in Mexico." *Current History* (April) 160–65.

Archibald, Randall. 2013. "In Trek North, First Lure Is Mexico's Other Line." *New York Times,* April 27, A1, A8.

Arendt, Hannah. [1951] 1966. *The Origins of Totalitarianism.* New York: Schocken Books.

Ariès, Philippe. 1962. *Centuries of Childhood: A Social History of Family Life.* Trans. R. Baldock. New York: Knopf.

Ashbrook, Tom. 2014. *On Point*. National Public Radio, June 9.

"Asylum Officer Basic Training Manual." U.S. Citizenship and Immigration Services–RAIO–Asylum Division. Rev. March 9, 2009. Available at www .uscis.gov. Accessed November 15, 2012.

Baum, Jennifer, Alison Kamhi, and C. Mario Russell. 2012. "The Most in Need and the Least Served." *Family Court Review* 50 (4): 621–28.

Benson, Christi Jo. 2008–9. "Crossing Borders: A Focus on Treatment of Transgender Individuals in U.S. Asylum Law and Society." *Whittier Law Review* 30: 41–66.

Berger, Judson. 2013. "Judge Claims DHS Delivering Smuggled Children to Illegal Parents." Available at www.foxnews.com/politics/2013/12/19/judge-claims-dhs-parents-smuggle. Accessed December 22, 2013.

Bersani, Michael G. 1992. "*Flores v. Meese*: Playing Hide and Seek with the Right to Physical Freedom—Children Teach the INS the ABC's of Due Process." *Syracuse Law Review* 43: 867–900.

Bhabha, Jacqueline. 2006. "Not a Sack of Potatoes: Moving and Removing Children across Borders." *Public Interest Law Journal* 15: 197–217.

———. 2014. *Child Migration and Human Rights in a Global Age*. Princeton: Princeton University Press.

Bhabha, Jacqueline, and Susan Schmidt. 2006. *Seeking Asylum Alone in the United States: Unaccompanied and Separated Children and Refugee Protection in the U.S.* Cambridge, MA: Human Rights at Harvard.

———. 2007a. "Kafka's Kids: Children in U.S. Immigration Proceedings: Part I: Seeking Asylum Alone." *Immigration Briefings* 07–01(1).

———. 2007b. "Kafka's Kids: Children in U.S. Immigration Proceedings: Part II: Beyond and Besides Asylum." *Immigration Briefings* 07–02(1).

———. 2011. "From Kafka to Wilberforce: Is the U.S. Government's Approach to Child Migrants Improving?" *Immigration Briefings* 11–02.

Bluebond-Langner, Myra, and Jill Korbin, eds. 2007. "Challenges and Opportunities in the Anthropology of Childhood: An Introduction to Children, Childhoods, and Childhood Studies." *American Anthropologist* 109 (2): 241–46.

Boehm, Deborah A. 2012. *Intimate Migrations: Gender, Family, and Illegality among Transnational Mexicans*. New York: New York University Press.

Bonilla-Silva, Eduardo. 2006. *Racism without racists: Color-Blind Racism and the Persistence of Racial Inequality in the United States*. 2nd ed. Lanham, MD: Rowman and Littlefield.

Braune, Nick. 2008. "Interview, Border Lawyer for Undocumented Minors." *Texas Civil Rights Review*. Available at http://texascivilrightsreview.org /phpnuke/Modules.php?name=News&file=print&sid=1298. Accessed December 3, 2013.

Byrne, Olga. 2008. *Unaccompanied Children in the United States: A Literature Review*. New York: Vera Institute of Justice.

Byrne, Olga, and Elise Miller. 2012. *The Flow of Unaccompanied Children through the Immigration System: A Resource for Practitioners, Policy Makers, and Researchers*. Center on Immigration and Justice. New York: Vera Institute of Justice.

Capps, Randolph, et al. 2007. "Paying the Price: The Impact of Immigration Raids on America's Children." Urban Institute. Available at www.urban.org/publications/411566.html. Accessed March 16, 2013.

Carbado, Harris, and Kimberle Crenshaw. 2013. "Racial Profiling Lives On." *New York Times,* August 15, A21.

Carrier, Joseph. 1995. *De los otros: Intimacy and Homosexuality among Mexican Men.* New York: Columbia University Press.

Carroll, Susan. 2014. "Crossing Alone: Children Fleeing to U.S. Land in Shadowy System." *Houston Chronicle,* May 24 and 29. Available at www.houstonchronicle.com/ News/investigations/article/Crossing-alone-Children-fleeing-to-U-S-land-in-5503127.php. Accessed May 30, 2014.

Castenada, Ernesto, and Leslie Buck. 2012. "Addressing the Effects of Separation within Transnational Families." Paper presented at On Their Own: Unaccompanied Children National Conference, U.S. Committee for Refugees and Immigrants, April 25, 2012, Washington, DC.

Cave, Damien. 2013. "A Salvation Army of One." *New York Times Magazine,* April 21, 33.

———. 2014a. "An American Life Lived in the Shadows." *New York Times,* June 9. Available at www.nytimes.com/2014/06/09/us/for-illegal-immigrants-america/lifelived-in-shadows.html. Accessed June 11, 2014.

———. 2014b. "Complaints of Abuse by Border Agents Often Ignored, Records Show." *New York Times,* May 5. Available at www.nytimes.com/2014/05/06/Us/complaints-of-abuse-by-border-agents-often-ignored-records-show.html. Accessed June 7, 2011.

Cavendish, Betsy, and Maru Cortazar. 2011. "Children at the Border: The Screening, Protection and Repatriation of Unaccompanied Mexican Minors." Available at appleseednetwork.org/wp-Content/uploads/2012/05/Children-At-The-Border1.pdf. Accessed February 12, 2013.

Center for Human Rights and Constitutional Law, Latham and Watkins, and National Center for Youth Law. 2003. "Flores Status Report" (April 7), author's files.

Chaffetz, Jason. 2014. The Asylum Reform and Border Protection Act, H.R. 5137. Available at www.congress.gov/bill/113th-congress/house-bill/5137. Accessed July 30, 2014.

Chapparo, James M. 2010. "U.S. Immigration and Customs Enforcement, to Field Office Directors and Deputy Field Office Directors." U.S. Immigration and Customs Enforcement (February 22). Available at http://media.washingtonpost.com/wp-srv/politics/documents/ICEdocument032710.pdf. Accessed January 7, 2014.

Chavez, Leo R. 2008. *The Latino Threat: Constructing Immigrants, Citizens, and the Nation.* Stanford, CA: Stanford University Press.

Constable, Pamela, and Scott Clement. 2014. "Despite Hurdles, Hispanics Cling Tightly to American Dream." *Washington Post,* January 31, A1, A8.

Coutin, Susan Bibler. 2000. *Legalizing Moves: Salvadoran Immigrants' Struggle for U.S. Residency.* Ann Arbor: University of Michigan Press.

———. 2005. "Being en Route." *American Anthropologist* 107 (2): 195–206.

————. 2007. *Nation of Emigrants: Shifting Boundaries of Citizenship in El Salvador and the United States.* Ithaca, NY: Cornell University Press.

Crow, Melissa. 2013. "Groups File Legal Claims against Border Patrol in Abuse Cases." National Immigration Project, Northwest Immigrant Rights Project, ACLU of San Diego and Imperial Counties. Available at http://immigration-impact.com/2013/03/13/groups-file-legal-claims-against-border-patrol-in-abuse-cases/. Accessed October 20, 2013.

De Genova, Nicholas. 2002. "Migrant 'Illegality' and Deportability in Every-day Life." *Annual Review of Anthropology* 31: 419–47.

De Genova, Nicholas, and Natalie Peutz, eds. 2010. *The Deportation Regime: Sovereignty, Space, and the Freedom of Movement.* Durham, NC: Duke University Press.

Dow, Mark. 2004. *American Gulag: Inside U.S. Immigration Prisons.* Berkeley: University of California Press.

Dwyer, Jim. 2014. "A 12-Year-Old's Trek of Despair Ends in a Noose at the Border." *New York Times,* April 19. Available at www.nytimes.com/2014/04/20 /nyregion/a-12-year-olds-trek-of-despair-ends-in-a-noose-at-the-border.html. Accessed June 11, 2014.

Executive Office of Immigration Review (EOIR). 2012. *EOIR FY 2011 Statistical Yearbook.* Falls Church, VA: Office of Planning, Analysis, and Technology.

————. 2013. "Using the Friend of the Court Model for Unaccompanied Minors and Respondents with Indicia of Mental Incompetence." Draft document.

Fassin, Didier. 2005. "Compassion and Repression: The Moral Economy of Immigration Policies in France." *Cultural Anthropology* 20 (3): 362–87.

Ferguson, Ann Arnette. 2001. *Bad Boys: Public Schools in the Making of Black Masculinity.* Ann Arbor: University of Michigan Press.

Finnegan, William. 2013. "The Deportation Machine: A Citizen Trapped in the System." *New Yorker,* April 29, 24–29.

First Focus. 2013. "Immigration Reform and Implications for Children: An Analysis of Border Security, Economic Opportunity, and Immigration Modernization Act of 2013 (S.744)." April. Available at www.firstfocus.net /library/legislative-comparisons/immigration-reform-and-the-implications-for-children-and-families-an. Accessed January 20, 2014.

Foucault, Michel. 1982. "The Subject and the Power." In *Michel Foucault: Beyond Structuralism and Hermeneutics,* ed. Hubert L. Dreyfus and Paul Rabinow, 208–26. Brighton: Harvester.

————. 1997. "Security, Territory, and Population." In *Michel Foucault: Ethics, Subjectivity, and Truth,* ed. Paul Rabinow, 67–71. New York: New Press.

Frankel, Elizabeth M. 2011. "Detention and Deportation with Inadequate Due Process: The Devastating Consequences of Juvenile Involvement with Law Enforcement for Immigrant Children." *Duke Forum for Law and Social Change* 3: 63–107.

Frydman, Lisa, Elizabeth Dallam, and Blaine Bookey. 2014. "A Treacherous Journey: Child Migrants Navigating the U.S. Immigration System" (February). Center for Refugee Studies and Kids in Need of Defense. Available at www.uchastings.edu/centers/cgrsdocs/treacherous_journey_cgrs_kind_report.pdf. Accessed March 20, 2014.

Good, Anthony. 2007. *Anthropology and Expertise in the Asylum Courts.* London: Routledge/Clarendon.

Gordon, Ian. 2014. "70,000 Kids Will Show Up Alone at Our Border This Year: What Happens to Them?" *Mother Jones,* July–August. Available at www.motherjones.com/politics/2014/06/child-migrants-surge-unaccompanied-central-america. Accessed June 3, 2014.

Gorman, Erin Eileen. 1993. "*Reno v. Flores:* The INS' Automatic Detention Policy for Alien Children." *Georgia Immigration Law Journal* 7: 435–71.

Gozdziak, Elzbieta. 2010. "In the Best Interest of the Child: Perceptions, Responses, and Challenges in Providing Assistance to Trafficked Children in the United States." In *Children and Migration: At the Crossroads of Resiliency and Vulnerability,* ed. Maria Ensor and Elzbieta Gozdziak, 166–86. New York: Palgrave Macmillan.

Graythorn, Dennis, Daniel Glad, and Seth Goldstein. 2009. "Assembly Line Injustice: Blueprint to Reform America's Immigration Courts." *Appleseed.* Available at http://appleseednetwork.org/wp-content/uploads/2012/05/Assembly-Line-Injustice-Blueprint-to-Reform-Americas-Immigration-Courts1.pdf. Accessed January 20, 2013.

Greulich, William, and S. Idell Pyle. 1959. *Radiographic Atlas of Skeletal Development of the Hand and Wrist.* Stanford, CA: Stanford University Press.

"Guidelines for Children's Asylum Claims." December 10, 1998. Available at www.uscis.gov/files/pressrelease/ChildrensGuidelines121098.pdf. Accessed December 12, 2013.

Gupta, Vanita. 2013. "How to Really End Mass Incarceration." *New York Times,* August 15, A21.

Haddal, Chad C. 2007. "Unaccompanied Alien Children: Policies and Issues." Congressional Research Service Report for Congress. Available at www.rcusa.org/uploads/pdfs/CRS%20UAC%20Report%202007.pdf. Accessed August 15, 2010.

———. 2010. "Border Security: The Role of the U.S. Border Patrol." Congressional Research Service. Available at www.fas.org/sgp/crs/homesec/RL32562.pdf. Accessed February 6, 2013.

Harding, Susan Friend. 2000. *The Book of Jerry Falwell: Fundamentalist Language and Politics.* Princeton: Princeton University Press.

Hartigan, John, Jr. 2010. *Race in the 21st Century: Ethnographic Approaches.* New York: Oxford University Press.

Hazeldean, Susan. 2011–12. "Confounding Identities: The Paradox of LGBT Children under Asylum Law." *University of California, Davis Law Review* 45: 373–443.

Heidbrink, Lauren. 2014. *Migrant Youth, Transnational Families, and the State: Care and Contested Interests.* Philadelphia: University of Pennsylvania Press.

Hernandez, Sandra. 2010. "Complaints Targets Immigration Judge." *L.A. Daily Journal,* March 8.

Heymann, Josiah. 2011. "Drugs, Guns, and Money: Tackling the Real Threats to Border Security." Immigration Policy Center. Available at immigrationpolicy .org/sites/default/files/docs/Heyman_-_Drugs_Guns_and_Money_091211 .pdf. Accessed October 12, 2013.

Human Rights Watch and ACLU. 2010. *Deportation by Default: Mental Disability, Unfair Hearings and Indefinite Detention in the US Immigration System.* New York.

Huntington, Samuel P. 2004. "The Hispanic Challenge." *Foreign Policy* (March–April): 30–45.

Illegal Immigration Reform and Immigrant Responsibility Act of 1996. 1996. P.L. No. 104–208, 110 Stat. 3009–546.

Immigrant Legal Resource Center. 2010. "Practice Advisory: One Parent Special Immigrant Juvenile Status Claims." Available at www.immigrationadvocates.org/nonprofit/library/item.327648-Practice_Advisory_OneParent_ Special_ImmigrantJuvenileStatusClaims. Accessed January 3, 2011.

Jackson, Kristen. 2012. "Special Status Seekers." *Los Angeles Lawyer* (February): 20–26.

Jenkins, Ellen A. 2009. "Taking the Square Peg out of the Round Hole: Addressing the Misclassification of Transgendered Asylum Seekers." *Golden Gate University Law Review* 40 (1): 67–95.

Junck, Angie. 2012. "Special Immigrant Juvenile Visa: Relief for Neglected, Abused, and Abandoned Undocumented Children." *Juvenile and Family Court Journal* 63 (1): 48–62.

Kanstroom, Daniel. 2007. *Deportation Nation: Outsiders in American History.* Cambridge, MA: Harvard University Press.

Keener, Dana M., and Denise N. Slavin. 2002. "An Independent Immigration Court: An Idea Whose Time Has Come." Immigration Reform and the Reorganization of Homeland Defense. Hearing before the Subcommittee on Immigration of the Senate Judicairy Committee, 107th Cong.

Kennedy, Elizabeth. 2014. "No Childhood Here: Why Central American Children Are Fleeing Their Homes." American Immigration Council, July 1. Available at www.americanimmigrationcouncil.org/perspectives/no-childhood-here-why-central-american-children-are-fleeing-their-homes. Accessed July 12, 2014.

Kids in Need of Defense. 2013. "The Time Is Now: Understanding and Addressing the Protection of Immigrant Children Who Come Alone to the United States." Available at www.supportkind.org/en/about-us/resources. Accessed June 12, 2013.

Krogstad, Jens, Ana Gonzalez-Barrera, and Mark Lopez. 2014. "Children 12 and Under Are the Fastest Growing Group of Unaccompanied Minors at the U.S. Border." Available at www.pewresearch.org/fact-tank/2014/07/22/children-12-and-Under-are-fastest-growing-group-of-unaccompanied-minors-at-u-s-border/. Accessed July 24, 2014.

Kubrin, Charles E., Marjorie S. Zatz, and Ramiro Martinez Jr., eds. 2012. *Punishing Immigrants: Policy, Politics, and Injustice.* New York: New York University Press.

Lacayo, Elena A. 2010. "The Impact of Section 287(g) of the Immigration and Nationality Act on the Latino Community." Available at www.nclr.org /images/uploads/Publications/287gReportFinal.pdf. Accessed November, 1, 2013.

Lancaster, Roger. 1998. *Life Is Hard: Machismo, Danger, and the Intimacy of Power in Nicaragua.* Berkeley: University of California Press.

———. 2010. "Republic of Fear: The Rise of Punitive Governance in America." In *The Insecure American: How We Got Here and What We Should Do about It,* ed. Hugh Gusterson and Catherine Besteman, 63–76. Berkeley: University of California Press.

Lawyers Committee for Human Rights. 1990. *The Detention of Asylum Seekers in the United States: A Cruel and Questionable Policy.* New York: Lawyers Committee for Human Rights.

Le Vine, Robert A. 2007. "Ethnographic Studies of Childhood: A Historical Overview." *American Anthropologist* 109 (2): 246–60.

Lloyd, Angela. 2006. "Regulating Consent: Protecting Undocumented Immigrant Children from Their (Evil) Step-Uncle Sam, Or How to Ameliorate the Impact of the 1997 Amendments to the SIJ Law." *Public Interest Law Journal* 15: 237–61.

López, Rebeca M. 2012. "Codifying the Flores Settlement Agreement: Seeking to Protect Immigrant Children in U.S. Custody." *Marquette Law Review* 95: 1635–77.

Lustig, Stuart L., et al. 2008. "Burnout and Stress among United States Immigration Judges." *Bender's Immigration Bulletin* 13 (January 1): 22–36.

Lutheran Immigration and Refugee Services (LIRS). 2010. *Family Reunification Best Practices: A Guidance Manual for the Suitability Assessment Background Investigation Process.* Baltimore, MD.

Lyall, James. 2014. "The Constitution-Free Agency: How the Border Patrol Is Running and Making a Mockery of the Rule of Law." *Politico,* July 29. Available at www.politico.com/magazine/story/2014/07/border-patrol-constitution-free-agency-109375.html. Accessed August 4, 2014.

Markham, Lauren. 2013. "First the Fence, Then the System." *Virginia Quarterly Review* (Summer): 170–91.

Marks, Dana L. 2008. "An Urgent Priority: Why Congress Should Establish an Article I Immigration Court." *Bender's Immigration Bulletin* 13 (3): 3–21.

———. 2012. "Still a Legal 'Cinderella'? Why the Immigration Courts Remain an Ill-Treated Step-Child Today." *Federal Lawyer* (March): 25–33.

Marks, Dana L. and Denise N. Slavin. 2011. "Conflicting Roles of Immigration Judges: Do You Want Your case Heard by a 'Government Attorney' or by a 'Judge'?" *Bender's Immigration Bulletin* 16: 1785–92.

———. 2012. "A View through the Looking Glass: How Crimes Appear from the Immigration Court Perspective." *Fordham Law Journal.* Available at http://lawprofessors.typepad.com/files/a-view-through-the-looking-glass-fordham-urban-law-journal.pdf. Accessed January 22, 2013.

McKenna, Megan. 2014. "Report: U.S. Immigration System Failing Unaccompanied Children." *KIND* blog (February). Available at www.supportkind

.org/en/blog/810-report-us-immigration-system-failing-unaccompanied-children.

Medina, Jennifer. 2014. "Fearing Lawsuits, Sheriffs Balk at U.S. Request to Hold Noncitizens for Extra Time." *New York Times,* July 5. Available at http://nytims/1xwS2hD. Accessed July 5, 2014.

Mehta, Suketu. 2011. "Annals of Immigration: The Asylum Seeker." *New Yorker,* August 1, 32–37.

Meissner, Doris, et al. 2013. *Immigration Enforcement in the U.S.: The Rise of a Formidable Machinery.* Washington, DC: Migration Policy Institute.

Menjívar, Cecilia, and Daniel Kanstroom, eds. 2013. *Constructing Illegality in America: Immigrant Experiences, Critiques, and Resistance.* New York: Cambridge University Press.

Merjan, Armen. 2009. "A Guinean Refugee's Odyssey: In Re Jarno, the Biggest Asylum Case in U.S. History and What It Tells Us about Our Broken System." *Georgetown Immigration Law Journal* 23: 649–90.

Morgan, Deborah A. 2006. "Not Gay Enough for the Government: Racial and Sexual Stereotypes in Sexual Orientation Asylum Cases." *Law and Sexuality Review: Lesbian, Gay, Bisexual and Legal Issues* 15: 135–61.

Morgenthau, Robert. 2013. "A Plea to Carry out a Principled Immigration Policy." *New York Times,* December 4. Available at www.nytimes. com/2013/12/05/opinion/a-plea-to-carry-out-a-principled-immigration-policy.html?_r=0. Accessed January 24, 2014.

Nakamura, David, Jerry Marken, and Manuel Roig-Franken. 2014. "Obama Aides Were Warned of Brewing Border Crisis." *Washington Post,* July 19. Available at www.washingtonpost.com/politics/obama-aides-were-warned-of-brewing-border-crisis/2014/07/19/8b5d2282-0d1b-11e4-b8e5-d0de80767fc2_story.html. Accessed July 19, 2014.

Napolitano, Janet. 2013. Testimony, U.S. Senate Judiciary Committee. "Comprehensive Immigration Reform Legislation." April 19.

National Center for Border Security and Immigration, University of Texas at El Paso. 2014. Unaccompanied Alien Children Project. March 20. Available at http://ncbsi.utep.edu/documents/UAC%20Project%20Site%20Visits/UTEP%20NCBSI%20Final%20Report%20March%2020%202014.pdf. Accessed July 21, 2014.

National Immigrant Justice Center, Esperanza Immigrant Rights Project, Americans for Immigrant Justice, Florence Immigrant and Refugee Rights Project, and ACLU Border Litigation Project. 2014. "Systematic Abuse of Unaccompanied Immigrant Children by U.S. Customs and Border Protection." Available at FINAL_DHS_Complaint_re_CBP_Abuse_of_UICs_2014_06_11. Accessed June 11, 2014.

Nazario, Sonia. 2013. "The Heartache of an Immigrant Family." *New York Times,* October 15, A23.

Neal, David. 2007. Chief Immigration Judge, U.S. Department of Justice, Executive Office of Immigration Review. "Operating Policies and Procedures Memorandum 07–01: Guidelines for Immigration Court Cases Involving Unaccompanied Alien Children." May 22. Available at www.usdoj.gov /eoir/efoia/ocij/oppm07/07-01.pdf. Accessed March 1, 2010.

Neilson, Victoria, and Aaron Morris. 2005. "The Gay Bar: The Effect of the One-Year Filing Deadline on Lesbian, Gay, Bisexual, Transgender, and HIV-Positive Foreign Nationals Seeking Asylum or Withholding of Removal." *New York University Law Review* 8: 233–82.

Ngai, Mae. 2004. *Impossible Subjects: Illegal Aliens and the Making of Modern America*. Princeton: Princeton University Press.

No More Deaths/No Mas Muertes. 2011. "Culture of Cruelty: Abuse and Impunity in Short-Term U.S. Border Patrol Custody." Available at www.nomoredeathsvolunteers.org/Print%20Resources/Abuse%20Doc%20Reports/Culture%20of%20Cruelty/CultureofCrueltyFinal.pdf. Accessed April 3, 2013.

Nugent, Christopher. 2005–6. "Whose Children Are These? Towards Ensuring the Best Interests and Empowerment of Unaccompanied Alien Children." *Boston University Public Interest Journal* 15: 219–35.

NYU School of Law and New York Civil Liberties Union. 2011. "Justice Derailed: What Raids on New York Trains and Buses Reveal about Border Patrols' Internal Enforcement Practices." Available at www.nyclu.org/publications/report-justice-Derailed-what-raids-trains-and-buses-reveal-about-border-patrols-interi. Accessed January 3, 2014.

Office of the Inspector General (OIG). 2001. "Unaccompanied Juveniles in INS Custody." Report No. I-2001–009. Available at www.justice.gov/oig/reports/INS/e0109/index.htm. Accessed March 1, 2009.

———. 2004. "Unaccompanied Juveniles in INS Custody." Report No. 04–18. Available at www.oig.dhs.gov/assets/OIG_juvenile.pdf. Accessed March 3, 2009.

———. 2005. "A Review of DHS' Responsibilities for Alien Juveniles." Report No. 05–45. Available at www.oig.dhs.gov/assets/Mgmt/OIG_05–45_Sep05.pdf. Accessed March 30, 2009.

———. 2010. "CBP's Handling of Unaccompanied Alien Children." Report No. 10– 117. Available at www.oig.dhs.gov/assets/Mgmt/OIG_10–117_Sep10.pdf. Accessed April 3, 2011.

Olivas, Michael A. 1990. "Unaccompanied Refugee Children: Detention, Due Process, and Disgrace." *Stanford Law and Policy Review* 2: 159–66.

Paz, Octavio. 1961. *The Labryinth of Solitude: Life and Thought in Mexico*. New York: Grove Press.

Perry, Tony. 2013. "Border Patrol Tracker and Child-Survival Trainer." *Washington Post*, September 29, C9.

Peutz, Natalie, and Nicholas DeGenova. 2010. Introduction to *The Deportation Regime: Sovereignty, Space, and the Freedom of Movement*, ed. Nicholas DeGenova and Natalie Peutz, 1–29. Durham, NC: Duke University Press.

Preston, Julia. 2014. "U.S. Setting up Emergency Shelters in Texas as Youths Cross Border Alone." *New York Times*, May 16. Available at www.nytimes.com/2014/05/17/us/us-sets-up-crisis-shelter-as-children-flow-across-border-alone. Accessed June 11, 2014.

Priest, Dana. 2013. "Mexico's Changes in Anti-Drug Fight Imperil U.S. Role." *Washington Post*, April 28, A1, A12–13.

Ranji-Nogales, Jay, Andrew Schoenholtz, and Philip Schrag. 2007. "Refugee Roulette: Disparities in Asylum Adjudication." *Stanford Law Review* 60: 295–412. Available at www.durbin.senate.gov/DREAMERS. Accessed November 30, 2012.

Redfield, Peter. 2005. "Doctors, Borders, and Life in Crisis." *Cultural Anthropology* 20 (3): 328–61.

Robles, Frances. 2014. "Fleeing Gangs, Children Head to U.S. Border." *New York Times,* July 9. Available at RoblesFleeing%20Gangs,%20Children%20Head%20to%20U.S.%20Border%20-%20NYTimes.com.webarchive. Accessed July 10, 2014.

Rogers, David. 2014. "Flood of Child Immigrants: A Neglected Challenge." *Politico,* May 28. Available at www.politico.com/story/2014/05/flood-of-child-migrants-a-neglected-challenges-107198.html. Accessed June 11, 2014.

Rosenblum, Marc R., and Doris Meissner. 2014. *The Deportation Dilemma: Reconciling Tough and Humane Enforcement.* Washington, DC: Migration Policy Institute.

Roth, John. 2014. "Oversight of Unaccompanied Alien Children." Office of the Inspector General, Department of Homeland Security. Available at www.oig.dhs.gov/assets/Mgmt/2014/Over_Un_Ali_Chil.pdf. Accessed August 2, 2014.

Saulny, Susan. 2012. "After Recession, More Young Adults Are Living on Street." *New York Times,* December 19, A14, A17.

Scheper-Hughes, Nancy, and Carolyn Sargent, eds. 1998. *Small Wars: The Cultural Politics of Childhood.* Berkeley: University of California Press.

Schrag, Peter. 2011. *Not Fit for Our Society: Immigration and Nativism in America.* Berkeley: University of California Press.

Scott, Elizabeth S. and Laurence Steinberg. 2003. "Blaming Youth." *Texas Law Review* 81: 799–840.

Scott, Stephanie H. 2009. "Resilience in Undocumented, Unaccompanied Children: Perceptions of the Past and Future Outlook." PhD diss., Catholic University of America.

Semple, Kirk. 2014. "Youths Facing Deportation to Be Given Legal Counsel." *New York Times,* June 6, A11, A14.

Sen, Rinku. 2012. "Immigrants Are Losing the Policy Fight, but That's Beside the Point." *Colorlines,* September 17. Available at http://colorlines.com/archives/2012/09/Immigrants_are_losing_the_political_fight_but_thats_beside_the_point.html. Accessed February 26, 2013.

Shear, Michael D. 2013. "Obama's Defender of Borders Reverts to Voice for Migrants." *New York Times,* May 4, A1, A9.

Slack, Jeremy, et al. 2013. *In the Shadow of the Wall: Family Separation, Immigration Enforcement, and Security.* Tucson: Center for Latin American Studies, University of Arizona.

Somers, Aryah M., et al. 2010a. "Constructions of Childhood and Unaccompanied Children in the Immigration System in the United States." *UC Davis Journal of Juvenile Law and Policy* 14: 311–80.

———. 2010b. "Voice, Agency, and Vulnerability: The Immigration of Children through Systems of Protection and Enforcement." *International Migration,* special issue. Available at 10.111/j.1468–2435.2010.00653.x.

Southam, Keith. 2011. "Who Am I and Who Do you Want Me to Be? Effectively Defining a Lesbian, Gay, Bisexual, and Transgender Social Group in Asylum Applications." *Chicago-Kent Law Review* 86: 1363–87.

Stephen, Lynn. 2007. *Transborder Lives: Indigenous Oaxacans in Mexico, California, and Oregon.* Durham, NC: Duke University Press.

Stephens, Sharon, ed. 1995. *Children and the Politics of Culture.* Princeton: Princeton University Press.

Stoll, David. 2013. *El Norte or Bust! How Migration Fever and Microcredit Produced a Financial Crash in a Latin American Town.* Lanham, MD: Rowman and Littlefield.

Stryker, Rachael. 2010. *The Road to Evergreen: Adoption, Attachment Therapy, and the Promise of Family.* Ithaca, NY: Cornell University Press.

Terrio, Susan J. 2008. "New Barbarians at the Gates of Paris? Prosecuting Undocumented Minors in the Juvenile Court—The Problem of the 'Petits Roumains.'" *Anthropological Quarterly* 81 (4): 873–901.

———. 2009. *Judging Mohammed: Juvenile Delinquency, Immigration, and Exclusion at the Paris Palace of Justice.* Stanford, CA: Stanford University Press.

———. 2014. "Life Ended Here." *Politico,* July 10. Available at www.politico.com/magazine/story/2014/07/children-border-detention-108788.html#.U789vY1yF8Y.

Theodoredis, Pamela. 1994–95. "Detention of Alien Juveniles: *Reno v. Flores.*" *New York Law School Journal of Human Rights* 12: 393.

Thronson, David B. 2002. "Kids Will Be Kids? Reconsidering Conceptions of Children's Rights Underlying Immigration law." *Ohio State Law Journal* 63 (3): 979–1016.

———. 2006. "You Can't Get There from Here: Toward a More Child-Centered Immigration Law." *Virginia Journal of Social Policy and the Law* 14: 58–86.

———. 2007. "Custody and Contradictions: Exploring Immigration Law as Federal Family Law in the Context of Child Custody." *Hastings Law Journal* 59 (3): 453–514.

———. 2008. "Creating Crisis: Immigration Raids and the Destabilization of Immigrant Families." *Wake Forest Law Review* 43: 391–421.

———. 2010–11. "Entering the Mainstream: Making Children Matter in Immigration Law." *Fordham Urban Law Journal* 38: 393–413.

Ticktin, Miriam. 2011. "Casualties of Care." In *Immigration and the Politics of Humanitarianism in France.* Berkeley: University of California Press.

TRAC Immigration Reports. 2012. ICE, Prosecutorial Discretion Program. June 28. Available at http://trac.syr.edu/immigration/reports/287/. Accessed July 30, 2012.

———. 2014. "Immigration Court Backlogs, Juvenile Cases Help Push Immigration Court Backlog to All-Time High." July 10. Available at trac.syr.edu/whatsnew/email.140710.html.

Uehling, Greta L. 2008. "The International Smuggling of Children: Coyotes, Snakeheads, and the Politics of Compassion." *Anthropological Quarterly* 81 (4): 833–71.

United Nations High Commissioner on Refugees (UNHCR). 2014. "Children on the Run: Unaccompanied Children Leaving Central America and Mexico and the Need for International Protection." Executive Summary. Available at www.unhcrwashington.org/sites/default/files/UAC_Children%20On%20 the%20Run_Executive%20Summary_May2014.pdf. Accessed May 9, 2014.

United States Conference of Catholic Bishops (USCCB). 2014. "Mission to Central America: The Flight of Unaccompanied Children to the United States." Report of the Committee on Migration of the USCCB. Washington, DC.

U.S. Customs and Border Protection. 2014. "Southwest Border Unaccompanied Alien Children." Available at www.cbp.gov/newsroom/stats/southwest-border-unaccompanied-children. Accessed July 24, 2014.

U.S. Department of Health and Human Services. Office of the Inspector General, Department of Unaccompanied Alien Children's Services. 2008. "Efforts to Serve Children." Available at http://oig.hhs.gov.oei/reports/oei-07–06–00290.pdf. Accessed September 12, 2013.

———. Administration for Children and Families. Office of Refugee Resettlement, Division of Children's Services. 2008. Provisional Policy and Procedures Manual.

———. 2010. Power Point Presentation, ORR conference (April). Author's files.

———. 2012, 2013. "Statistics on Operation."

U.S. Department of Justice. 2014. "The Department of Homeland Security's Authority to Prioritize Removal of Certain Aliens Unlawfully Present in the United States and to Defer Removal of Others." Available at www.justice. gov/sites/default/files/olc/opinions/attachments/2014/11/20/2014–11–19-auth-prioritize-removal.pdf. Accessed November 20, 2014.

U.S. Immigration and Customs Enforcement (ICE). 2009. "Secure Communities: A Comprehensive Plan to Identify and Remove Criminal Aliens." Available at www.ice.gov/doclib/foia/secure_communities/securedcommunitiesstrategiesp lano9.pdf. Accessed January 17, 2014.

———. 2011. "Civil Immigration Enforcement: Priorities for the Apprehension, Detention, and Removal of Aliens." Amended and updated by the memorandum of the same title, issued March 2. Available at www.ice.gov /doclib/news/releases/2011/110302washingtondc.pdf. Accessed January 7, 2013.

———.2014. "Fact Sheet: Delegation of Immigration Authority Section 287(g) Immigration and Nationality Act." Available at www.ice.gov/news/library /factsheets/287g.htm. Accessed April 3, 2014.

Urrea, Luis Alberto. 2004. *The Devil's Highway: A True Story*. New York: Little, Brown.

Vigh, Henrik. 2006. *Navigating Terrains of War: Youth and Soldiering in Guinea-Bissau*. New York: Berghahn Books.

Vogt, Wendy A. 2013. "Crossing Mexico: Structural Violence and the Commodification of Undocumented Central American Migrants." *American Ethnologist* 40 (4): 764–80.

Ward, Peter. 2004. "From the Marginality of the 1960s to the 'New Poverty' of Today." *Latin American Research Review* 39 (1): 183–87.

Weiss, Jeff. 1998. "Guidelines for Children's Asylum Claims." INS Office of International Affairs. Available at www.uscis.gov/USCIS/Humanitarian/ Refugees%. Accessed December 15, 2013.

Welch, Michael. 2012. "Panic, Risk, Control: Conceptualizing Threats in a Post-9/11 Society." In *Punishing Immigrants: Policy, Politics, and Injustice,* ed. Charis E. Kubrin, Marjorie Zatz, and Ramiro Martinez Jr., 19–41. New York: New York University Press.

Wessler, Seth Freed. 2011. "Shattered Families: The Perilous Intersection of Immigration Enforcement and the Child Welfare System." Applied Research Center. Available at www.atlanticphilanthropies.org/sites/default/files /Uploads/ARC_Report_Shattered_Families_Full_Report_Nov2011Release. pdf. Accessed January 10, 2014.

———. 2012. "Nearly 205K Deportations of Parents of U.S. Citizens in Just over Two Years." *Colorlines.* Available at www.colorlines.com/archives /2012/12/advocates_and.html. Accessed December 21, 2012.

The White House. Office of the Press Secretary. 2014. "Fact Sheet: Immigration Accountability Executive Action." November 20. Available at www.white-house.gov/the-press-office/2014/11/20/fact-sheet-immigration-accountabil-ity-executive-action. Accessed November 20, 2014.

Winerip, Michael, and Michael Schwartz. 2014. "Riker's: Where Mental Illness Meets Brutality in Jail." *New York Times,* July 14. Available at http://nyti .ms/1r9SgLa. Accessed July 14, 2014.

Women's Commission for Refugee Women and Children. 2002. "Prison Guard or Parent? INS Treatment of Unaccompanied Refugee Children." New York. Available at www.womensrefugeecommission.org/.

———. 2009. "Halfway Home: Unaccompanied Children in Immigration Cus-tody." Orrick Herrington & Sutcliffe LLP, New York. Available at www .womensrefugeecommission.org/.

Women's Commission for Refugee Women and Children and Lutheran Immigra-tion and Refugee Service. 2007. "Locking up Family Values: The Detention of Immigrant Families." Available at www.womensrefugeecommission.org/.

Women's Refugee Commission. 2010. "Torn Apart by Immigration Enforce-ment: Parental Rights and Immigration Detention." New York. Available at www.womensrefugeecommission.org/.

———. 2012. "Forced from Home: The Lost Boys and Girls of Central Amer-ica." New York. Available at www.womensrefugeecommission.org/.

World Bank. 2011. *Crime and Violence in Central America: A Development Challenge.* Washington, DC: World Bank.

Young, Wendy. 2014. "Urgent: Child Migration Emergency—Please Help." June 2. www.supportkind.org/en/blog/853-urgent-child-migration-emer-gency-please-help. Accessed June 10, 2014.

Young, Wendy, and M. McKenna. 2010. "The Measure of a Society: The Treatment of Unaccompanied Refugee and Immigrant Children in the United States." *Harvard Civil Rights–Civil Liberties Law Review* 45: 247–60.

Zatz, Marjorie S., and Nancy Rodriguez. 2015. *Dreams and Nightmares: Immigration Policy, Youth and Families.* Berkeley, CA: University of Cali-fornia Press.

Zatz, Marjorie, and Hilary Smith. 2012. "Immigration, Crime, and Victimization: Rhetoric and Reality." *Annual Review of Law and Social Science* 8: 141–59.

Zilberg, Elana. 2011. *Space of Detention: The Making of a Transnational Gang Crisis between Los Angeles and San Salvador.* Durham, NC: Duke University Press.

Index